BARCODE ON
NEXT PAGE

The Pauline Writings

BIBLIOGRAPHIES

Craig A. Evans
General Editor

1. The Pentateuch
2. The Historical Books
3. Poetry and Wisdom
4. Prophecy and Apocalyptic
5. Jesus
6. The Synoptic Gospels
7. The Johannine Writings
8. Luke–Acts and New Testament Historiography
9. The Pauline Writings
10. Hebrews and the General Epistles
11. Old Testament Introduction
12. New Testament Introduction
13. Old Testament Theology
14. New Testament Theology

BIBLIOGRAPHIES No. 9

The Pauline Writings

An Annotated Bibliography

Mark A. Seifrid
Randall K. J. Tan

 Baker Academic

A Division of Baker Book House Co
Grand Rapids, Michigan 49516

Published by Baker Academic
a division of Baker Book House Company
P.O. Box 6287, Grand Rapids, MI 49516-6287

Printed in the United States of America

Library of Congress Cataloging-in-Publication Data
Seifrid, Mark A.
    The Pauline writings : an annotated bibliography / Mark A. Seifrid, Randall K. J. Tan.
      p.   cm. — (IBR bibliographies ; no. 9)
    Includes index.
    ISBN 0-8010-2482-X (pbk.)
    1. Bible. N.T. Epistles of Paul—Bibliography. I. Tan, Randall K. J., 1974– II. Title. III. Series.

Z7772.P1 S45 2003
[BS2650.52]
016.227—dc21   2002026038

For information about Baker Academic, visit our web site:
www.bakeracademic.com

Contents

Series Preface   9
Authors' Preface   11
Abbreviations   13

1. Bibliographical Tools and Surveys   17
2. History of Modern Interpretation   20
3. Paul's Conversion and Call   27
4. History and Chronology of Paul's Mission   31
5. Overviews of Paul's Life and Thought   38
6. Paul and First-Century Judaism   42
7. Paul and the Greco-Roman World   48
   7.1   Religious and Philosophical Background   49
   7.2   Social Background   51
8. Paul and Jesus   58
9. Paul and Earliest Christianity   63
   9.1   Paul and the Hellenists   63
   9.2   Hymns, Creeds, and Confessions   66
   9.3   Paul and His Opponents   72
   9.4   Paul and James   75
10. Paul's Influence on Early Christian Tradition   79
11. The Letters of Paul   83
   11.1 Literary Studies   83
   11.2 Linguistics and Discourse Analysis   84
   11.3 Rhetorical Criticism   87
        11.3.1 General Orientation   88
        11.3.2 Greco-Roman/
               Historical Model   91
        11.3.3 Modern Rhetoric   92
        11.3.4 Style and Forms   93
   11.4 Epistolography   94

11.5   Pseudonymity   99
11.6   The Pauline Corpus   102
11.7   Paul and the Old Testament   105
11.8   The Paul of the Letters
       and the Paul of Acts   109
11.9   Commentaries   111
       11.9.1   Romans   111
       11.9.2   1 Corinthians   113
       11.9.3   2 Corinthians   114
       11.9.4   Galatians   115
       11.9.5   Ephesians   117
       11.9.6   Philippians   118
       11.9.7   Colossians and Philemon   120
       11.9.8   1 and 2 Thessalonians   121
       11.9.9   The Pastoral Epistles   123
12.   Special Studies   126
12.1   Romans   126
12.2   1 Corinthians   129
12.3   2 Corinthians   131
12.4   Galatians   133
12.5   Ephesians   134
12.6   Philippians   135
12.7   Colossians   136
12.8   1 and 2 Thessalonians   137
12.9   Pastoral Epistles   139
13.   Pauline Theology   141
13.1   Comprehensive Treatments   141
13.2   Narrative Framework   144
13.3   God   146
13.4   Christ   148
13.5   The Spirit   155
13.6   Salvation   159
       13.6.1   Promise   160
       13.6.2   The Law   160
       13.6.3   Sin, Suffering, and Death   166
       13.6.4   The Human Being before God
                (Anthropology)   168
       13.6.5   The Cross and Atonement   171
       13.6.6   Redemption, Adoption (Sonship),
                Freedom   176
       13.6.7   The Gospel, Proclamation,
                and Mission   177

13.6.8 Faith   180
13.6.9 Justification   183
13.6.10 Reconciliation   186
13.6.11 Participation   188
13.6.12 Holiness   190
13.6.13 Final Judgment   191
13.7 Eschatology   192
13.8 Israel   199
13.9 The Church   203
  13.9.1 General Orientation   204
  13.9.2 Metaphors and Other Characterizations   205
  13.9.3 Apostle, Church Organization, and Ministry   208
  13.9.4 Baptism   212
  13.9.5 Lord's Supper   215
  13.9.6 Discipline   217
  13.9.7 Worship   218
  13.9.8 Male and Female Relations and Women in Ministry   220
13.10 Ethics   225
  13.10.1 General Orientation   226
  13.10.2 Sexual Ethics and Homosexuality   230
  13.10.3 Marriage/Celibacy and Divorce and Remarriage   231
  13.10.4 Relations to Civil Authorities   232

Name Index   235

Series Preface

With the proliferation of journals and publishing houses dedicated to biblical studies, it has become impossible for even the most dedicated scholar to keep in touch with the vast materials now available for research in all the different parts of the canon. How much more difficult for the minister, rabbi, student, or interested layperson! Herein lies the importance of bibliographies and in particular this series—IBR Bibliographies.

Bibliographies help guide students to works relevant to their research interests. They cut down the time needed to locate materials, thus providing the researcher with more time to read, assimilate, and write. These benefits are especially true for the IBR Bibliographies. First, the series is conveniently laid out along the major divisions of the canon, with four volumes planned on the Old Testament, six on the New Testament, and four on methodology (see the listing of series titles on page 2). The compiler of each volume must select only the most important and helpful works for inclusion and arrange entries under various topics to allow for ease of reference. Furthermore, the entries are briefly annotated in order to inform the reader about the works' contents more specifically, once again giving guidance to the appropriate material and saving time by preventing the all too typical "wild goose chase" in the library.

Since the series is designed primarily for American and British students, the emphasis is on works written in English. Fortunately, a number of the most important foreign-language works have been translated into English, and wherever this is the case this information is included along with the original publication data. Again keeping in mind the needs of the student, we have decided to list the English translation before the original title.

These bibliographies are presented under the sponsorship of

the Institute for Biblical Research (IBR), an organization of evangelical Christian scholars with specialties in both Old and New Testaments and their ancillary disciplines. The IBR has met annually since 1970; its name and constitution were adopted in 1973. Besides its annual meetings (normally held the evening and morning prior to the annual meeting of the Society of Biblical Literature), the institute publishes a journal, *Bulletin for Biblical Research*, and conducts regional study groups on various biblical themes in several areas of the United States and Canada. The Institute for Biblical Research encourages and fosters scholarly research among its members, all of whom are at a level to qualify for a university lectureship. Finally, the IBR and the series editor extend their thanks to Baker Book House for its efforts to bring this series to publication. In particular, we would like to thank David Aiken for his wise guidance in giving shape to the project.

Craig A. Evans
Acadia Divinity School

Authors' Preface

A colleague once warned that assembling a bibliography is a thankless task: it is never cited and often criticized. Whether that judgment is true or not, the production of a bibliography certainly is difficult. Not that the collection of titles is onerous: one now may easily download many more entries than we have listed here in an afternoon or less. The hard work lies in selection, assessment, and annotation. In accord with the aim of this series, we have endeavored to provide a guide that will make the research easier and more efficient for all serious students of Scripture. We are quite aware that our bibliography is incomplete. Many important works could not be included in this bibliography, which already has gone well beyond the original limits set for it. We therefore have attempted to produce a representative bibliography, which will introduce the various topics of study on Paul, and lead to works that themselves provide further bibliography. Generally, our selection has been weighted toward works in the English language and toward recent studies that themselves describe the state of research and/or supply their own bibliographies. Anyone who studies Paul will (or, at least, ought to) quickly recognize that the whole of his thought hangs together. If one pulls on any one string of it, one finds oneself unraveling the whole. That means that especially in the theological sections of this bibliography a good deal of cross-referencing is necessary in order to get a good grasp of any particular topic. We should not neglect to remind the users of this bibliography of several excellent reference works, the *Anchor Bible Dictionary* (*ABD*), the *Dictionary of Paul and His Letters* (*DPL*), and, for those who use German, the *Theologische Realenzyklopädie* and *Die Religion in Geschichte und Gegenwart* (now appearing in its

11

fourth edition). We have frequently referred to articles in these works. Even where we have not, they should be consulted.

Finally, *todoth eleph* (literally, nearly) to Noel Rabinowitz, who patiently brought our entries into conformity with the stylistic guidelines for the series, without any kvetching whatsoever. Thanks, too, to Jim Hamilton, who cheerfully volunteered to proofread our work.

Mark A. Seifrid
Randall K. J. Tan

Abbreviations

AB	Anchor Bible
ABD	*Anchor Bible Dictionary.* Edited by D. N. Freedman. 6 vols. New York, 1992
AGJU	Arbeiten zur Geschichte des antiken Judentums und des Urchristentums
AnBib	Analecta biblica
ATANT	Abhandlungen zur Theologie des Alten und Neuen Testaments
ATDan	Acta theologica danica
ATLA	American Theological Library Association
BBR	*Bulletin for Biblical Research*
BECNT	Baker Exegetical Commentary on the New Testament
BETL	Bibliotheca ephemeridum theologicarum lovaniensium
BHT	Beiträge zur historischen Theologie
Bib	*Biblica*
BJRL	*Bulletin of the John Rylands University Library of Manchester*
BJS	Brown Judaic Studies
BNTC	Black's New Testament Commentaries
BZ	*Biblische Zeitschrift*
BZNW	Beihefte zur Zeitschrift für die neutestamentliche Wissenschaft
CBET	Contributions to Biblical Exegesis and Theology
CBQ	*Catholic Biblical Quarterly*
ConBNT	Coniectanea biblica: New Testament Series
CJT	*Canadian Journal of Theology*
CRINT	Compendia rerum iudaicarum ad Novum Testamentum

DLNT	*Dictionary of the Later New Testament and Its Developments.* Edited by R. P. Martin and P. H. Davids. Downers Grove, Ill., 1997
DNTB	*Dictionary of New Testament Background.* Edited by C. Evans and S. Porter. Downers Grove, Ill., 2000
DPL	*Dictionary of Paul and His Letters.* Edited by G. F. Hawthorne and R. P. Martin. Downers Grove, Ill., 1993
ECC	Eerdmans Critical Commentary
EFN	Estudios de filología neotestamentaria. Cordova, Spain, 1988–
ETR	*Etudes théologiques et religieuses*
ETS	Erfurter theologische Studien
EvQ	*Evangelical Quarterly*
EvT	*Evangelische Theologie*
ExAud	*Ex auditu*
ExpT	*Expository Times*
FN	*Filología Neotestamentaria*
FRLANT	Forschungen zur Religion und Literatur des Alten und Neuen Testaments
GBS	Guides to Biblical Scholarship
GTA	Göttinger theologischer Arbeiten
GTJ	*Grace Theological Journal*
HBT	*Horizons in Biblical Theology*
HDR	Harvard Dissertations in Religion
HNT	Handbuch zum Neuen Testament
HTKNT	Herders theologischer Kommentar zum Neuen Testament
HTR	*Harvard Theological Review*
HUT	Hermeneutische Untersuchungen zur Theologie
ICC	International Critical Commentary
IKaZ	*Internationale katholische Zeitschrift*
Int	*Interpretation*
JAC	*Jahrbuch für Antike und Christentum*
JBL	*Journal of Biblical Literature*
JETS	*Journal of the Evangelical Theological Society*
JRE	*Journal of Religious Ethics*
JSJSup	Supplements to the Journal for the Study of Judaism
JSNT	*Journal for the Study of the New Testament*

JSNTSup	Journal for the Study of the New Testament: Supplement Series
JTS	*Journal of Theological Studies*
KEK	Kritisch-exegetischer Kommentar über das Neue Testament (Meyer-Kommentar)
LEC	Library of Early Christianity
NA[27]	*Novum Testamentum Graece*, Nestle-Aland, 27th ed.
NCB	New Century Bible
NICNT	New International Commentary on the New Testament
NIGTC	New International Greek Testament Commentary
NovT	*Novum Testamentum*
NovTSup	Novum Testamentum Supplements
NTAbh	Neutestamentliche Abhandlungen
NTG	New Testament Guides
NTOA	Novum Testamentum et Orbis Antiquus
NTS	*New Testament Studies*
NTTS	New Testament Tools and Studies
PNTC	Pelican New Testament Commentaries
PRSt	*Perspectives in Religious Studies*
PSB	*Princeton Seminary Bulletin*
RB	*Revue biblique*
ResQ	*Restoration Quarterly*
RevExp	*Review and Expositor*
SBEC	Studies in Bible and Early Christianity
SBJT	*The Southern Baptist Journal of Theology*
SBL	Society of Biblical Literature
SBLDS	SBL Dissertation Series
SBLMS	SBL Monograph Series
SBLRBS	SBL Resources for Biblical Study
SBLSBS	SBL Sources for Biblical Study
SBM	Stuttgarter biblische Monographien
SBS	Stuttgarter Bibelstudien
SBT	Studies in Biblical Theology
SD	Studies and Documents
SJT	*Scottish Journal of Theology*
SNT	Studien zum Neuen Testament
SNTSMS	Society for New Testament Studies Monograph Series

ST	*Studia theologica*
SUNT	Studien zur Umwelt des Neuen Testaments
TJ	*Trinity Journal*
TJT	*Toronto Journal of Theology*
TLZ	*Theologische Literaturzeitung*
TNTC	Tyndale New Testament Commentaries
TRu	*Theologische Rundschau*
TS	*Theological Studies*
TSAJ	Texte und Studien zum antiken Judentum
TynBul	*Tyndale Bulletin*
UBS[4]	*The Greek New Testament,* United Bible Societies, 4th ed.
UNT	Untersuchungen zum Neuen Testament
VE	*Vox evangelica*
WBC	Word Biblical Commentary
WEC	Wycliffe Exegetical Commentary
WMANT	Wissenschaftliche Monographien zum Alten und Neuen Testament
WTJ	*Westminster Theological Journal*
WUNT	Wissenschaftliche Untersuchungen zum Neuen Testament
ZNW	*Zeitschrift für die neutestamentliche Wissenschaft und die Kunde der älteren Kirche*
ZTK	*Zeitschrift für Theologie und Kirche*

1

Bibliographical Tools and Surveys

Recent reports of research are listed here along with the usual reference works. Beyond the resources listed, the invaluable access to library catalogs that is now available through the Internet should not be overlooked. Bibliographic websites, which are still in their infancy, may be located through a search engine.

1 *Elenchus Bibliographicus Biblicus*. Rome: Pontifical Biblical Institute, 1920–present.

  EBB is the most thorough bibliography covering the field of biblical studies. Published annually, the volumes generally appear two or more years after the contents they index. Volumes 1–48 (1920–67) were issued as a part of *Biblica*, and were not as complete or as well-organized as *EBB*.

2 *ATLA Biblical Studies CD-ROM*. Evanston, Ill.: American Theological Library Association, 1949–present.

  This relatively affordable CD-ROM contains approximately 130,000 citations drawn from the annual ATLA religion database: *Religion Index One: Periodicals* (*RIO*, including the *Index to Religious Periodical Literature* [*IRPL*]; 1949–present); *Religion Index Two: Multi-author Works* (*RIT*; 1960–present); and *Index to Book Reviews in Religion* (*IBRR*; 1949–present). These materials generally will be available in theological libraries, primarily in the form of the *ATLA Religion Indexes CD-ROM* (*RIO/RIT/IBRR*; 1975–present), or as hard-copy indexes (formerly released semiannually).

3 *New Testament Abstracts*. Weston, Mass.: 1956–present.

  Abstracts of selected, significant articles and monographs.

4 K. Schelkle. *Paulus: Leben, Briefe, Theologie*. Erträge der

Forschung 152. Darmstadt: Wissenschaftliche Buchgesellschaft, 1981.

> A report of research. A number of the French and German titles
> listed are available in English.

5   P. Petersen, ed. *Paul the Apostle and Pauline Literature: A
       Bibliography Selected from the ATLA Religion Database.*
       4th ed. Chicago: American Theological Library Associa-
       tion, 1984.

> A complete subject and author index of the ATLA material (de-
> scribed in #2) having to do with Paul, up to June 1984. Al-
> though it is now out of print, it is available in a number of
> libraries.

6   G. Borchert. *Paul and His Interpreters: An Annotated Bib-
       liography.* TSF-IBR Bibliographic Study Guides. Madison,
       Wisc.: Theological Students Fellowship, 1985.

> Numerous entries, brief annotation.

7   H. Hübner. "Paulusforschung seit 1945: Ein kritischer Lit-
       eraturbericht." Pp. 2649–840 in *Aufstieg und Niedergang
       der römischen Welt.* II: *Principat.* Edited by W. Haase and
       H. Temporini. Vol. 25/4. Berlin: de Gruyter, 1988.

> An extensive survey of recent research, with special attention
> given to theological topics.

8   A. Hultgren. "The Epistles of Paul." Pp. 296–311 in *New
       Testament Christology: A Critical Assessment and Anno-
       tated Bibliography.* Biographies and Indexes in Religious
       Studies 12. New York: Greenwood, 1988.

> One hundred twenty-five annotated entries on the Christology
> of the Pauline letters.

9   O. Merk. "Paulus-Forschung, 1936–1985." *TRu* 53 (1988):
       1–81.

> A continuation of Bultmann's earlier reports of research (see
> #20), it is useful not only as a bibliographical aid, but also as a
> guide to current issues.

10   G. Hawthorne, R. P. Martin, and D. G. Reid, eds. *Dictio-
       nary of Paul and His Letters.* Downers Grove, Ill., and
       Leicester, England: InterVarsity, 1993.

> An indispensable collection of more than two hundred articles,
> many of which are of outstanding quality. The bibliographies
> included with the articles are superb. The user needs only to be
> alerted that a great diversity of opinion appears here.

11   W. Mills. *An Index to Periodical Literature on the Apostle
       Paul.* NTTS 16. Leiden: Brill, 1993.

An update and considerable expansion of B. Metzger, *Index to Periodical Literature on the Apostle Paul*, NTTS 1 (Leiden: Brill, 1960). On the letters of Paul, see also his *Bibliographies for Biblical Research: New Testament Series* (Lewiston, N.Y.: Mellen Biblical Press, 1993–).

2

History of Modern Interpretation

Although others earlier had questioned the traditional ascription of Pauline authorship to the Pastorals (e.g., Schleiermacher), the modern period of interpretation of Paul had its real foundation in the "positive criticism" of Ferdinand Christian Baur (see Kümmel, #23). Baur, taking a new step, sought to place each of the NT writings in its "proper" historical framework. While his idealistic conception of history (substantially shaped by Hegel's thought) did not endure, the impetus he provided toward independent historical treatment of Acts and the Pauline letters did. The questions that his historical paradigm raised remain to this day, especially that of the relation between Paul and earliest Jewish Christianity (see Munck's complaint regarding the undue influence of Baur, #24), and the reliability of Acts (see Ramsay, #15; Ellis, #26; §11.8; and chapters 4 and 9 below). The subsequent period of study saw the dismantling of Baur's work (to which both Albrecht Ritschl and the British scholar J. B. Lightfoot made important contributions [cf. Kümmel, #23; and Neill and Wright, #37]). Baur's antithesis between a universalistic Paul and a particularistic Judaism was replaced by a dualistic Paul, whose thought contained irreconcilable differences due to the influences of Judaism and philosophical Hellenism. Paul's doctrine, conditioned by its age, was dispensable. He was appropriated by means of his universalistic religious experience of inner freedom. By this means, most liberals in the late nineteenth century still saw Paul as the true disciple of Jesus. The distance between Jesus and Paul (and the recognition that earliest Christianity is the decisive middle term) became a central matter of investigation for the twentieth century (on this period see Schweitzer, #17, and Bultmann, #20). The liberal categories for interpreting Paul were dismantled by a series of studies, which included those of Gunkel (#13), Kabisch (#14), and, especially, the essay by Wrede (#16). Paul again was recognized as a theologian, in whose thought eschatology played a decisive role (see Schweitzer, #21). Fresh questions regarding Paul's background emerged to become central to twentieth-century debate. Heitmüller, R. Reitzenstein, and Bousset (#18) saw "mystery religions" deriving from popular Hellenism and Gnosticism as formative for Paul's thought. The idea of a Hellenistic Gentile Christianity prior to Paul in which these syncretizing influences were at work was taken up into Bultmann's influential treatment of Paul's theology (#22). Much of the interpretation of Paul in the middle part of the twentieth century centered on this reconstruction and the questions it raised. Scholarship generally has moved away from these issues. The first break with Bultmann came from within his own school, through Ernst Käsemann (#675), who recast Paul's theology in terms of God the creator rather than the existence of the human being. Even Käsemann's approach largely has been set aside since the late 1970s, when a rereading of Paul's Judaism and its relationship to his gospel came to dominate the discussion (see chapters 3 and 6). The current study of Paul has broadened into an array of approaches, including rhetorical criticism of his letters (in various forms), the social setting of the communities he addressed, and the narrative character of his theology. The manner in which Paul's thought is appropriated nevertheless tends to fall into recurring patterns. Furthermore, Adolf Schlatter's observation still holds true that biblical research is not driven by its own questions, but by those brought to it from without. Research into the history of modern interpretation therefore promises to provide perspective and to warn against some dead-ends that have been traveled already.

12 F. Baur. *Paul, the Apostle of Jesus Christ*. Translated by A. Menzies. 2 vols. London: Williams & Norgate, 1875.
First published in 1845, Baur was engaged in a thorough revision of it at the time of his death. Zeller completed the work, using large sections from the first edition. This second edition

is the one generally available: *Paulus, der Apostel Jesu Christi,* ed. E. Zeller, 2d ed., 2 vols. (Leipzig: Fues's Verlag, 1866–67).

13   H. Gunkel. *The Influence of the Holy Spirit: The Popular View of the Apostolic Age and the Teaching of the Apostle Paul.* Translated by R. A. Harrisville and P. Quanbeck II. Philadelphia: Fortress, 1979. German edition: *Die Wirkungen des heiligen Geistes nach der populären Anschauung der apostolischen Zeit und der Lehre des Apostels Paulus.* Göttingen: Vandenhoeck & Ruprecht, 1888.

Gunkel sounded a death knell for the rationalistic moralism of the post-Baur era: for Paul (and the rest of the NT) the Spirit is a supernatural power, not an ideal.

14   R. Kabisch. *Die Eschatologie des Paulus in ihren Zusammenhängen mit dem Gesamtbegriff des Paulinismus.* Göttingen: Vandenhoeck & Ruprecht, 1893.

Critical of the neglect of eschatology by nineteenth-century NT scholarship, Kabisch asserts that it was foundational to Paul's theology and ethics.

15   W. Ramsay. *St. Paul the Traveller and the Roman Citizen.* New York: G. P. Putnam's Sons; London: Hodder & Stoughton, 1896.

Standing at the opposite pole to Baur, Ramsay seeks to confirm the reliability of the book of Acts on the basis of geographical and historical detail.

16   W. Wrede. *Paul.* Translated by E. Lummis. Lexington, Ky.: American Theological Library Association, 1962. German edition: *Paulus.* Religionsgeschichtliche Volksbücher 1. Tübingen and Halle: Mohr, 1904. A reprint appears in *Das Paulusbild in der neueren deutschen Forschung,* pp. 1–97 (see #28).

Decisively influenced by Jewish apocalyptic expectations of the Messiah and not by Jesus or the earliest believing community, Paul was an independent theologian, the second founder of Christianity.

17   A. Schweitzer. *Paul and His Interpreters: A Critical History.* Translated by W. Montgomery. New York: Schocken, 1964. German edition: *Geschichte der Paulinische Forschung von der Reformation bis auf die Gegenwart.* Tübingen: Mohr (Siebeck), 1911. The summary chapter is reprinted in *Das Paulusbild in der neueren deutschen Forschung* (see #28).

Essential reading. Schweitzer was gifted at demolition, and the problems of interpretation he exposes perennially reappear in new forms.

18 W. Bousset. *Kyrios Christos: A History of Belief in Christ from the Beginnings of Christianity to Irenaeus.* Translated by J. Steely. Nashville: Abingdon, 1970. German edition: *Kyrios Christos: Geschichte des Christusglaubens von den Anfängen des Christentums bis Irenaeus.* FRLANT 21. Göttingen: Vandenhoeck & Ruprecht, 1913.

Influential attempt to find the basis of Paul's thought in the veneration of a cultic god (κύριος) of popular Hellenistic religion, rather than in Jesus and the earliest Palestinian believing community. See "Gentile Christian Primitive Community," 119–52, and his treatment of Paul, 153–210.

19 J. G. Machen. *The Origin of Paul's Religion.* New York: Macmillan, 1921.

A comprehensive and significant response to the history-of-religions interpretation of Paul (especially Wrede and Bousset). It is reviewed and rejected by Bultmann largely on the basis of the presupposition that historical work must operate with naturalistic premises, *TLZ* 1 (1924): 13–14.

20 R. Bultmann. "Zur Geschichte der Paulus-Forschung." *TRu* 1 (1929): 26–59.

Important assessment of critical interpretation of Paul. Continuing reports by Bultmann appear in *TRu* 6 (1934): 229–46; 8 (1936): 1–22. The original article is reprinted in *Das Paulusbild in der neueren deutschen Forschung* (see #28).

21 A. Schweitzer. *The Mysticism of Paul the Apostle.* Translated by W. Montgomery. New York: Seabury, 1968. German edition: *Die Mystik des Apostels Paulus.* Tübingen: Mohr (Siebeck), 1930.

A continuation of the line of thought initiated by H. Lüdemann, in which Pauline soteriology is interpreted in material terms. Unlike Heitmüller and Bousset, Schweitzer finds the source of Paul's thought in the eschatological expectations of first-century Judaism.

22 R. Bultmann. *Theology of the New Testament.* Translated by K. Grobel. Scribner Studies in Contemporary Theology. New York: Scribner's, 1951. German edition: *Theologie des Neuen Testaments.* Vol. 1. Tübingen: Mohr (Siebeck), 1948.

"The Kerygma of the Hellenistic Church aside from Paul," 33–183, and "The Theology of Paul," 185–366. See the important review by Nils Dahl, *TLZ* 22 (1954): 21–43.

23   W. Kümmel. *The New Testament: The History of the In-
      vestigation of Its Problems* (esp. pp. 120–404). Translated
      by S. Gilmour and H. Kee. Nashville: Abingdon, 1972. Ger-
      man edition: *Das Neue Testament: Geschichte der Er-
      forschung seiner Probleme.* Freiburg and München: Karl
      Alber, 1958.
          A standard critical history of research.
24   J. Munck. *Paul and the Salvation of Mankind* (esp. pp. 69–
      86). Translated by F. Clarke. Atlanta: John Knox, 1959.
      Danish edition: *Paulus und die Heilsgeschichte.* Århus,
      Denmark: Universitetsforlaget, 1954.
          An attack on the abiding influence of the Tübingen school's an-
          tithesis between Paul and early Jewish Christianity.
25   G. Delling. "Zum neueren Paulusverständnis." *NovT* 4
      (1960): 95–121.
          Penetrating discussion of midcentury study of Paul, anticipat-
          ing Käsemann's Oxford Congress address of the following year.
26   E. E. Ellis. *Paul and His Recent Interpreters.* Grand
      Rapids: Eerdmans, 1961.
          One of the few surveys that gives attention to British responses
          to German scholarship.
27   B. Rigaux. *The Letters of St. Paul: Modern Studies.* Edited
      and translated by S. Yonick. Chicago: Franciscan Herald,
      1968. French edition: *Saint Paul et ses Lettres: Etat de la
      Question.* Studia Neotestamentica Subsidia 2. Paris and
      Bruges: Desclée de Brouwer, 1962.
          A good summary of much of the research from Baur to the late
          1960s.
28   K. Rengstorf. *Das Paulusbild in der neueren deutschen
      Forschung.* 3d ed. Wege der Forschung 24. 1964; Darm-
      stadt: Wissenschaftliche Buchgesellschaft, 1982.
          A useful collection of essays by Wrede, Schlatter, Schweitzer,
          Heitmüller, Bultmann, Käsemann, and others.
29   J. Hyatt, ed. *The Bible in Modern Scholarship.* Nashville:
      Abingdon, 1965.
          Contains papers read at the one-hundreth meeting of the SBL
          by Johannes Munck ("Pauline Research since Schweitzer,"
          166–77), W. D. Davies ("Paul and Judaism," 178–86), and Hel-
          mut Koester ("Paul and Hellenism," 187–95). Although each
          stakes out his own turf rather than producing a historical sur-
          vey, the articles are a useful window to twentieth-century
          study of Paul.
30   H. Conzelmann. "Current Problems in Pauline Research."

Int 22 (1968): 171–86. German edition: "Heutige Probleme der Paulus-Forschung." *Der Evangelische Erzieher* 18 (1966): 241–52.
Enlightening discussion of midcentury debate from the perspective of the Bultmann school.

31 E. Best. "Recent Pauline Studies." *ExpT* 80 (1969): 164–67.
Concise, yet broad in scope.

32 W. Meeks, ed. *The Writings of St. Paul*. New York: W. W. Norton, 1972.
Pages 151–444 contain excerpts and essays by historians, biblical scholars, theologians, and cultural interpreters of Paul on such topics as grace and ethics, the influence of Paul, his relationship to Judaism, and his understanding of religious experience.

33 H. Harris. *The Tübingen School*. Oxford: Clarendon, 1975.
A bibliographical and theological portrait.

34 M. Brauch. "God's Righteousness in Recent German Discussion." Pp. 523–42 in *Paul and Palestinian Judaism*. Edited by E. P. Sanders. Philadelphia: Fortress; London: SCM, 1977.
Discusses reactions to Käsemann's understanding of "the righteousness of God" as a salvation-creating power.

35 J. Plevnik. *What Are They Saying about Paul?* New York: Paulist, 1986.
A brief survey of some recent trends in interpreting Paul's thought, described and assessed from a Catholic perspective.

36 L. E. Keck. "Paul's Theology in Historical Criticism." Pp. 126–58 in *Paul and His Letters*. 2d ed., revised and enlarged. Proclamation Commentaries. Philadelphia: Fortress, 1988.
Brief survey.

37 S. Neill and N. T. Wright. *The Interpretation of the New Testament: 1861–1986*. 2d ed. Oxford: Oxford University Press, 1988.
Pages 403–30 contain a readable critique of the study of Paul's thought from Schweitzer to Sanders, anticipating Wright's own covenantal thesis. This section is lacking in the original edition by Neill (1964).

38 S. J. Hafemann. "Paul and His Interpreters." Pp. 666–79 in *Dictionary of Paul and His Letters*. Downers Grove, Ill., and Leicester, England: InterVarsity, 1993.
Concludes with probing reflections on the current state of study.

39   S. E. Porter, ed. *The Pauline Writings*. The Biblical Seminar
       34. Sheffield: Sheffield Academic Press, 1995.
           Collection of significant essays on Paul and his thought.
40   B. Matlock. *Unveiling the Apocalyptic Paul: Paul's Inter-*
       preters and the Rhetoric of Criticism. JSNTSup 127.
       Sheffield: Sheffield Academic Press, 1996.
           A survey of the various ways in which the label "apocalyptic"
           has been used and abused by scholars. Somewhat cynical in
           tone, Matlock assumes a "postcritical" pose.
41   C. H. Cosgrove. "A History of New Testament Studies in
       the Twentieth Century." *RevExp* 96 (1999): 369–83.
           Brief survey of the issues.

3

Paul's Conversion and Call

Should Paul's encounter with Christ be regarded as a conversion or call? That is to ask, was it salvific for Paul himself, or was it merely a commission to preach to the Gentiles? Of what significance was this christophany for Paul's subsequent view of Christ, God, the Law, faith? Paul's conversion will always remain a point of controversy, just as it was in his day. The literature on the topic is considerable. Here again, we have provided only a representative sample intended to lead the student into the present discussion. The topic is inseparable from discussions of early Judaism (chapter 6) and Paul's Christology (§13.4). Overviews of Paul's life and thought (chapter 5) naturally also contain discussions of his conversion. See also the important work by Seyoon Kim, *Paul and the New Perspective: Second Thoughts on the Origin of Paul's Gospel* (Grand Rapids and Cambridge, England: Eerdmans, 2002), which appeared too late to be included in this bibliography.

42　W. G. Kümmel. "Römer 7 und die Bekehrung des Paulus." Pp. 1–163 in *Römer 7 und das Bild des Menschen im Neuen Testament*. München: Chr. Kaiser, 1974. Original publication: Leipzig: J. G. Hinrichs'sche Buchhandlung, 1929.

> Influential argument that the chapter does not reflect the experience of Paul.

43　K. Stendahl. "The Apostle Paul and the Introspective Conscience of the West." *HTR* 56 (1963): 199–215.

> There is no evidence that Paul ever suffered from pangs of guilt. His gospel has to do with the inclusion of the Gentiles.

44   P. Stuhlmacher. " 'The End of the Law': On the Origin and
Beginnings of Pauline Theology." Pp. 134–54 in *Reconcili-
ation, Law, and Righteousness: Essays in Biblical Theol-
ogy*. Translated by E. R. Kalin. Philadelphia: Fortress, 1986.
Original publication: "Das Ende Des Gesetzes." *ZTK* 67
(1970): 14–39.
   Paul was entirely caught up in the Law until he met the risen
   Christ, who becomes for him "the end of the Law."

45   G. Bornkamm. "The Revelation of Christ to Paul on the
Damascus Road and Paul's Doctrine of Justification and
Reconciliation: A Study in Galatians 1." Pp. 90–103 in *Reconciliation and Hope: New Testament Essays on Atonement and Eschatology Presented to L. L. Morris on His Sixtieth Birthday*. Edited by R. Banks. Grand Rapids: Eerdmans,
1974.
   Justification as the central Pauline teaching derived from his
   conversion, from something of an existentialist perspective.

46   U. Wilckens. "Die Bekehrung des Paulus als Religionge-
schichtliches Problem." Pp. 11–32 in *Rechtfertigung als
Freiheit: Paulusstudien*. Neukirchen: Neukirchener, 1974.
   Apocalypticism as the fundamental structure around which
   Paul's interpretation of the "Christ-event" is formed. It
   remains questionable whether this paradigm suffices.

47   K. Haacker. "Die Berufung des Verfolgers und die Rechtfertigung des Gottlosen." *Theologische Beiträge* 6 (1975):
119.
   Brief but thorough survey of the evidence, in which it is argued
   that Paul's teaching on the justification of the ungodly is the
   inversion of his former persecution of the church.

48   A. Hultgren. "Paul's Pre-Christian Persecutions of the
Church: Their Purpose, Locale, and Nature." *JBL* 95 (1976):
97–111.
   Paul opposed the preaching of the crucified Jesus as Messiah in
   Judea, and attempted to discipline those wayward Jews who be-
   lieved in him.

49   S. Kim. *The Origin of Paul's Gospel*. WUNT 2/4. Tübin-
gen: Mohr (Siebeck), 1981; Grand Rapids: Eerdmans, 1982.
   Paul's gospel and theology derived from his vision of the risen
   Christ. This work was completed in the same year as E. P.
   Sanders's *Paul and Palestinian Judaism* (#106).

50   C. Dietzfelbinger. *Die Berufung des Paulus als Ursprung
seiner Theologie*. WMANT 58. Neukirchen-Vlyun: Neukirchener, 1985.

Not only the vision of the risen Christ, but the audition on the Damascus road was the basis of Paul's Law-free gospel.

51 P. Fredriksen. "Paul and Augustine: Conversion Narratives, Orthodox Traditions, and the Retrospective Self." *JTS* 37 (1986): 334.

Recollections of earlier events are notoriously subject to subsequent experience. We therefore have no access to Paul's conversion as it really was. But Paul does not recount his experience, does he?

52 B. R. Gaventa. *From Darkness to Light: Aspects of Conversion in the New Testament.* Philadelphia: Fortress, 1986.

Examination of New Testament conceptions. See also "Galatians 1 and 2: Autobiography as Paradigm," *NovT* 27 (1986): 309–26, in which Gaventa takes a minimalist reading of Paul's presentation of his conversion.

53 C. M. Tuckett. "Deuteronomy 21,23 and Paul's Conversion." Pp. 345–50 in *L'Apôtre Paul: Personalité, Style, et Conception du Ministère.* Edited by A. Vanhoye. BETL 73. Louvain: Louvain University Press, 1986.

Argues against associating the curse upon one "hanged on a tree" with Paul's conversion.

54 J. D. G. Dunn. " 'A Light to the Gentiles': The Significance of the Damascus Road Christophany for Paul." Pp. 251–66 in *The Glory of Christ in the New Testament: Studies in Christology in Memory of G. B. Caird.* Edited by L. D. Hurst and N. T. Wright. Oxford: Clarendon, 1987.

The vindication of the crucified Jesus signaled the acceptance of the Gentiles. See also Dunn's commentaries on Romans and Galatians, and his essay in #60.

55 H. Räisänen. "Paul's Conversion and the Development of His View of the Law." *NTS* 33 (1987): 404–19.

Paul only gradually became alienated from the Law.

56 T. L. Donaldson. "Zealot and Convert: The Origin of Paul's Christ-Torah Antithesis." *CBQ* 51 (1989): 655–82.

Important observations concerning the presence of the earliest community that confessed the crucified Jesus as Messiah.

57 A. Segal. "Conversion and Messianism: An Outline for a New Approach." Pp. 296–340 in *The Messiah: Developments in Early Judaism and Christianity.* Edited by J. H. Charlesworth. Minneapolis: Fortress, 1992.

Background to conversion, particularly in early Judaism. Examination of Paul's terminology for conversion and transformation.

58   M. Seifrid. " 'Justification by Faith' and Paul's Conver-
          sion." Pp. 136–81 in *Justification by Faith: The Origin and
          Development of a Central Pauline Theme*. NovTSup 68.
          Leiden: Brill, 1992.
          Argument that Paul's teaching on justification was rooted in
          his conversion. See also #688.

59   L. Hurtado. "Convert, Apostate, or Apostle to the Nations:
          The 'Conversion' of Paul in Recent Scholarship." *Studies
          in Religion/Sciences Religieuses* 22 (1993): 273–84.
          Useful outline and analysis of the issues presently under debate.

60   R. N. Longenecker, ed. *The Road from Damascus: The Im-
          pact of Paul's Conversion on His Life, Thought, and Min-
          istry*. Grand Rapids: Eerdmans, 1997.
          Important collection of essays from various perspectives on
          Paul's conversion and its entailments.

4

History and Chronology
of Paul's Mission

The reconstruction of a chronology of Paul's ministry is essential not only to understanding Paul and his letters, but the growth of earliest Christianity. Theories of development in Paul's understanding of the Law and justification, eschatology and ethics are contingent upon various chronologies. As the following list of sources indicates, we are at a rather uncertain moment in the history of research. Current scholarship is tending to greater disagreement regarding the course of Paul's mission. As Riesner has shown in his indispensable survey (#82, pp. 1–26), once the reliability of Acts is dismissed, little possibility for consensus remains. This observation is no argument for the automatic acceptance of the historicity of Acts, of course. But it is an indication of the subjectivity inherent in each proposal, and cautions that the results of modern researchers must be treated with greater skepticism than they have been. Perennial problems undoubtedly will continue to receive attention in the future: (1) the date of the crucifixion; (2) correlation of the Jerusalem visits of Galatians 1–2 with those of Acts; (3) whether the three and fourteen years (Gal. 1:18 and 2:1) are counted from the same point in time or the latter added to the former; (4) the viability of linking the flight from Damascus to an external date; (5) the date of expulsion of Jews from Rome under Claudius; and (6) the date of the tribunal before Gallio. In addition to the works cited below, those listed in chapter 5, "Overview of Paul's Life and Thought," often contain detailed assessments of Pauline chronology.

61   J. Knox. *Chapters in a Life of Paul.* Rev. ed. Edited by D. R. A. Hare. Macon, Ga.: Mercer University Press, 1987. Original edition: Nashville: Abingdon, 1950.

        Advocating a radical skepticism of the historicity of Acts, Knox developed and subsequently modified a three-Jerusalem-visit chronology of Paul's ministry. Among other features, his proposal included a very late date for Galatians (after Romans!) on the supposition that conflict with opponents increased after the last Jerusalem visit. Although originally he equated the fourteen-year time span of 2 Cor. 12:2 with that of Gal. 2:1, he later discarded this questionable connection. Knox has influenced a number of scholars, including Hurd (#67) and Lüdemann (#71).

62   T. H. Campbell. "Paul's 'Missionary Journeys' as Reflected in His Letters." *JBL* 74 (1955): 80–87.

        A succinct demonstration, still worth attention, that "the general outline of Paul's missionary career as found in Acts is essentially in harmony with that which may be derived from his letters." Acts may therefore be appropriated as a reliable source for the reconstruction of Paul's ministry.

63   J. Finegan. *Handbook of Biblical Chronology.* Rev. ed. Peabody, Mass.: Hendrickson, 1998. Original edition: Princeton: Princeton University Press, 1964.

        Survey of methods of reckoning time in the ancient world with treatment of problems of biblical chronology, including Paul's ministry.

64   G. Ogg. *The Chronology of the Life of Paul.* London: Epworth, 1968.

        Conservative treatment of Acts, advocating a very long "third" missionary journey, A.D. 53–59.

65   K. Haacker. "Die Gallio-Episode." *BZ* 16 (1972): 252–55.

        Deißmann's claim that Paul must have appeared before Gallio near the end of Paul's stay in Corinth does not carry weight (cf. 18:18), nor is it necessary to think that the hearing came near the beginning of Gallio's entrance into office.

66   A. Suhl. *Paulus und seine Briefe: Ein Beitrag zur Paulinischen Chronologie.* SNT 11. Gütersloh: Mohn, 1975.

        Suhl argues that the Jerusalem Conference took place at the time of the reported visit of Acts 11:27–30, so that all Paul's missionary activity took place after the Jerusalem Conference. See now also his major article, "Paulinische Chronologie im Streit der Meinungen," in *Aufstieg und Niedergang der römischen Welt,* ed. H. Temporini and W. Haase, vol. 26/2 (Berlin and New York: de Gruyter, 1995), 939–1188.

67 J. C. Hurd, Jr. "Chronology, Pauline." Pp. 166–67 in *Interpreter's Dictionary of the Bible: Supplement*. Nashville: Abingdon, 1976.

A significant representative of the Knox school. See also *The Origin of 1 Corinthians* (London: SPCK, 1965); "Pauline Chronology and Pauline Theology," in *Christian History and Interpretation* (Cambridge: Cambridge University Press, 1967), 225–48; and "The Sequence of Paul's Letters," *CJT* 14 (1968): 188–200.

68 R. Jewett. *A Chronology of Paul's Life*. Philadelphia: Fortress; London: SCM, 1979. U.K. title: *Dating Paul's Life*.

Jewett advances an important variant of the three-journey approach by accepting the identification of Paul's second visit to Jerusalem as the Apostolic Council (Gal. 2:1–10), and equating this meeting chronologically with the one reported in Acts 18:22. The Apostolic Council then takes place after the first mission to Europe. Among other results, this provides Jewett with an explanation for the lack of the problem of nomism in the Thessalonian correspondence and its apparent emergence as a recent problem in Galatians.

69 P. Klein. "Zum Verständnis von Gal 2:1." *ZNW* 70 (1979): 250–51.

Paul's aim in Gal. 1:11–2:1 is to demonstrate his independence from Jerusalem. The length of his lack of contact with Jerusalem plays an important role in this argument. This consideration suggests that the "fourteen years" of Gal. 2:1 has its starting point in Paul's call, otherwise he would have used the larger number.

70 B. C. Corley, ed. *Colloquy on New Testament Studies: A Time for Reappraisal and Fresh Approaches*. Macon, Ga.: Mercer University Press, 1983.

A 1980 seminar moderated by John C. Hurd, with contributions by Robert Jewett and Gerd Lüdemann, and a subsequent response from John Knox.

71 G. Lüdemann. *Paul, Apostle to the Gentiles: Studies in Chronology*. Translated by F. S. Jones. Philadelphia: Fortress, 1984. German edition: *Paulus, der Heidenapostel*, vol. 1: *Studien zur Chronologie*. FRLANT 123. Göttingen: Vandenhoeck & Ruprecht, 1980.

Proceeding from the assumption that Paul's letters must be used prior to and independently of Acts, Lüdemann argues for an unconventional three-visit chronology. The mission with Barnabas to South Galatia continued in a founding missionary visit to Macedonia and Achaia in 39–41 (1 Thessalonians, Philippians). The Antioch incident took place in this period, prior to the Jerusalem conference. Following the conference, Paul set forth to organize the collection within the congregations he had planted. Troubles within his congregations prompted the writing of 1 Corinthians, 2 Cor. 1–9, 2 Cor. 10–13, and Galatians at this time. On completion of his work, prior to his journey to Jerusalem, he wrote Romans. Among other interesting proposals, Lüdemann postulates that Acts 18:1–17 represents a conflation of earlier and later visits to Corinth. See the critiques by Jewett (#68, p. 82) and Riesner (#82, pp. 18–21).

72   N. Hyldahl. *Die Paulinische Chronologie.* ATDan 19. Leiden: Brill, 1986.

The three-year (Gal. 1:18) and fourteen-year (Gal. 2:1) periods after Paul's calling overlap. The heavenly vision (2 Cor. 12:2) took place shortly before the flight from Damascus (2 Cor. 11:32–33). The eleven-year period between the first two Jerusalem visits therefore is closely tied to the fourteen-year period from the flight from Damascus until the writing of 2 Corinthians. The Sabbath year A.D. 54/55 provides a fixed point for the Jerusalem collection and the entire chronology. The result is a late date for Paul's call (ca. A.D. 39/40). This thesis entails an impossible dating of the flight from Damascus.

73   J. A. Fitzmyer. "The Pauline Letters and the Lucan Account of Paul's Missionary Journeys." Pp. 82–89 in *Society of Biblical Literature 1988 Seminar Papers.* Edited by D. J. Lull. Atlanta: Scholars Press, 1988.

A useful reconsideration of the value of Acts for Pauline chronology, highlighting the correlation of sequences between the letters and Acts, information about Paul's early mission, and an important assessment of the tribunal before Gallio, which Fitzmyer places in early A.D. 52.

74   F. F. Bruce. *The Acts of the Apostles.* 3d ed., revised and enlarged. Grand Rapids: Eerdmans; Leicester, England: Apollos, 1990. [See esp. pp. 46–59, 92–93.] Original edition: London: Tyndale, 1951.

Pithy correlation of Acts and Paul.

75   C. J. Hemer. "Acts and Epistles." Pp. 244–76 in *The Book of Acts in the Setting of Hellenistic History.* Edited by C. Gempf. Winona Lake, Ind.: Eisenbrauns, 1990.

Warning against an a priori prejudice against the historicity of Acts, Hemer argues against the Knox reconstruction of a three-Jerusalem-visit ministry of Paul and Jewett's linking a 37–39 dating of the Damascus escape to a seventeen-year span between the first and second Jerusalem visits (thus placing the

Apostolic Council after the first mission to Macedonia and Achaia). Hemer develops his own chronology from two integrated sequences in Acts which may be linked to external dating: Paul's arrival and ministry in Corinth (50–52) and his last voyage to Jerusalem through his Roman imprisonment (57–62). This leaves two gaps which must be correlated with the evidence of Paul's letters: the pre-50 activities of Paul and the period from 52–57.

76   J. Knox. "On the Pauline Chronology: Buck-Taylor-Hurd Revisited." Pp. 258–74 in *The Conversation Continues: Studies in Paul and John in Honor of J. Louis Martyn.* Edited by R. T. Fortna and B. R. Gaventa. Nashville: Abingdon, 1990.
      A final assessment of the skeptical use of Acts by a pioneer of the method.

77   D. A. Carson, D. J. Moo, and L. Morris. "Paul: The Man and His Letters." Pp. 215–37 in *An Introduction to the New Testament.* Grand Rapids: Zondervan, 1992.
      A five-visit chronology of Paul's ministry, based on a correlation of the information of Acts and Paul's letters, including bibliography.

78   K. P. Donfried. "New Testament Chronology." Vol. 1, pp. 1012–22 in *The Anchor Bible Dictionary.* Edited by D. N. Freedman. New York: Doubleday, 1992.
      A cautious treatment of Pauline chronology. While acknowledging the traditional critical view that correlates Acts 15:1–29 with Gal. 2:1–10, Donfried regards the Knox-Lüdemann approach as a viable alternative.

79   J. Taylor. "The Ethnarch of King Aretas at Damascus: A Note on 2 Cor 11,32–33." *RB* 99 (1992): 719–28.
      Argues from epigraphic evidence of the association of the titles στρατηγός and ἐθνάρχος that Paul refers to the (Nabatean) tribal title of the governor (στρατηγός) of Damascus in 2 Cor. 11:32–33. The Pauline text provides the only evidence for Nabatean rule of Damascus in this period, yet is corroborated by the extent of Nabatean influence (Mommsen). This conclusion reinforces Jewett's location of Paul's flight in the frame of A.D. 37–39. Cf. E. A. Knauf, "Zum Ethnarchen des Aretas 2 Kor 11:32," *ZNW* 74 (1983): 145–47, who argues that there is no evidence that Aretas IV held Damascus and that the dating of Paul's flight is difficult. Taylor seems to have the better case.

80   L. C. A. Alexander. "Chronology of Paul." Pp. 115–23 in *Dictionary of Paul and His Letters.* Downers Grove, Ill., and Leicester, England: InterVarsity, 1993.

Inclined somewhat toward Jewett's three-visit chronology: a sequential reading of Gal. 1:18, 2:1, a solid dating of the Aretas incident (37–39), a probable three- to four-year period of travel and mission between Antioch and the first arrival in Corinth, and placement of the Antioch incident and Apostolic Council after the first Macedonian mission. With Lüdemann, suggests a close chronological link between Gal. 2:10 and Paul's organizing a collection. Yet the author draws no firm conclusion and includes thorough presentations of alternative reconstructions and opposing views.

81 D. Wenham. "Acts and the Pauline Corpus: II. The Evidence of Parallels." Pp. 215–58 in *The Book of Acts in Its Ancient Literary Setting.* Edited by B. W. Winter and A. D. Clarke. Grand Rapids: Eerdmans; Carlisle, England: Paternoster, 1993.

A survey of the historical links between Acts and the letters of Paul, with large space given to the argument that the equation of Acts 11:20 and Gal. 2:1–10 is plausible. See also Longenecker, #414, pp. lxxii–lxxxviii.

82 R. Riesner. *Paul's Early Period: Chronology, Mission Strategy, Theology.* Translated by D. Stott. Grand Rapids: Eerdmans, 1998. German edition: *Die Frühzeit des Apostels Paulus: Studien zur Chronologie, Missionsstrategie und Theologie.* WUNT 71. Tübingen: Mohr (Siebeck), 1994.

A thorough treatment of Pauline chronology, with special attention to the founding of the Thessalonian church. Especially valuable for its close attention to historical background relevant to the reports of Acts. Riesner argues for a relative, not absolute priority for Paul's letters in reconstructing chronology. The letters do not provide the basis for a solid external dating, not even by means of the Aretas incident (2 Cor. 11:32, 33). Riesner therefore calls for a return to the relative "consensus" that prevailed from 1910–80, on the basis of the Gallio inscription and acceptance of the Acts framework.

83 C. Breytenbach. *Paulus und Barnabas in der Provinz Galatien: Studien zu Apostelgeschichte 13f.; 16,6; 18,23 und den Adressaten des Galaterbriefes.* AGJU 38. Leiden: Brill, 1996.

Fresh defense of the South Galatian hypothesis, with attention to local geographical and historical data.

84 M. Hengel and A. M. Schwemer. *Paul between Damascus and Antioch: The Unknown Years.* Translated by J. Bowden. Louisville: Westminster John Knox, 1997. German edition: *Paulus zwischen Damascus und Antiochien: Die*

unbekannte Jahre des Apostels. WUNT 108. Tübingen:
Mohr (Siebeck), 1998.

Reconstruction of Paul's conversion and early missionary activity on the basis of Acts and the early letters of Paul and external sources, suggestive at many points, rich in historical detail and imagination.

5

Overviews of Paul's Life and Thought

Portraits of Paul, in which history, chronology, and theology are brought together, are exceedingly useful. There is always a danger of failing to see how individual exegetical or historical decisions affect our overall image of the apostle. Syntheses, which are generally the province of mature scholars, provide precisely this opportunity. It is interesting to note how many of the recent overviews of Paul's life and thought have continued to insist that Paul's encounter with the risen Christ shaped his understanding of the Law and of justification, despite the challenge of a "new perspective on Paul" (on which, see below). Often those who take up the task of writing an overview regard Paul as a singular figure in the early church, and retain many features of Protestant critical scholarship from the earlier part of the century.

85　R. Bultmann. "Paulus." Vol. 4, cols. 1019–45 in *Die Religion in Geschichte und Gegenwart*. Edited by H. Gunkel and L. Zscharnack. 2d ed. Tübingen: Mohr (Siebeck), 1930.
　　Still of historical interest as the conclusion of the history-of-religions approach to Paul.

86　M. Dibelius. *Paul*. Edited and completed by W. G. Kümmel. Translated by F. Clarke. Philadelphia: Westminster, 1953; London: Longmans, 1951. German edition: *Paulus*. Sammlung Göschen 1160. Berlin: de Gruyter, 1949.
　　A dense, compact synthesis. Paul's persecution of the earliest church was his response to the perceived threat of a crucified Messiah to "aristocratic Pharisaism." This interpretation of Paul overturns the claim that "Lutheranism" has always relied

on a false image of Jewish guilt in constructing its portrait of him.

87 G. Bornkamm. *Paul*. Translated by D. M. G. Stalker. Minneapolis: Fortress, 1995. Original edition: New York: Harper & Row; Toronto: Fitzhenry & Whiteside, 1971. German edition: *Paulus*. 7th ed. Urban-Taschenbücher 119. 1969; Stuttgart: Kohlhammer, 1993.

Lengthy treatment of the background and mission of Paul, with an equally weighty treatment of Paul's theology. Like Bultmann, Bornkamm argues that Paul persecuted a purely Hellenistic community of believers in Damascus. Paul's thought is guided by the unfolding of Christology in terms of justification.

88 O. Kuss. *Paulus: Die Rolle des Apostels in der theologischen Entwicklung der Urkirche*. Auslegung und Verkündigung 3. Regensburg: Friedrich Pustet, 1971.

A massive synthesis by a Catholic scholar. A sketch of Paul's life and ministry based on a critical treatment of Acts, followed by a brief exposition of the "authentic" letters of Paul, then history of interpretation of Paul, followed by a lengthy description of his theology (pp. 270–469). Paul is the "ecumenical herald of salvation at the last hour."

89 F. F. Bruce. *Paul: Apostle of the Heart Set Free*. Grand Rapids: Eerdmans, 1977. U.K. title: *Paul: Apostle of the Free Spirit*. Exeter, England: Paternoster, 1977.

Remarkably thorough treatment of nearly every question that has engaged scholars in the past century.

90 R. Longenecker. *Paul, Apostle of Liberty: The Origin and Nature of Paul's Christianity*. Grand Rapids: Baker, 1976. Original edition: New York: Harper & Row, 1964.

A study of Paul in terms of a "legality-liberty" dialectic. Longenecker seeks to bring together Paul's Jewish background, his apostolic ministry, and the record of Acts. He draws a distinction between "reacting nomism" and "acting legalism." Paul was converted from the latter. The "Jewishness" of the Paul of Acts corresponds with his ethic of love espoused in the letters.

91 J. A. Fitzmyer. *Paul and His Theology: A Brief Sketch*. Englewood Cliffs, N.J.: Prentice Hall, 1989.

As the title indicates, a brief sketch.

92 S. Legasse. *Paul Apotre: Essai de Biographie Critique*. Paris: Cerf, 1991.

Although appreciative of the historical value of Acts, the author places the Antioch incident after the second missionary journey.

93   E. P. Sanders. *Paul.* Past Masters. Oxford: Oxford University Press, 1991.

A condensed presentation of Sanders's Paul. A large portion of the work is taken up with a defense of Sanders's views. Righteousness language, in its "deeper meaning" (76), signifies merely that one dies with Christ and becomes a new person.

94   H. D. Betz. "Paul." Vol. 5, pp. 186–201 in *The Anchor Bible Dictionary.* New York: Doubleday, 1992.

A concise critical treatment of Paul's life, letters, and thought in which the theme of justification by faith is accorded a central role. Although there is development in Paul's thought, his earlier understanding of the offer of righteousness in Christ apart from Torah remained unchanged.

95   J. Becker. *Paul: Apostle to the Gentiles.* Translated by O. C. Dean. Louisville: Westminster John Knox, 1993. German edition: *Paulus: Der Apostel der Völker.* Tübingen: Mohr (Siebeck), 1989.

A noteworthy treatment of background, chronology, and interpretation of the Pauline letters by a mature scholar. Each letter that the author regards as authentic is treated in its historical setting prior to a synthesis of Paul's thought. Paul's understanding of the Law and justification derives from his calling and remains constant throughout his ministry, setting him apart from much of early Christianity. The communal aspect of salvation, shaped by "Paul's experience," is nevertheless integral to his thought, and is expressed in a theology of election.

96   C. K. Barrett. *Paul: An Introduction to His Thought.* Louisville: Westminster John Knox; London: Geoffrey Chapman, 1994.

A brief treatment of Paul's background and mission, followed by a lengthy essay on his theology, and a shorter discussion of Colossians, Ephesians, the Pastoral Epistles, and Acts as the "sequel" to this theology. Paul's thought is largely shaped by controversy with Judaizers, who interpreted the promises of God in the light of the Law. In contrast, he guards the *solus Christus* of salvation through his theology of justification. Barrett is aware of the "new perspective on Paul," but holds his ground.

97   K. Haacker. *Paulus: Der Werdegang eines Apostels.* SBS 71. Stuttgart: Katholisches Bibelwerk, 1997. Original publication: "Zum Werdegang des Apostels Paulus: Bibliographische Daten und ihre theologische Relevanz." Pp. 815–938, 1924–33 in *Aufstieg und Niedergang der römischen Welt.*

Edited by H. Temporini and W. Haase. Vol. II.26.2. Berlin and New York: de Gruyter, 1995.

Survey of the background, conversion, and calling (Haacker rightly insists that the word "conversion" must be retained), and early mission of Paul.

98 J. Gnilka. *Paulus von Tarsus: Apostel und Zeuge.* HTKNT, Supplements 6. Freiburg: Herder, 1996.

A thorough synthesis, which, although it bypasses much of post-Sanders discussion of Paul, is otherwise quite up-to-date in the literature, and displays everywhere the careful work of a mature critical scholar.

99 E. Lohse. *Paulus: Eine Biographie.* Munich: C. H. Beck, 1996.

Critical interpretation of Paul's life and theology by a mature scholar, who maintains distance from the "new perspective" on Paul.

100 A. N. Wilson. *Paul: The Mind of the Apostle.* New York: W. W. Norton; London: Sinclair Stevenson, 1997.

Portrait of Paul by a journalist, à la Wrede (see #16).

101 C. J. den Heyer. *Paul: A Man of Two Worlds.* Translated by J. Bowden. Harrisburg, Pa.: Trinity Press International; London: SCM, 2000. Dutch edition: *Paulus: Man van twee werelden.* Zoetermeer, the Netherlands: Uitgeverij Meinema, 1998.

Critical interpretation of Paul for a popular audience, with much space given to the analysis of individual letters.

102 C. J. Roetzel. *Paul: The Man and the Myth.* Columbia: University of South Carolina Press, 1998.

A biographical treatment of Paul on the basis of topical depictions: early life, apostle to the Gentiles, letter-writer, theologizer, ascetic, and his influence ("the mythic apostle").

103 B. Witherington III. *The Paul Quest: The Renewed Search for the Jew of Tarsus.* Downers Grove, Ill.: InterVarsity, 1998.

Not a survey of research, but a portrait of Paul's person and thought using categories of social description.

104 J. B. Polhill. *Paul and His Letters.* Nashville: Broadman & Holman, 1999.

Balanced, conservative treatment of Paul and his mission, with measured responses to current scholarship and excellent bibliography and considerable attention to history and background.

6

Paul and First-Century Judaism

From about the middle of this century until recently, scholarship increasingly turned to a Jewish and Palestinian background for the interpretation of the core of Paul's thought. The current discussion has been shaped considerably by Sanders's work (#106), so much so that James Dunn has spoken of a prevailing "new perspective on Paul" (see the article under this title in *BJRL* 66 [1983]: 95–122). There are various dimensions in which Paul might be viewed in relation to the Judaism of his day, particularly in his ethical instruction, his "mysticism," and his "apocalypticism." The following bibliography is by no means complete, but should provide an introduction to the range of questions currently in discussion. See also various entries in C. Evans and S. Porter, eds., *Dictionary of New Testament Background* (Downers Grove, Ill.: InterVarsity, 2000).

105 W. D. Davies. *Paul and Rabbinic Judaism.* 4th rev. ed. Philadelphia: Fortress, 1980. Original edition: New York: Harper & Row, 1948.

In a period in which Paul was still interpreted against the backdrop of Hellenism, Davies insisted that the proper background was Palestinian, or "rabbinic," Judaism. He sees a great deal of continuity between Paul and early Judaism, particularly in Jewish eschatological expectations of a change in the Torah. Although this point is questionable, there is much to be gained from this work. The fourth edition is especially important, since it contains the article by Davies mentioned above (see #29), and a response to the work of E. P. Sanders.

106 E. P. Sanders. *Paul and Palestinian Judaism: A Compar-*

ison of Patterns of Religion. Philadelphia: Fortress, 1977.

A demolition of the picture of "life under the Law" as entailing merit and uncertainty of salvation, upon which the history-of-religions portraits of Paul (and liberal ones before them) rested. Sanders characterizes early Judaism as "covenantal nomism," which viewed divine mercy as outweighing any requirement for strict retribution of misdeeds. Paul, in contrast, works from the basic conviction that Christ is Savior of all, by virtue of a saving union with him ("participationist eschatology"). See also Sanders's portrait of Paul (#93); comparison of Jesus and Paul (#179); *Paul, the Law, and the Jewish People* (Philadelphia: Fortress, 1983); and *Judaism: Practice and Belief, 63 BCE–66 CE* (Philadelphia: Trinity Press International; London: SCM, 1992).

107 D. A. Hagner. "Paul in Modern Jewish Thought." Pp. 143–68 in *Pauline Studies: Essays Presented to Professor F. F. Bruce on His Seventieth Birthday.* Edited by D. A. Hagner and M. Harris. Grand Rapids: Eerdmans; Exeter, England: Paternoster, 1980.

While earlier Jewish interpretation of Paul tended to question Paul's familiarity with Palestinian Judaism, more recent Jewish studies have affirmed Paul's Jewishness. According to C. G. Montefiore, Paul did not know the religion represented by rabbinic Judaism, as his pessimism regarding human ability and his understanding of the Law reveal. He has a different soteriology, mysticism, and religious psychology. Similarly, for J. Klausner, Paul was torn between Palestinian Judaism and Jewish Hellenism. For Buber, Paul was thoroughly Hellenized in his understanding of intellectual faith, *fides qua creditur,* over against *emunah,* covenantal trust. For S. Sandmel, Paul's background is to be found in Philo and the Stoics (*The Genius of Paul: A Study in History* [1958; Philadelphia: Fortress, 1979]). Standing in distinction to these are more recent studies by L. Baeck, H. J. Schoeps (*Paulus: Die Theologie des Apostels im Lichte der jüdischen Religionsgeschichte* [Tübingen: Mohr (Siebeck), 1959]), and S. Ben-Chorin, who insist on Paul's Jewishness, which nevertheless is permeated by Hellenism. Treatment of the seemingly undigestible blocks of Paul's Christology and soteriology largely depends on what one does with the Damascus-road encounter with Christ. See now, D. A. Hagner, "Paul and Judaism: The Jewish Matrix of Early Christianity: Issues in the Current Debate," *BBR* 3 (1993): 111–30; and "Paul's Quarrel with Judaism," in *Anti-Semitism and Early Christianity,* ed. C. A. Evans and D. A. Hagner (Minneapolis: Fortress, 1993), 128–50.

108 F. Thielman. *From Plight to Solution: A Jewish Framework*

*for Understanding Paul's View of the Law in Galatians
and Romans.* NovTSup 61. Leiden: Brill, 1989.

> First-century Jews awaited a divine intervention which would
> end Israel's rebelliousness and create new obedience. One such
> Jew was Paul, who interpreted Jesus' death and resurrection as
> constituting this eschatological act of God. This is both a re-
> sponse to Sanders (#106) and an attempt to find continuity be-
> tween Paul and early Judaism in a posited widespread lament
> over a continuing "exile." On this latter topic see N. T. Wright
> (#522; esp. pp. 147–279).

109 A. Segal. *Paul the Convert: The Apostolate and Apostasy
of Saul the Pharisee.* New Haven: Yale University Press,
1990.

> On the basis of a sociological perspective, Segal, a Jewish
> scholar, affirms that Paul indeed underwent a conversion. Paul
> was a Jewish apocalyptic mystic who had an ecstatic experi-
> ence, like Ezekiel's throne vision. He transferred the character-
> istics of conversion-oriented sectarian Judaism to the Diaspora.
> Yet for Paul, faith, not Torah, was the mark of the community.
> He was not against the Law, but ritual boundaries. Segal has
> difficulty accounting for Rom. 7, although he attempts it.

110 M. Bockmuehl. *Revelation and Mystery in Ancient Judaism and Pauline Christianity.* WUNT 2/36. Tübingen:
Mohr (Siebeck), 1990.

> Paul's understanding of mystery and revelation is structurally
> similar to that of early Judaism, in which "mystery" designated
> the content of revelation given to inspired interpreters of
> Torah. Paul's thought, however, evidences a decisive shift.
> Torah for him is a witness to Christ, in whom the final revela-
> tion of God's righteousness has been given.

111 P. Tomson. *Paul and the Jewish Law: Halakha in the Letters of the Apostle to the Gentiles.* CRINT 3/1. Assen, the
Netherlands: Van Gorcum; Minneapolis: Fortress, 1990.

> An excellent study, in the line of W. D. Davies, uncovering par-
> allels between Paul's moral directives and early Jewish tradi-
> tion. Paul expected Gentiles to adhere to the Noachian com-
> mandments, and therefore provides them with *halakhah*. Yet
> Tomson underplays the paradoxical character of the "impera-
> tive" in Paul's letters: it is contained within the indicative.
> "Christ," not the Law (and *halakhah*), is the controlling para-
> digm for Paul's appropriation of—the word that Paul chooses is
> significant—"Scripture" (e.g., 1 Cor. 9:21, Gal. 6:2).

112 M. Hengel. *The Pre-Christian Paul.* In collaboration with
R. Deines. Philadelphia: Trinity Press International, 1991.

Paul had Pharisaic training in Jerusalem, and yet was acquainted with the Diaspora synagogue. He persecuted Hellenistic Jewish believers who adopted a critical stance in relation to cultic requirements of the Law.

113 T. Laato. *Paul and Judaism: An Anthropological Approach.* South Florida Studies in the History of Judaism 115. Atlanta: Scholars Press, 1995. German and Finnish edition: *Paulus und das Judentum: Anthropologische Erwägungen.* Turku, Finland: Åbo Akademis Förlag, 1991.

Laato clearly sets forth the "pessimism" of Paul—his radical diagnosis of the state of the fallen human being—as the fundamental difference between Paul and his Jewish contemporaries.

114 S. Westerholm and P. Richardson. *Law in Religious Communities in the Roman Period: The Debate over Torah and Nomos in Post-biblical Judaism and Early Christianity.* Studies in Christianity and Judaism 4. Waterloo, Ont.: Wilfrid Laurier University Press, 1991. [See esp. pp. 19–92.]

The several essays by Westerholm on (mainly) Protestant interpretation of "the Law" and of Paul provide an excellent introduction to current issues.

115 W. Stegner. "Paul the Jew." Pp. 503–11 in *Dictionary of Paul and His Letters.* Downers Grove, Ill., and Leicester, England: InterVarsity, 1993.

Paul's education, use of the Old Testament, apocalyptic worldview, and elements of mysticism in his thought reveal his continuing Jewish identity.

116 J. M. Scott. "Restoration of Israel." Pp. 796–805 in *Dictionary of Paul and His Letters.* Downers Grove, Ill., and Leicester, England: InterVarsity, 1993.

Paul stood in the stream of eschatological Judaism that looked forward to the restoration of Israel from exile. This idea was fundamental to his theology and mission.

117 D. Boyarin. *A Radical Jew: Paul and the Politics of Identity.* Berkeley: University of California Press, 1994.

A provocative reading of Paul by a Jewish scholar. Paul, living in tension between Jewish monotheism and Hellenistic universalism, thinks in Platonic terms, interprets Scripture allegorically, and embraces a "disembodied ethic." Despite the questionability of this thesis, Boyarin rightly perceives the implicit dangers in the "new perspective on Paul." The form of Pauline universalism which the new perspective on Paul generally presupposes eliminates ethnic particularism and its signs and thereby threatens the domination of minorities.

118 F. Avemarie. *Tora und Leben: Untersuchungen zur Heils-*

bedeutung der Tora in der frühen rabbinischen Literatur.
TSAJ 55. Tübingen: Mohr (Siebeck), 1996.

Remarkable in both its thoroughness and careful handling of the materials, this work will be the standard by which all other treatments of rabbinic views on salvation are judged for a long time. Rabbinic utterances regarding the Law must be understood "aspectually," without forcing a systematic unity on them. This means, among other things, that Sanders's theory fails to account for the sayings in which participation in the age to come, or in eternal life, is contingent on obedience, just as Weber and P. Billerbeck failed to account for sayings that stress another way to eternal life other than that of weighing merit (and larger purposes for the Law as well).

119   R. Deines. *Die Pharisäer: Ihr Verständnis im Spiegel der christlichen und jüdischen Forschung seit Wellhausen und Graetz.* WUNT 101. Tübingen: Mohr (Siebeck), 1997.

Penetrating study of the history of research; essential reading. See also Deines's essay in #123.

120   T. Donaldson. *Paul and the Gentiles: Remapping the Apostle's Convictional World.* Minneapolis: Fortress, 1997.

Gentiles could share in Israel's means of righteousness and hope of salvation, but only by being "in Christ" and thus becoming members of a redefined, eschatological Israel. As with Wilckens (#46), above, it remains questionable whether this paradigm is adequate.

121   T. Eskola. *Theodicy and Predestination in Pauline Soteriology.* WUNT 2/100. Tübingen: Mohr (Siebeck), 1998.

Early Judaism was characterized by a crisis of theodicy that issued in a "predestinarian" soteriology, according to which those who repented and kept the Law would be saved. It may therefore be characterized as a "synergistic nomism." In contrast, Paul adopted a predestination of judgment (according to which all are under condemnation) and Christocentric predestinarianism (according to which God calls to salvation through the gospel).

122   M. Elliott. *The Survivors of Israel: A Reconsideration of the Theology of Pre-Christian Judaism.* Grand Rapids: Eerdmans, 2000.

Over against the prevailing paradigm of "covenantal nomism," Elliott finds that the main pseudepigraphal writings expect divine judgment to fall on an apostate Israel. The soteriology is exclusivistic: only those who lived by the "true" interpretation of Scripture (which often involved calendrical disputes) would be saved. In Second Temple "remnant groups," such dualistic covenantal soteriology prevailed. They expected the time of judgment in which the wicked (within Israel!) would be destroyed and the righteous preserved, as in the flood narrative (which became a significant paradigm in such early Jewish writings). Only the remnant, "the survivors of Israel," will be saved and vindicated before the rest of the nation.

123 D. A. Carson, P. O'Brien, and M. Seifrid, eds. *Justification and Variegated Nomism*. Vol. 1: *The Complexities of Second Temple Judaism*. Grand Rapids: Baker; Tübingen: Mohr (Siebeck), 2001.

Collection of essays that reexamines early Jewish writings in light of E. P. Sanders's theory of "covenantal nomism."

7

Paul and the Greco-Roman World

There was considerable interest at the beginning of the twentieth century in the relation of earliest Christianity to the Greco-Roman world. German scholars in particular produced a number of studies (inter alia, A. Deissmann, E. Norden [#210], J. Weiss, A. Bonhöffer, H. Wendland, H. Lietzmann). This concern diminished for several decades, only to resurge in the last fifteen years or so. In considerable measure, theological interpretation in the middle part of the twentieth century was set over against and displaced such historical work. Furthermore, any response to the history-of-religions school (in which Christianity was regarded as a syncretistic phenomenon) had to be drawn from Jewish sources. Likewise, early sociological studies tended to claim too much explanatory power (as if the rise of early Christianity could be fully comprehended sociologically), and consequently fell into neglect. The study of Paul, his letters, and his churches within the context of the Greco-Roman world will undoubtedly play an increasingly large, if not dominant, role in research for some time to come. The breadth and variety of topics within this field, and the rapid growth of the number of publications dealing with these aspects of Paul and his letters, allow only a representative sampling of publications. It is useful to divide current study into three general areas (even if they overlap one another): religious and philosophical, social, and rhetorical backgrounds. We reserve the last of these areas for a later, separate section of the bibliography (see §11.3, "Rhetorical Criticism"). Here we shall treat the first two in independent subsections.

A word of introduction to the study of the social background of Paul's letters is in order. A range of approaches currently compete with one another. At the one end are those who insist on attention to the "realia," the hard data derived from ancient sources, and require that all syntheses arise from the details: Edwin Judge, a classical scholar, and those under his influence stand out here in particular. At the other end are those who approach the materials with an overarching sociological model. Both approaches have their dangers. We all operate with presupposed "models," so that a completely neutral position is not attainable. On the other hand (and here lies the greater danger), we also may be tempted to stretch data to fit our framework, or to ignore aspects of the text that contradict a modern approach. Eclectic use of sociological models may often prove useful. Obviously those studies best able to synthesize primary data with comprehensive frameworks (however they might be derived) will always be the most persuasive and illuminating. In addition to the works listed below, dictionary articles should be consulted. In *ABD*, see D. Balch, "Household Codes," 3:318–20; H. D. Betz, "Hellenism," 3:127–35; B. Fiore, "Parenesis and Protreptic," 5:162–65; and J. Fitzgerald, "Haustafeln," 3:80–81. In *DPL*, see P. Towner, "Households and Household Codes," 417–19; D. Aune, "Religions, Greco-Roman," 786–96; T. Paige, "Philosophy, Greco-Roman," 713–18; E. Yamauchi, "Hellenism," 383–88; and idem, "Gnosis, Gnosticism," 350–54. See also various entries in C. Evans and S. Porter, eds., *Dictionary of New Testament Background* (Downers Grove, Ill.: InterVarsity, 2000).

7.1 Religious and Philosophical Background

124 J. Sevenster. *Paul and Seneca*. NovTSup 4. Leiden: Brill, 1961.
> Comparison of Paul with the Stoicism of Seneca, in the areas of theology, anthropology, social relations, and eschatology. Sevenster draws sharp distinctions between the two.

125 R. McL. Wilson. *Gnosis and the New Testament*. Oxford: Basil Blackwell, 1968. [See esp. pp. 31–59.]
> Gnostic motifs may be traced to the pre-Christian period, but not fully developed Gnosticism.

126 E. Yamauchi. *Pre-Christian Gnosticism: A Survey of the Proposed Evidences*. Grand Rapids: Baker; London: Tyndale, 1973.
> Survey of the evidence and criticism of the method of the history-of-religions school: Gnosticism is represented by late

sources and was a diverse phenomenon. There is no solid evidence for a fully developed "pre-Christian gnosticism."

127 D. Wiens. "Mystery Concepts in Primitive Christianity and Its Environment." Pp. 1248–84 in *Aufstieg und Niedergang der römischen Welt*. Edited by H. Temporini and W. Haase. Vol. 23/2. Berlin and New York: de Gruyter, 1980.

Extremely useful treatment of history of research, current questions, and the significance of the mystery religions for earliest Christianity. See also Wedderburn (#705).

128 W. Schmithals. "The Corpus Paulinum and Gnosis." Pp. 107–24 in *The New Testament and Gnosis*. Edited by A. H. B. Logan and A. J. M. Wedderburn. Edinburgh: T. & T. Clark, 1983.

Survey of Paul from a scholar who sees Gnosticism everywhere.

129 J. Fitzgerald. *Cracks in an Earthen Vessel: An Examination of the Catalogues of Hardships in the Corinthian Correspondence*. SBLDS 99. Atlanta: Scholars Press, 1988.

Thorough history of research. Reassertion of the Hellenistic background of the "catalogs of hardships," over against Schrage's insistence on a Jewish background. Paul's use of *peristasis* catalogs shows an awareness of their similar use by moral philosophers. He is distinctive in his use of OT traditions of the suffering righteous, and in his understanding of the crucified Christ.

130 A. Malherbe. *Paul and the Popular Philosophers*. Philadelphia: Fortress, 1989.

Series of essays comparing Paul with the traditions employed by Greco-Roman philosophers. See also #500.

131 D. Balch and W. Meeks. *Greeks, Romans, and Christians: Essays in Honor of Abraham J. Malherbe*. Minneapolis: Fortress, 1990.

Includes various articles on Paul: D. Balch, "The Areopagus Speech," 52–79; C. Holladay, "1 Corinthians 13: Paul as Apostolic Paradigm," 80–98; S. Garrett, "The God of This World and the Affliction of Paul: 2 Cor 4:1–2," 99–117; J. Neyrey, "Acts 17: Epicureans and Theodicy," 118–34; B. Fiore, "Passion in Paul and Plutarch," 135–43; J. Fitzgerald, "Paul, the Ancient Epistolary Theorists, and 2 Cor 10–13," 190–200; M. White, "Morality between Two Worlds: A Paradigm of Friendship in Philippians," 210–15; T. Olbricht, "An Aristotelian Rhetorical Analysis of 1 Thessalonians," 216–36; D. Lührmann, "The Beginnings of the Church at Thessalonica," 237–52; S. Stowers, "Paul on the Use and Abuse of Reason," 253–86; W. Meeks,

"The Circle of Reference in Pauline Morality," 305–17; and B. Lategan, "Is Paul Developing a Specifically Christian Ethics in Galatians?" 318–28.

132 D. Balch. "Neopythagorean Moralists and the New Testament Household Codes." Pp. 380–411 in *Aufstieg und Niedergang der römischen Welt*. Edited by H. Temporini and W. Haase. Vol. 26/1. Berlin and New York: de Gruyter, 1992.
Neo-Pythagorean texts are closer to the New Testament texts than Stoic or Hellenistic Jewish parallels usually suggested.

133 A. Malherbe. "Hellenistic Moralists and the New Testament." Pp. 267–333 in *Aufstieg und Niedergang der römischen Welt*. Edited by H. Temporini and W. Haase. Vol. 26/1. Berlin and New York: de Gruyter, 1992.
Essential reading for advanced study. Includes a history of research, treatment of 1 Thessalonians as a "parenetic letter," discussion of the household codes (*Haustafeln*), the diatribe, *topoi* (stock treatments of moral subjects), virtue and vice lists, and other matters.

134 M. E. Boring, K. Berger, and C. Colpe. *Hellenistic Commentary to the New Testament*. Nashville: Abingdon, 1995.
Suggested parallels to NT texts. See also #135.

135 G. Strecker and U. Schnelle. *Neuer Wettstein: Texte zum Neuen Testament aus Griechentum und Hellenismus*. Vol. 2. Pts. 1 and 2. Berlin and New York: de Gruyter, 1996.
Fresh collection of Greco-Roman materials relevant to NT texts in the tradition of Johann Jakob Wettstein, *Novum Testamentum Graece* (1751–52).

7.2 Social Background

136 E. Judge. *The Social Pattern of the Christian Groups in the First Century*. London: Tyndale, 1960.
Overview of social relations in early Christianity, which included persons of high status.

137 A. N. Sherwin-White. *Roman Society and Roman Law in the New Testament*. Oxford: Clarendon, 1963.
Displays the close connections between the account of Acts and Roman law. See now Tajra (#152).

138 E. Judge. "St. Paul and Classical Society." *JAC* 13 (1972): 19–36.
An appeal for the study of the social and historical urban background of Paul's Christianity.

139 S. Bartchy. *MAΛΛΟΝ ΧΡΗΣΑΙ: First-Century Slavery and*

the Interpretation of 1 Corinthians 7:21. SBLDS 11. Missoula, Mont.: Society of Biblical Literature, 1973.
> Interpretation of this verse against the background of slavery in the Greco-Roman world.

140 F. F. Bruce. "The New Testament and Classical Studies." *NTS* 22 (1976): 229–42.
> Brief overview and appeal for the relevance of classical studies, especially for the study of the Book of Acts.

141 E. Judge. "'Antike und Christentum': Towards a Definition of the Field, A Bibliographical Survey." Pp. 3–85 in *Aufstieg und Niedergang der römischen Welt.* Edited by H. Temporini and W. Haase. Vol. 23/1. Berlin and New York: de Gruyter, 1979.
> Account of F. J. Dölger's founding the journal *Jahrbuch für Antike und Christentum (JAC)*, and the subsequent preparation of the *Reallexikon für Antike und Christentum*, followed by a survey of classical studies relevant to early Christianity.

142 R. Hock. *The Social Context of Paul's Ministry: Tentmaking and Apostleship.* Philadelphia: Fortress, 1980.
> Paul's practices and instructions to the Thessalonians reflect moral traditions of Greco-Roman philosophers, and their view of status.

143 J. P. Sampley. *Pauline Partnership in Christ: Christian Community and Commitment in Light of Roman Law.* Philadelphia: Fortress, 1980.
> Along with other, larger models of Christian community, Paul used the Roman legal terminology and concepts of *societas*, consensual partnership among various Christians. See the critique from L. Bormann (#161).

144 D. Balch. *Let Wives Be Submissive: The Domestic Code in I Peter.* SBLMS 26. Chico, Calif.: Scholars Press, 1981.
> Pressure for the adoption of the household code came from Greco-Roman society, which was suspicious of Eastern cults. The usual Greco-Roman demand is addressed to Christian wives, who are encouraged to maintain their own religion, and therefore the motive of the exhortation is both missionary and apologetic. This study surpasses that of J. E. Crouch, *The Origin and Intention of the Colossian Haustafel,* FRLANT 109 (Göttingen: Vandenhoeck & Ruprecht, 1972).

145 W. Meeks. *The First Urban Christians: The Social World of the Apostle Paul.* New Haven: Yale University Press, 1983.
> Important work in the resurgence of study of the social back-

ground of earliest Christianity. Meeks gives attention both to the historical data and various sociological models. Exploration of the "social world" of the first Christians: both the world in which they lived and the "world" they constructed.

146 D. Verner. *The Household of God: The Social World of the Pastoral Epistles.* SBLDS 71. Chico, Calif.: Scholars Press, 1983.

The church of the Pastoral Epistles is large, and tended to be led by those who came from the ranks of the wealthy. There were gnosticizing tendencies, which may have arisen in reaction to the dominant patriarchal structure. These views are quite popular now, even if they are questionable.

147 E. Judge. "Cultural Conformity and Innovation in Paul: Some Clues from Contemporary Documents." *TynBul* 35 (1984): 324.

Paul's relation to the patronal system. See also Judge's *Rank and Status in the World of the Caesars and St. Paul,* University of Canterbury Publication 29 (Canterbury, England: University of Canterbury Press, 1984).

148 N. Peterson. *Rediscovering Paul: Philemon and the Sociology of Paul's Narrative World.* Philadelphia: Fortress, 1985.

Approach to Paul through the model of Clifford Geertz's "symbolic" world. The problem of returning the converted slave to Paul brings a shift from equality between Paul and Philemon, to Paul's assertion of translocal authority. Paul puts his case at the "cosmic" level, which he expects the congregation shares with him.

149 J. Stambaugh and D. Balch. *The New Testament in Its Social Environment.* LEC 2. Philadelphia: Westminster; London: SPCK, 1986. U.K. title: *The Social World of the First Christians.*

Useful overview of the structures of first-century society.

150 P. Marshall. *Enmity in Corinth: Social Conventions in Paul's Relations with the Corinthians.* WUNT 2/23. Tübingen: Mohr (Siebeck), 1987.

Marshall seeks to reconstruct the stormy relations between Paul and the Corinthians on the basis of Greco-Roman understandings of friendship and patronage. Paul's refusal of support from a wealthy faction within the Corinthian church caused a breach in friendship and led to the formation of an alliance with the "false" ("excessive, hybristic") apostles. Paul's skilled response suggests that he was well-trained in rhetoric, and of relatively high social status, but deliberately set it aside on the basis of his understanding of the gospel.

151 M. MacDonald. *The Pauline Churches: A Socio-historical Study of Institutionalization in the Pauline and Deutero-Pauline Writings.* SNTSMS 60. Cambridge: Cambridge University Press, 1988.

Working from P. Berger and T. Luckmann's sociology of knowledge and Weberian analysis of routinization of charisma (with correction from Holmberg), MacDonald argues that social structure of the Pauline churches changed in the post-Pauline period, with increasing emphasis on the stabilization of the community (Colossians and Ephesians) and protection from false teaching (Pastoral Epistles). The Greco-Roman household, already important as a model for the church with Paul, took on increasing significance and provided more rigid structures for the churches. The desire to evangelize and tensions with outsiders also helped shape the Christian communities. See, however, U. Brockhaus, *Charisma und Amt* (Wuppertal, Germany: R. Brockhaus, 1972); Ellis (#760); and Clarke (#157), who develop good arguments against this traditional interpretation.

152 H. Tajra. *The Trial of St. Paul.* WUNT 2/35. Tübingen: Mohr (Siebeck), 1989.

A new treatment like that of Sherwin-White (see #137). Luke's account of Paul's trial implies detailed knowledge of legal practices and language in the Roman empire.

153 B. Holmberg. *Sociology and the New Testament: An Appraisal.* Minneapolis: Fortress, 1990.

Employs church-sect typology (Weber) and perspectives from the sociology of knowledge to correlate Christian beliefs and their social context. Social level of the first Christians and early Christianity viewed as a millenarian sect, with much critical discussion of various recent proposals.

154 D. Martin. *Slavery as Salvation: The Metaphor of Slavery in Pauline Christianity.* New Haven and London: Yale University Press, 1990.

Ancient slavery did not necessarily mean low status. The notion of an "enslaved leader" appears as a rhetorical *topos* in antiquity for populist leaders. Paul takes it up in order to undermine the assumptions of privilege among those of high status in the Corinthian congregation, and thereby establishes his authority.

155 J. Neyrey. *Paul, in Other Words: A Cultural Reading of His Letters.* Louisville: Westminster John Knox, 1990.

A reading of Paul on the basis of the work of the anthropologist Mary Douglas, in which holy/profane distinctions order the world. See Mary Douglas, *Purity and Danger: An Analysis of Concepts of Pollution and Taboo* (1969; London: Routledge and Kegan Paul, 1978).

156 G. Theissen. *Social Reality and the Early Christians: Theology, Ethics, and the World of the New Testament.* Translated by M. Kohl. Minneapolis: Fortress, 1992.

See "Soteriological Symbolism in the Pauline Writings," 159–86; "Christology and Social Experience," 187–201; and "Judaism and Christianity in Paul," 202–30.

157 A. Clarke. *Secular and Christian Leadership in Corinth: A Socio-historical and Exegetical Study of 1 Corinthians 1–6.* AGJU 18. Leiden: Brill, 1993.

Representative of the "realia" approach, oriented toward the primary data. Paul confronts secular models of Christian leadership within the Corinthian congregation. Elite members of the congregation were taking others to court to enhance their status. The toleration of immorality might have been due to expediency, an unwillingness to challenge someone of high status. Critical of Weberian analysis that posits a rising institutionalism and Sohm's conclusion that there was no hierarchical leadership in the community.

158 B. Winter. *Seek the Welfare of the City: Christians as Benefactors and Citizens.* Grand Rapids: Eerdmans, 1994.

Paul's application of the gospel in the context of patronage.

159 D. Gill and C. Gempf. *The Book of Acts in Its Greco-Roman Setting.* Grand Rapids: Eerdmans, 1994.

Essays on the historical and social background of Acts.

160 B. Rapske. *The Book of Acts and Paul in Roman Custody.* The Book of Acts in Its First-Century Setting. Grand Rapids: Eerdmans; Carlisle, England: Paternoster, 1994.

In a manner which fits contemporary practices and views, Luke portrays the dissonant element of Paul's status, showing how it has led to his mistreatment, ultimately intending to show that he enjoys divine approval.

161 L. Bormann. *Philippi: Stadt und Christengemeinde zur Zeit des Paulus.* NovTSup 78. Leiden: Brill, 1995.

The patron-client relation with Paul and the Philippians' political understanding in light of contemporary materials.

162 W. Deming. *Paul on Marriage and Celibacy: The Hellenistic Background of 1 Corinthians 7.* SNTSMS 83. Cambridge: Cambridge University Press, 1995.

Paul's treatment of marriage is similar to Stoic thought, and the position he counters bears similarities to Cynic ideas on marriage and social obligations.

163   T. Engberg-Pedersen, ed. *Paul in His Hellenistic Context.* Minneapolis: Fortress, 1995.

Essays on the rhetorical, moral-philosophical, and social background to Paul's thought and practice in the Hellenistic world, with an excellent introductory essay by the editor. Mystical elements in Paul's thought became the focus of the history-of-religions school—but this interest, focused on Gnosticism, moved toward Jewish backgrounds. A reassessment is overdue.

164   J. Harrill. *The Manumission of Slaves in Early Christianity.* HUT 32. Tübingen: Mohr (Siebeck), 1995.

Survey of slavery in the ancient world, confirmation of Bartchy's reading of μᾶλλον χρῆσαι in 1 Cor. 7:21 as "use freedom," and argument that corporate manumission was widespread in the ancient world.

165   J. Taylor, S.M. "St Paul and the Roman Empire: Acts of the Apostles 13–14." Pp. 1189–1231 in *Aufstieg und Niedergang der römischen Welt.* Edited by H. Temporini and W. Haase. Vol. 26/2. Berlin and New York: de Gruyter, 1995.

Historical and geographical background.

166   B. Witherington III. *Conflict and Community in Corinth: A Socio-rhetorical Commentary on 1 and 2 Corinthians.* Grand Rapids: Eerdmans; Carlisle, England: Paternoster, 1995.

Combines analysis in terms of classical rhetoric with attention to the social realities of the Corinthian situation. Thorough bibliography. See also Witherington's shorter commentary, *Friendship and Finances in Philippi,* The New Testament in Context (Valley Forge, Pa.: Trinity Press International, 1994).

167   B. Malina and J. Neyrey. *Portraits of Paul: An Archaeology of Ancient Personality.* Louisville: Westminster John Knox, 1996.

Paul interpreted in terms of a "collectivist" understanding of culture, in which group aims have priority over individual aims. Ironically, Malina and Neyrey's work is rather individualist in nature, not taking into account the broader community of scholarship, which finds a rising individualism in the Hellenistic period (cf. M. Hengel, *Judaism and Hellenism* [Philadelphia: Fortress, 1974], 1:116–17).

168   R. Strelan. *Paul, Artemis, and the Jews in Ephesus.* BZNW 80. Berlin and New York: de Gruyter, 1996.

Paul's missionary work in Ephesus against the background of the Artemis cult. Paul had very little success, and that success he did see was probably among Jews. This is the evidence of Paul himself and Luke. A wealth of information of the religious and social context of Ephesus.

169 C. Wansink. *Chained in Christ: The Experience and Rhetoric of Paul's Imprisonments.* JSNTSup 130. Sheffield: Sheffield Academic Press, 1996.
First-century imprisonment, Paul's presentation of it, and the tradition of it in the early church.

170 R. A. Horsley, ed. *Paul and Empire: Religion and Power in Roman Imperial Society.* Harrisburg, Pa.: Trinity Press International, 1997.
Collection of essays.

171 B. Winter. *Philo and Paul among the Sophists.* Cambridge: Cambridge University Press, 1997.
Philo and Paul both shared the *paideia* on which the sophistic movement was based. Just as Philo rejected the movement in Alexandria, Paul did so in Corinth, where the church wrongly conceptualized its relation to him as that of disciples of a Sophist.

172 F. G. Downing. *Cynics, Paul, and the Pauline Churches: Cynics and Christian Origins.* London: Routledge, 1998.
On the basis of the embodiment of Gal. 3:28 as a lifestyle, Paul would have been regarded as a Cynic by his Greco-Roman contemporaries.

173 T. Engberg-Pedersen. *Paul and the Stoics.* Edinburgh: T. & T. Clark, 2000.
The main lines of Paul's theology in Philippians, Galatians, and Romans interpreted in terms of Stoic thought.

174 B. Winter. *After Paul Left Corinth: The Influence of Secular Ethics and Social Change.* Grand Rapids: Eerdmans, 2001.
Exploration of the origin and nature of the problems concerning discipleship, incest, ligitation, homosexuality, and idol meats which erupted only after Paul's departure from Corinth.

8

Paul and Jesus

The question of continuity between Paul and Jesus was elevated to the status of a "problem" in the critical scholarship of the late nineteenth century. In contrast to Jesus' so-called ethical religion, Paul offered a religion of redemption, and therefore could be described as the second founder of Christianity (see #16). Skepticism regarding the historicity of the gospel traditions raised the problem of how "the proclaimer became the proclaimed" (Bultmann; see his essays "Jesus and Paul," in *Existence and Faith*, edited and translated by S. Odgen, Living Age Books [New York: World, 1960; London: Hodder & Stoughton, 1961], 183–201; and "The Significance of the Historical Jesus for the Theology of Paul," in *Faith and Understanding*, translated by L. Smith, vol. 1 [New York: Harper & Row, 1969], 220–46.) Clearly, the relation between Paul and Jesus involves questions of both historical and theological continuity. The lines of questioning run in at least four directions: (1) the particularity of Paul's letters directed to post-Easter Gentile churches and their needs (to which Jesus' words did not always speak directly); (2) the purpose of Jesus and his own understanding of his mission and death; (3) the salvation-historical significance of the cross and resurrection; and (4) the importance and stability of the traditions of Jesus' words and deeds in the earliest church.

175 E. Jüngel. *Paulus und Jesus*. 6th ed. HUT 2. Tübingen: Mohr (Siebeck), 1986. Original edition: 1962.
   A comparison of Paul's teaching on justification with Jesus' parables of the kingdom.

176 D. L. Dungan. *The Sayings of Jesus in the Churches of Paul: The Use of the Synoptic Tradition in the Regulation of Early Church Life.* Philadelphia: Fortress; Oxford: Basil Blackwell, 1971.

Detailed examination of two passages in which Paul cites Jesus explicitly (1 Cor. 9:4–18; 1 Cor. 7:1–7) in comparison with the Gospels shows how allusive his usage is, and suggests that he supposed his congregations knew a great deal of the sayings contained in the Synoptic tradition.

177 F. F. Bruce. *Paul and Jesus.* Grand Rapids: Baker, 1974; London: SPCK, 1977.

Brief survey and discussion of the issues.

178 D. Allison, Jr. "The Pauline Epistles and the Synoptic Gospels: The Pattern of the Parallels." *NTS* 28 (1982): 1–32.

References to Jesus' sayings turn up in a few distinct sections of Paul's letters (Rom. 12–14; 1 Thess. 4–5; Col. 3–4; 1 Corinthians), and draw upon distinct discourse material found in the Gospels (missionary discourse, Mark 9:33–50; Luke 6:27–38). On this topic see also Davies (#105, pp. 136–46).

179 E. P. Sanders. "Jesus, Paul, and Judaism." Pp. 390–450 in *Aufstieg und Niedergang der römischen Welt.* Edited by H. Temporini and W. Haase. Vol. 25/1. Berlin: de Gruyter, 1982.

Jesus expected the imminent reign of God (this is what the cleansing of the temple signified) and included the outcasts in the covenantal hope of salvation. Paul radicalized Jesus' inclusivity by insisting on the inclusion of the Gentiles, and thereby assigned the Law to a limited role.

180 P. Richardson and J. C. Hurd, eds. *From Jesus to Paul: Studies in Honor of Francis Wright Beare.* Waterloo, Ont.: Wilfrid Laurier University Press, 1984.

Collection of essays from a variety of perspectives on Paul's relation to Jesus. See especially the overview by S. G. Wilson, "From Jesus to Paul: The Contours and Consequences of a Debate," 1–21.

181 E. Schweizer. "The Testimony to Jesus in the Early Christian Community." *HBT* 7 (1985): 77–98.

Acute reflections on the unity and diversity of the Christian tradition regarding Jesus' teaching and the confession of him as Christ.

182 F. Neirynck. "Paul and the Sayings of Jesus." Pp. 265–321 in *L'Apôtre Paul: Personnalité, Style et Conception du*

Ministère. Edited by A. Vanhoye. BETL 73. Louvain: Louvain University Press, 1986.

> Aside from 1 Cor. 7:10–11 and 9:14 there are no explicit references to commands of the Lord in Paul's letters. There is no certain trace of a conscious use of Jesus' sayings.

183   A. J. M. Wedderburn, ed. *Paul and Jesus: Collected Essays.* JSNTSup 37. Sheffield: JSOT Press, 1989.

> Useful collection, with a number of essays by the editor (which appear elsewhere as journal articles). See especially the article by V. P. Furnish, "The Jesus-Paul Debate: From Baur to Bultmann," 17–50.

184   J. D. G. Dunn. "Paul's Knowledge of the Jesus Tradition." Pp. 193–207 in *Christus Bezeugen: Für Wolfgang Trilling.* Edited by K. Kertelge, T. Holtz, and C.-P. März. Freiburg: Herder, 1990.

> Paul alluded to Jesus as a model for Christians in writing to house churches in Rome that he had not planted. He must therefore have assumed such knowledge on these churches' part. Yet the Jesus-tradition was not fixed. It was a "living tradition."

185   T. Holtz. "Paul and the Oral Gospel Tradition." Pp. 380–93 in *Jesus and the Oral Gospel Tradition.* Edited by H. Wansbrough. JSNTSup 64. Sheffield: Sheffield Academic Press, 1991.

> Two modes of transmission: both fixed and free. That is not to say that there are two kinds of tradition, but that the early church put the sayings of Jesus having to do with ethics in words related to its own situation. Sayings related to the coming of the kingdom remained relatively fixed.

186   S. Patterson. "Paul and the Jesus Tradition: It Is Time for Another Look." *HTR* 84 (1991): 23–41.

> The author proposes the *Gospel of Thomas* as a help to seeing how the sayings of Jesus were used in the early Christian community, and hence how Paul received them.

187   M. Thompson. *Clothed with Christ: The Example and Teaching of Jesus in Romans 12.–15.13.* JSNTSup 59. Sheffield: JSOT Press, 1991.

> Thompson draws a distinction between "allusions" (i.e., conscious reference) and "echoes" (where influence may be detected, but need not be conscious usage). At most there is one allusion to Jesus' sayings in this section, at Rom. 14:14. A number of echoes are likely. The example of Christ in the flesh is of crucial importance to Paul. Through transformation by the Spirit, believers are to follow Christ's pattern. Thoughtful

analysis of the lack of direct reference to Jesus' teaching, and call for reassessment by "maximalists."

188 J. M. G. Barclay. "Jesus and Paul." Pp. 492–503 in *Dictionary of Paul and His Letters*. Downers Grove, Ill., and Leicester, England: InterVarsity, 1993.

Insightful survey of the history of research. Nevertheless, the author seems to undervalue allusions to Jesus' words in Paul's letters, to overlook Jesus' own vision for a worldwide mission, and to diminish the meaning of the gospel by the claim that "Jewish nationalism" was at stake for both Jesus and Paul.

189 V. P. Furnish. *Jesus according to Paul*. Understanding Jesus Today. Cambridge: Cambridge University Press, 1993.

Survey from a critical perspective for a popular audience.

190 S. Kim. "Sayings of Jesus." Pp. 474–92 in *Dictionary of Paul and His Letters*. Downers Grove, Ill., and Leicester, England: InterVarsity, 1993.

Echoes of Jesus' sayings are discernible in all the major themes of Paul's theology. As apostle, Paul "re-presented" the sayings of Jesus in a new setting. Eleven certain or probable sayings of Jesus in Paul's letters, thirty-one further possible echoes.

191 D. Wenham. *Paul: Follower of Jesus or Founder of Christianity?* Grand Rapids and Cambridge, England: Eerdmans, 1995.

Comparison of themes and connection of traditions in eight areas: understanding the kingdom; the identity of Jesus; the meaning of Jesus' death; the community of faith; ethics; eschatology; and life and ministry of Jesus. A thorough and significant treatment of Paul's relation to Jesus, concluding that Paul saw himself as a follower of Jesus.

192 R. Riesner. "Paulus und die Jesus-Überlieferung." Pp. 347–65 in *Evangelium, Schriftauslegung, Kirche: Festschrift für Peter Stuhlmacher zum 65. Geburtstag*. Edited by Å. Jostein, S. Hafemann, and O. Hofius. Göttingen: Vandenhoeck & Ruprecht, 1997.

Important discussion of the history of research, and eight theses concerning Jesus-tradition: (1) Until the middle of the second century, early Christian writings do not use the Jesus-tradition in a different manner from the NT, despite highly valuing it. (2) In the second century and even beyond, along with the fixed tradition in the Gospels there was an oral tradition of Jesus-tradition used in instruction in the congregations. (3) In many NT writings the substantial lack of expressly cited Jesus-tradition is even more astonishing than is the case with

Paul. (4) Letters, preaching, and apocalypses were not designated for the practice of transmitting Jesus-tradition. (5) Paul also practiced, in his instruction of the congregations, an independent transmission of the Jesus-tradition in which its verbal form was preserved. (6) Paul knew more Jesus-tradition than what he cites in the particular situations called for in his letters. (7) The expectation of finding Jesus-tradition in Paul's letters is determined both by the biography/theology of the apostle, and by the transmission of Jesus-tradition in a controlled form through distinct persons. (8) Even an optimistic view of the familiarity of Paul with Jesus-tradition must demonstrate itself on the basis of clear criteria. Call for the assembling of parallels as a tool for research.

193 M. J. Harris. *Slave of Christ: A New Testament Metaphor for Total Devotion to Christ*. New Studies in Biblical Theology 8. Downers Grove, Ill.: InterVarsity, 2001.

Paul's usage against its Greco-Roman background.

9

Paul and Earliest Christianity

The tracing of Paul's relation to the earliest church falls basically into four lines: (1) the analysis of the reports of Acts; (2) the location and examination of early Christian tradition in Paul's letters; (3) the reconstruction of his opponents from his letters; and (4) his relationship with James (according to Acts, Galatians, and the Letter of James).

9.1 Paul and the Hellenists

The term "Hellenists" is found in three places in Acts, the third of which (if original, as seems likely) clearly refers to Gentiles (Acts 6:1, 9:29, 11:20), the first two to Jews. The term probably signifies the adoption of Greek language or culture (see #199), and therefore is sufficiently broad to describe both Jews and Greek-speaking Orientals. Greek-speaking Jews who believed in Christ naturally formed a bridge to the proclamation to the Gentiles. Over against the history-of-religions school, and Bultmann in particular, it is important to recognize Paul's connection with the Jerusalem church. Moreover, there are remarkable parallels between Stephen's speech and the Letter to the Hebrews. The church at Rome reflects a Law-free Christianity apart from Paul. Nevertheless, the question remains as to whether or how the "Hellenists" provided a historical and theological link from Jesus to Paul.

194 H. J. Cadbury. "The Hellenists." Pp. 59–74 in *The Beginnings of Christianity*. Edited by K. Lake and F. J. F. Jackson. Vol. 5. London: Macmillan, 1933.

Cadbury's argument, now discounted, is that the Hellenists were Greeks.

195 E. Blackman. "The Hellenists of Acts vi.1." *ExpT* 48 (1937): 524–25.

"Hellenists" are Gentile proselytes converted to Judaism, now converted to faith in Christ.

196 M. Simon. *St. Stephen and the Hellenists in the Primitive Church*. London: Longman, Green, 1958.

Stephen as a radical, a bridge to Pauline Christianity.

197 M. Scharlemann. *Stephen: A Singular Saint*. AnBib 34. Rome: Pontifical Biblical Institute, 1968.

Stephen stands as an isolated figure in the story of the earliest church. Paul moves beyond him, although they both regard the promises of God as central.

198 R. Scroggs. "The Earliest Hellenistic Christianity." Pp. 176–206 in *Religions in Antiquity: Essays in Memory of Erwin Ramsdell Goodenough*. Edited by J. Neusner. Studies in the History of Religions (Supplements to Numen) 14. Leiden: Brill, 1968.

"Stephen" is a Lukan construction reflecting a Samaritan mission, by a temple-critical group.

199 E. Ferguson. "The Hellenists in the Book of Acts." *ResQ* 12 (1969): 159–80.

Useful survey of research. Hellenists are those who follow a "Greek manner of life" (following B. B. Warfield, those at Antioch 11:20 are "Graecizing Syrians"), and are more inclined to be critical of Law and temple.

200 I. H. Marshall. "Palestinian and Hellenistic Christianity: Some Critical Comments." *NTS* 19 (1973): 271–87.

Critical questions to those who interpret Paul against the background of a fully Hellenized Christianity. Incidentally, an excellent introduction to the history of research.

201 R. Pesch et al. " 'Hellenisten' und 'Hebräer.' " *BZ* 23 (1979): 87–92.

"Hellenists," Greek-speaking Jews, formed a group inside the synagogue community.

202 M. Hengel. *Between Jesus and Paul: Studies in the Earliest History of Christianity*. Translated by J. Bowden. Philadelphia: Fortress; London: SCM, 1983.

See especially "The Hellenists," 1–29. Greek-speaking Jewish Christians, "Hellenists," link Paul and his theology to the earliest believing community, including his understanding of the Law and his Christology. The hymns to Christ which appear in his letters have their origin here.

203 H.-W. Neudorfer. *Der Stephanuskreis in der Forschungsgeschichte seit F. C. Baur.* Giessen, Germany: Brunnen, 1983.

Thorough survey of research, and defense of the thesis that Paul did indeed take up the theology of the "Stephen circle."

204 E. Larsson. "Die Hellenisten und die Urgemeinde." *NTS* 33 (1987): 202–25.

The Hellenists were conservative with respect to the Law. Only in debate with other Diaspora Jews was Jesus-tradition regarding the temple taken up and only after being scattered by persecution did Hellenists turn to the Gentiles.

205 C. Hill. *Hellenists and Hebrews: Reappraising Division within the Earliest Church.* Minneapolis: Fortress, 1992.

Hill shows the improbability of a severe persecution directed against a Hellenistic faction of the church, and dismisses attempts at finding criticism of the Law or temple in the charges against Stephen or in Stephen's speech. Both the Greek-speaking Jewish believers and the Christian Jews of Palestine experienced persecution, both offered compromises on the acceptance of Gentiles, and both groups were ideologically diverse.

206 T. W. Martin. "Hellenists." Pp. 135–36 in *The Anchor Bible Dictionary.* Edited by D. N. Freedman. Vol. 3. New York: Doubleday, 1992.

Useful survey of the interpretive questions.

207 H. Räisänen. "Die 'Hellenisten' der Urgemeinde." Pp. 1468–514 in *Aufstieg und Niedergang der römischen Welt.* Edited by H. Temporini and W. Haase. Vol. 26/2. Berlin: de Gruyter, 1995.

Hellenists as Law-free, temple-critical movement whose experience Luke shifts to an earlier period in the Acts narrative. Indeed, it was early in the history of Greek-speaking, non-Aramaic-speaking Christians that Jesus' death was proclaimed. A response to Hill.

208 K. Haacker. "Die Stellung des Stephanus in der Geschichte des Urchristentums." Pp. 1515–53 in *Aufstieg und Niedergang der römischen Welt.* Edited by H. Temporini and W. Haase. Vol. 26/2. Berlin: de Gruyter, 1995.

Stephen's martyrdom was due to tensions between Hellenistic Jewish Christians and their Jewish environment, yet the older model of a theological break (or "heresy") is inadequate. Rather, Acts suggests that Stephen's opponents projected their struggles with Hellenism onto him and his group.

209 W. Kraus. *Zwischen Jerusalem und Antiochia: Die "Hellenisten," Paulus und die Aufnahme der Heiden in das* *endzeitliche Gottesvolk.* SBS 63. Stuttgart: Katholisches Bibelwerk, 1999.

The missionary practice of the Greek-speaking Jewish believers, together with their criticism of the temple and their self-understanding as the eschatological people of God, brought them into conflict with their contemporaries and with the Pharisees in particular.

9.2 Hymns, Creeds, and Confessions

The attempt to trace the theology of "pre-Pauline" Christianity and Paul's relation to it through the isolation of hymnic and confessional material in his letters is an old one, going back to the rise of form criticism at the beginning of the twentieth century. Obviously his letters contain confessional material, which is occasionally clearly designated (e.g., 1 Cor. 11:23–25; 15:3–5, Eph. 5:14), and sometimes suggested by form and context (e.g., Rom. 1:2–4). We know that the earliest assemblies of Christians included the singing of "psalms, hymns, and spiritual songs" (Col. 3:16; cf. 1 Cor. 14:26), and that the practice was in place at the beginning of the second century (Pliny the Elder to Trajan: "[T]hey meet before dawn and sing a hymn to Christ as God" [*ante lucem convenire carmenque Christo quasi deo dicere*]; cf. Ignatius, *Eph* 4:1–2; *Mag* 1:2). Nevertheless, much scholarship has operated with too great a confidence in form-critical analysis as a means of distinguishing Paul's thought from earlier ideas (see, among others, Bultmann [#22]). We have these materials, after all, only in the form that Paul presents them. And only rarely do scholars take into account the creativity of Paul himself as an instructor of the congregations, which is precisely what such hymns and confessions were composed to do (1 Cor. 14:19). The following works make considerable use of confessional material (variously discerned) in tracing the background to Paul's thought in earliest Christianity. As with most other sections of this bibliography, the list here is representative, but not complete. Furthermore, as is apparent, it is bound up with the discussion of Pauline Christology, on which see §13.4 and also Hengel, "The Atonement" (#626).

210 E. Norden. *Agnostos Theos: Untersuchungen zur Formengeschichte religiöser Rede.* Leipzig and Berlin: Teubner, 1913. [See esp. pp. 250–76.]

Early, influential work. Comparative stylistic study shows that liturgical elements of Hellenistic speech penetrated early Judaism and turn up in hymnic material in the Pauline letters. Examination of Col. 1:15-20, 1 Tim. 3:16.

211 E. Stauffer. *New Testament Theology.* Translated by J. Marsh. London: SCM, 1963. German edition: *Die Theologie des Neuen Testaments.* 4th ed. Kohlhammer: Stuttgart, 1948. First edition: Gütersloh: Bertelsmann.

See "Die Glaubensformel der Urkirche," 212–34. "Dogma is as old as the church itself" (and not a later, Hellenistic corruption as von Harnack and others had claimed).

212 C. H. Dodd. *The Apostolic Preaching and Its Developments.* London: Hodder & Stoughton, 1950.

Distinction (highly questionable) between proclamation and instruction that developed from it.

213 E. Käsemann. "A Critical Analysis of Phil 2:5–11." Pp. 45–88 in *God and Christ: Existence and Providence.* Edited by R. Funk. New York: Harper & Row, 1968. First published as "Kritische Analyse von Phil. 2:5–11," *ZTK* 47 (1950): 313–60. It also appears in *Exegetische Versuche und Besinnungen* (Göttingen: Vandenhoeck & Ruprecht, 1964), 1:51–95.

The passage represents an acclamation of Christ's lordship in the face of the threat of other powers, a hymn which drew upon, but christianized, Gnostic themes. It is to be interpreted in the first place soteriologically, rather than ethically. This reading influenced Martin (#218), and has also called forth challenges (see the commentaries and, e.g., Hofius [#224] and Fee [#238]).

214 O. Cullmann. *The Christology of the New Testament.* Rev. ed. Translated by S. Guthrie and C. Hall. Philadelphia: Westminster, 1959. Original edition: *Die Christologie des Neuen Testaments* (Tübingen: Mohr [Siebeck], 1957).

The early community had to deal immediately with the first, not the second, coming of the Lord, and his earthly work was at the center of all development of Christology. The NT in many forms approximates the dogmatic confession of the deity of Jesus.

215 F. Hahn. *The Titles of Jesus in Christology: Their History in Early Christianity.* Translated by H. Knight and G. Ogg. New York: World; London: Lutterworth, 1969. German edition: *Christologische Hoheitstiteln: Ihre Geschichte im frühen Christentum.* Vandenhoeck & Ruprecht, 1963. Third edition: Göttingen: Vandenhoeck & Ruprecht, 1996.

Investigation of the individual titles. In the oldest Christology,
the motif of exaltation fails entirely; likewise, in the early eschatologically oriented community Jesus' life was not mes-
sianized. In Hellenistic Jewish Christianity, the theme of exaltation is developed and carried back to the earthly life of Jesus,
under Hellenistic influence (esp. the cult, and supposed conceptions of the "divine man" [θεῖος ἀνήρ]); this theme was further developed so that "Christ" was used less, "lord" and "son
of God" more. This Hellenistic conception determined the
Christology of the later ancient church.

216 W. Kramer. *Christ, Lord, Son of God.* Translated by
B. Hardy. SBT 50. Naperville, Ill.: Allenson; London: SCM,
1966. German edition: *Christos, Kyrios, Gottessohn: Untersuchungen zu Gebrauch und Bedeutung der christolo-
gischen Bezeichungen bei Paulus und den vorpaulinischen
Gemeinden.* ATANT 44. Zürich: Zwingli, 1963.
> The confessional materials in Paul's letters contain distinct
> forms and themes: the confession of faith in the Christ, accla-
> mation of the Lord, and the acknowledgment of him as son of
> God in the resurrection and sending formulas. Paul produced
> no new Christology, but employed the formulas given to him
> in proclamation, ecclesiology, and exhortation.

217 R. Deichgräber. *Gotteshymnus und Christushymnus in
der frühen Christenheit: Untersuchungen zu Form, Sprache
und Stil der frühchristlichen Hymnen.* SUNT 5. Göttingen: Vandenhoeck & Ruprecht, 1967.
> Important form-critical study of early Christian hymns, those
> addressed to God (including Rom. 11:33–36; Eph. 1:3–14; 1 Pet.
> 1:3–5; Col. 1:12–14) and those addressed to Christ (including
> Phil. 2:6–11; 1 Tim. 3:16; Heb. 1:3; 1 Pet. 2:21; Col. 1:15–20),
> which are united by a focus on God's saving deeds.

218 R. P. Martin. *A Hymn of Christ.* Downers Grove, Ill.: InterVarsity, 1997. Original title: *Carmen Christi: Philippians 2:5–11 in Recent Interpretation and in the Setting of
Early Christian Worship.* SNTSMS 4. Cambridge: Cambridge University Press, 1967. Revised edition: Grand
Rapids: Eerdmans, 1983.
> Following Käsemann, Martin argues that the passage is not to
> be interpreted ethically, but as a hymn (perhaps baptismal) to
> Christ as Lord, who has overcome the powers.

219 W. Rordorf. "La Confession de Foi et son 'Sitz im Leben'
dans L'Eglise Ancien." *NovT* 9 (1967): 225–38.
> Second-century worship, missionary preaching, and instruction
> as the "setting in life" for confessions.

220 K. Wengst. *Christologische Formeln und Lieder des Ur-christentums*. 2d ed. SNT 7. Gütersloh: Gütersloher Ver-lagshaus, 1973. Original edition: 1967.
   Survey and analysis.

221 J. T. Sanders. *The New Testament Christological Hymns: Their Historical Religious Background*. SNTSMS 15. Cambridge: Cambridge University Press, 1971.
   The hymns have their background in "Jewish Wisdom schools," and as thanksgiving developed into proclamation that sought to speak to outsiders.

222 A. Helmbold. "Redeemer Hymns—Gnostic and Christ-ian." Pp. 71–78 in *New Dimensions in New Testament Study*. Edited by R. N. Longenecker and M. C. Tenney. Grand Rapids: Zondervan, 1974.
   Differences observed.

223 L. Goppelt. *Theology of the New Testament*. Vol. 2: *The Variety and Unity of the Apostolic Witness to Christ*. Edited by J. Roloff. Translated by J. Alsup. Grand Rapids: Eerdmans, 1982. [See esp. pp. 65–106.] German edition: *Theologie des Neuen Testaments*. Göttingen: Vanden-hoeck & Ruprecht, 1976.
   On hymns/Christology.

224 O. Hofius. *Der Christushymnus Philipper 2, 6–11: Unter-suchungen zu Gestalt u. Aussage eines. Urchristl. Psalms*. 2d ed. WUNT 17. Tübingen: Mohr (Siebeck), 1991. Origi-nal edition: 1976.
   The hymn celebrates the revelation of the eschatological king-ship of God in the exaltation of the crucified Christ. Phil. 2:9–11 does not have to do with a triumph over the powers, but with universal mercy before Yahweh (cf. Isa. 45:23).

225 J. D. G. Dunn. *Christology in the Making: A New Testa-ment Inquiry into the Origins of the Doctrine of the In-carnation*. Philadelphia: Westminster, 1980.
   The decisive step to recognizing that God became incarnate in Jesus came only in the Johannine prologue. The confessional material in the Pauline letters allowed for, but did not require, this understanding. The "Wisdom Christology" of the later Pauline letters was crucial in the development of the idea of Christ's preexistence. See also Dunn's *Unity and Diversity in the New Testament* (#274).

226 P. Beasley-Murray. "Colossians 1:15–20: An Early Christ-ian Hymn Celebrating the Lordship of Christ." Pp. 169–83 in *Pauline Studies: Essays Presented to Professor F. F.*

Bruce on his Seventieth Birthday. Edited by D. Hagner and M. Harris. Grand Rapids: Eerdmans; Exeter, England: Paternoster, 1980.

Christ as creator and Christ as redeemer. Attention to background materials.

227 M. Hengel. "Hymns and Christology." Pp. 78–96 in *Between Jesus and Paul.* Translated by J. Bowden. London: SCM; Philadelphia: Fortress, 1983. Original publication: "Hymnus und Christologie." Pp. 1–23 in *Wort der Zeit: Festgabe für Karl Heinrich Rengstorf zum 75. Geburtstag.* Edited by W. Haubeck. Leiden: Brill, 1980.

Hymns to Christ were characteristic of the earliest Christian worship, bore an eschatological orientation, and served didactic purposes.

228 P. Stuhlmacher. *Reconciliation, Law, and Righteousness: Essays in Biblical Theology.* Translated by E. R. Kalin. Philadelphia: Fortress, 1986. German edition: *Versöhnung, Gesetz und Gerechtigkeit: Aufsätze zur biblischen Theologie.* Göttingen: Vandenhoeck & Ruprecht, 1981.

See especially "Jesus' Resurrection and the View of Righteousness in the Pre-Pauline Mission Congregations" (50–67). Rom. 4:25 and especially Rom. 3:25–26 as representative of the theology of the Stephen circle.

229 J. A. Fitzmyer. "κύριος." Pp. 329–31 in *Exegetical Dictionary of the New Testament.* Edited by H. Balz and G. Schneider. Vol. 2. Grand Rapids: Eerdmans, 1991. German edition: "κύριος." Pp. 811–20 in *Exegetisches Wörterbuch zum Neuen Testament.* Edited by H. Balz and G. Schneider. 2d ed. Vol. 2. Kohlhammer: Stuttgart, 1992. Original edition: 1981.

Especially good on the title "Lord" in early Judaism.

230 D. R. de Lacey. "'One Lord' in Pauline Christology." Pp. 191–203 in *Christ the Lord: Studies in Christology Presented to Donald Guthrie.* Edited by H. Rowdon. Downers Grove, Ill., and Leicester, England: InterVarsity, 1982.

Paul christianized the Shema (Deut. 6:4).

231 P. Stuhlmacher. "The Pauline Gospel." Pp. 1–25 in *The Gospel and the Gospels.* Edited by P. Stuhlmacher. Grand Rapids: Eerdmans, 1991. German edition: *Das Evangelium und die Evangelien.* Tübingen: Mohr (Siebeck), 1983.

Background to Paul's understanding of the expression "gospel" in earliest Christianity.

232 W. Gloer. "Homologie and Hymns in the New Testament: Form, Content, and Criteria for Identification." *PRSt* 11 (1984): 115–32.
> Good survey of research. It remains questionable whether one can distinguish between hymns and confessions as Gloer, along with others, supposes.

233 M. de Jonge. *Christology in Context: The Earliest Christian Response to Jesus.* Philadelphia: Westminster, 1988. [See esp. pp. 33–52.]
> Early Christian traditions appearing in Paul's letters.

234 S. E. Fowl. *The Story of Christ in the Ethics of Paul: An Analysis of the Function of the Hymnic Material in the Pauline Corpus.* JSNTSup 36. Sheffield: JSOT Press, 1990.
> The hymns found in Phil. 2:6–11, Col. 1:15–20, and 1 Tim. 3:16b are not used to defend a contested Christology, but to support ethical demands. See also Fowl's "Imitation of Paul/of Christ," *DPL* 428–31.

235 N. T. Wright. "Jesus Christ Is Lord: Phil 2.5–11" and "Poetry and Theology in Colossians 1.15–20." Pp. 56–98 and 99–119 in *The Climax of the Covenant: Christ and the Law in Pauline Theology.* Edinburgh: T. & T. Clark, 1991; Minneapolis: Fortress, 1992.
> Wright is inclined to read both as Pauline creations. His exegesis of the Philippians text is particularly significant. It has now been seriously challenged by S. Vollenweider, "Der 'Raub' der Gottgleichheit: Ein religionsgeschichtlicher Vorschlag zu Phil 2.6(–11)" *NTS* 45 (1999): 413–33, who has argued against the current tendency to read ἁρπαγμός ἡγήσατο as an idiom ("regard as an advantage") and to interpret the passage entirely in terms of a Jewish background.

236 J. Bailey and L. Vander Broek. *Literary Forms in the New Testament: A Handbook.* Louisville: Westminster John Knox, 1992. [See esp. pp. 76–87.]
> Includes hymns and creeds.

237 E. Best. "The Use of Credal and Liturgical Material in Ephesians." Pp. 53–69 in *Worship, Theology, and Ministry in the Early Church: Essays in Honor of Ralph P. Martin.* Edited by M. Wilkins and T. Paige. JSNTSup 87. Sheffield: JSOT Press, 1992.
> Examination of suggested hymnic material in Ephesians.

238 G. D. Fee. "'Philippians 2:5–11: Hymn or Exalted Pauline Prose?'" *BBR* 2 (1992): 29–46.
> Questioning of the claim that this passage represents a hymn.

239 R. P. Martin. "Hymns in the New Testament: An Evolving
Pattern of Worship Responses." *ExAud* 8 (1992): 33–44.
   A sketch of the background and development of New Testament hymns. NT hymns focus on Christ's saving work. In the
   later NT hymns, the descent/ascent motif replaces the theme
   of rejection/vindication. Spontaneous creation of hymns re-
   ceded in the second century.

240 R. P. Martin. "Hymns, Hymn Fragments, Songs, Spiritual
Songs." Pp. 419–23 in *Dictionary of Paul and His Letters.*
Downers Grove, Ill., and Leicester, England: InterVarsity,
1993.
   Overview and assessment of the significance of hymnic
   material in the Pauline letters. Confidence that hymns may be
   detected and that they disclose a pre-Pauline background. See
   also "Creed," 190–92.

241 K. Berger. "Hellenistische Gattungen im Neuen Testament." Pp. 1149–69 in *Aufstieg und Niedergang der römischen Welt.* Edited by H. Temporini and W. Haase. Vol.
25/2. Berlin: de Gruyter, 1995. See also his *Formgeschichte
des Neuen Testaments.* Heidelberg: Quelle & Meyer, 1984.
   Survey of Hellenistic literary forms in the New Testament.

242 G. Kennel. *Frühchristliche Hymnen? Gattungskritische
Studien zur Frage nach den Liedern der frühen Christenheit.* WMANT 71. Neukirchen-Vluyn: Neukirchener,
1995.
   Formal features of the Magnificat (Luke 1:46–55), Phil. 2:6–11,
   and Rev. 19:1–8 analyzed by means of Wolfgang Richter's linguistic method.

243 R. P. Martin and B. J. Dodd, eds. *Where Christology Began:
Essays on Philippians 2.* Louisville: Westminster John
Knox, 1998.
   Collection of essays on the genre, context, and meaning of Phil.
   2:5–11.

244 E. E. Ellis. *The Making of the New Testament Documents.*
Biblical Interpretation 39. Leiden: Brill, 1999.
   See pp. 69–116 for a discussion of pre-formed traditions in the
   Pauline letters.

9.3 Paul and His Opponents

   Theories about Paul's opponents are inseparable from reconstructions of the history of the earliest church. Several related
questions recur in the history of research: (1) Did the Jerusalem

apostles become adversaries of Paul? (2) Does Paul find himself battling a second front against pneumatic, Gnostic, or "wonder-working" opponents? (3) To what extent or in what way are the various opponents whom Paul attacks in his letters related to one another? The discussion of Paul's opponents in 2 Corinthians has played a large role here, since the opponents may be variously assessed. The abundant theories that the questions above have generated may be traced in all their variety in the works listed below. We have attempted to provide a sample of some of the important works on this topic; these works are representative of a larger body of literature. On this topic see also §9.4, "Paul and James," and chapter 10, "Paul's Influence on Christian Tradition."

245 D. W. Oostendorp. *Another Jesus: A Gospel of Jewish Christian Superiority in II Corinthians.* Kampen: Kok, 1967.

    Written against the thesis of Gnostic adversaries (Bultmann, Schmithals). The false apostles at Corinth taught that the restoration of Israel took place at Jesus' resurrection. The primacy of Israel over the Gentiles was now to be manifest. The reception of the Spirit takes place through the Law.

246 C. K. Barrett. "Paul's Opponents in II Corinthians." *NTS* 17 (1971): 233–54.

    Argues afresh for a distinction between the "false apostles" and the "super-apostles" (the roots of which go back to F. C. Baur). The latter represent "conservative Judaism," the former a "liberal Judaism" willing to adopt a Gnostic framework of thought.

247 J. J. Gunther. *St. Paul's Opponents and Their Background: A Study of Apocalyptic and Jewish Sectarian Teachings.* NovTSup 35. Leiden: Brill, 1973.

    Paul's opponents were ascetic, priestly, and separatistic, with developed angelology. A form of "non-conformist Judaism."

248 E. E. Ellis. "Paul and His Opponents: Trends in Research." Pp. 80–115 in *Prophecy and Hermeneutic in Early Christianity: New Testament Essays.* WUNT 18. Tübingen: Mohr (Siebeck); Grand Rapids: Eerdmans, 1978. Original publication: Pp. 264–98 in *Christianity, Judaism, and Other Greco-Roman Cults: Studies for Morton Smith at Sixty.* Pt. 1: *New Testament.* Edited by J. Neusner. Leiden: Brill, 1975.

    Indispensable survey of research from Calvin through Baur and

Lightfoot to Barrett and Schmithals. Acute observations at a number of points.

249 G. Lüdemann. *Opposition to Paul in Jewish Christianity.* Translated by M. E. Boring. Minneapolis: Fortress, 1983. German edition: *Paulus, der Heidenapostel: Antipaulinismus im frühen Christentum.* FRLANT 130. Göttingen: Vandenhoeck & Ruprecht, 1983.

Anti-Pauline attitude resulting from his Gentile mission has been shared by both liberal and conservative Jewish Christians since A.D. 50, an outgrowth of the attitude of the Jerusalem church. Survey of materials from the NT to Irenaeus.

250 D. Georgi. *The Opponents of Paul in Second Corinthians.* Philadelphia: Fortress, 1986. German edition: *Die Gegner des Paulus im 2. Korintherbrief: Studien zur religiösen Propaganda in der Spätantike.* WMANT 11. Neukirchen: Neukirchener, 1964.

The opponents are Hellenist Jews, who claim to be "divine men." See, however, C. R. Holladay, *"Theios Aner" in Hellenistic-Judaism: A Critique of the Use of This Category in New Testament Christology*, SBLDS 40 (Missoula, Mont.: Scholars Press, 1977).

251 J. M. G. Barclay. "Mirror-Reading a Polemical Letter: Galatians as a Test Case." *JSNT* 31 (1987): 73–93.

Scholarship generally has displayed undue selectivity and over-interpretation of the evidence, the mishandling of polemical statements, and excessive attention to particular words or phrases. Barclay's work represents an attempt to employ better criteria, which are taken up in the author's monograph *Obeying the Truth* (#828).

252 J. D. G. Dunn. "The Relationship between Paul and Jerusalem according to Galatians 1 and 2." Pp. 108–26 in *Jesus, Paul, and the Law: Studies in Mark and Galatians.* Louisville: Westminster John Knox; London: SPCK, 1990. Originally published in *NTS* 28 (1982): 461–78.

Paul's argument in Galatians shows that, although he once recognized the authority of the Jerusalem apostles, he came to regard his gospel and apostleship as independent. His change in attitude was the result of the incident at Antioch (on which see "The Incident at Antioch," 129–81, in the same volume).

253 J. L. Sumney. *Identifying Paul's Opponents: The Question of Method in 2 Corinthians.* JSNTSup 40. Sheffield: JSOT Press, 1990.

Examination of the methods employed by representatives of

the major hypotheses concerning Paul's opponents in 2 Corinthians. Insistence on the priority of the primary text and on flexibility and reserve in historical reconstructions. The opponents in 2 Cor. 10–13 may be identified as pneumatics, on the basis of their appeal to visions. Since a number of issues involving opponents are the same in 2 Cor. 1–9 (manifestation of the divine, financial support of apostles, evidence of apostolic status), the two groups may be identified.

254 P. Barnett. "Opponents of Paul." Pp. 644–53 in *Dictionary of Paul and His Letters*. Downers Grove, Ill., and Leicester, England: InterVarsity, 1993.

Useful survey of research followed by the author's own reconstruction of opposition to Paul in the earliest church, which, although suggestive, is not entirely convincing. Aside from Colossians, that opposition is to be regarded as Judaizing missionaries, who did not represent the Jerusalem apostles.

255 J. L. Sumney. *"Servants of Satan," "False Brothers," and Other Opponents of Paul*. JSNTSup 188. Sheffield: Sheffield Academic Press, 1999.

Paul faced a "spectrum" of opposition, not a single group. The Corinthian opponents were anti-Pauline Jewish Christian missionaries who claimed superiority but did not require circumcision. The opponents in Galatia, in contrast, claimed to agree with Paul, but demanded circumcision. Philippians may reveal a second anti-Pauline group. There is no evidence of a unified group (supported by Jerusalem) that sought to undermine Paul.

9.4 Paul and James

The relationship between Paul and James obviously bears fundamental significance for both the history of the earliest church and the theology of the New Testament. Not surprisingly, therefore, it remains one of the perennial topics of New Testament studies on which there is little consensus. The discussion of faith and works in the Letter of James on which we have concentrated our bibliographic entries plays a central role in the assessment of the issues. Further useful information may be found in treatments of the figure of James (esp. W. Pratscher, *Der Herrenbruder Jakobus und die Jakobustradition*, FRLANT 139 [Göttingen: Vandenhoeck & Ruprecht, 1987]; J. Painter, *Just James the Brother of Jesus in History and Tradition*, Studies on Personalities of the New Testament [Columbia: University of South Carolina Press, 1997]; B. Chilton and C. A. Evans, *James the Just and Christian Origins,* NovTSup 98 [Leiden: Brill, 1999]). See also Schlatter, *Glaube,* 453–69 (#660), Lindemann (#276), and the entries under §9.3, "Paul and His Opponents."

256   J. Jeremias. "Paul and James." *ExpT* 66 (1954–55): 368–71.
      Paul and James do not materially contradict one another, but differ in their understanding of the terms *faith, works,* and *justification.*

257   G. Eichholz. *Glaube und Werk bei Paulus und Jakobus.* Theologische Existenz Heute, n. s., 88. Munich: Chr. Kaiser, 1961.
      "Faith" for Paul is always measured against God's action in Jesus. He unmasks any attempt at self-justification. James attacks the "faith" that is content to remain without works—not that works must be added to faith, but that faith must have its own works. It is best to leave attempts at harmonization aside.

258   J. B. Lightfoot. "St. Paul and the Three." Pp. 292–374 in *St. Paul's Epistle to the Galatians with Introduction, Notes, and Dissertations.* Peabody, Mass.: Hendrickson, 1981. Original edition: London: Macmillan, 1866.
      James attacks a barren monotheism, and seems to direct his attack against the "self-complacent orthodoxy of a Pharisaic Christian." He is unlike the Ebionite "James" of the pseudo-Clementine literature, who could not have promoted the apostolic decree or have given Paul the right hand in fellowship.

259   L. Goppelt. "The Epistle of James." Pp. 199–211 in *Theology of the New Testament,* vol. 2: *The Variety and Unity of the Apostolic Witness to Christ.* Edited by J. Roloff. Translated by J. E. Alsup. Grand Rapids: Eerdmans, 1982.
      James did not understand faith in terms of its content, as Paul did, but simply as the act of believing. His statements are not directed against Paul, but against a slogan derived from Paul.

260   J. Reumann. *Righteousness in the New Testament: "Justification" in the United States Lutheran–Roman Catholic Dialogue.* Philadelphia: Fortress; New York: Paulist, 1982. [See pp. 148–58.]
      The Letter of James represents pseudonymous parenesis. James argues for "faith and works" in justification. He defends the centrality of justification involving faith.

261   M. Hengel. "Der Jakobusbrief als antipaulinische Polemic." Pp. 248–78 in *Tradition and Interpretation in the New Testament: Essays in Honor of E. Earle Ellis for His Sixtieth Birthday.* Edited by G. F. Hawthorne and O. Betz. Grand Rapids: Eerdmans, 1987.

James the brother of the Lord writes against the apostle Paul. See now Hengel's *Paulus und Jakobus: Kleine Schriften III,* WUNT 141 (Tübingen: Mohr [Siebeck], 2002).

262 M. Lautenschlager. "Der Gegenstand des Glaubens im Jakobusbrief." *ZTK* 87 (1990): 163–84.

The object of faith is Christ as judge. Faith is the essential precondition, but not the effective cause, for works (like blueprint and house). Therefore, James 2:24 does not presuppose a justification from faith and works (a synergism), but from works. Lautenschlager takes works of mercy as effecting atonement, for which he finds evidence in Jewish literature (e.g., Sir. 3:30b; Tob. 4:8–11). Works of mercy could compensate for evil deeds and, by means of a *iustitia distributiva,* avert damnation. James therefore has a radically optimistic nomism, which is diametrically opposed to Paul. For the author of James, Paul would be the "foolish man" (James 2:20). For Paul, the author of James would be cursed as one bringing another gospel. Luther keeps his "Doktorhut," James is not Tridentine, since he knows of no righteousness given through Christ.

263 P. H. Davids. "James and Paul." Pp. 457–61 in *Dictionary of Paul and His Letters.* Downers Grove, Ill., and Leicester, England: InterVarsity, 1993.

Very useful overview of the discussion. James and Paul not finally in contradiction with one another.

264 H. Frankemölle. *Der Brief des Jakobus.* Vol. 2. Gütersloh: Gütersloher; Würzburg: Echter, 1994. [See pp. 461–74.]

The New Testament presents a multiplicity of conceptions, including those concerning believing, doing, and justification. Paul and James do not interact with one another. Each fights his own battle: Paul concerning the possible ways of salvation, James concerning the realization of faith in works. Extensive discussion of current ecumenical trends in Protestant and Roman Catholic thought.

265 L. T. Johnson. *The Letter of James: A New Translation with Introduction and Commentary.* New York: Doubleday, 1995.

James and Paul share much of the same thought-world and language. Yet they do not address one another, but their own particular concerns. In opposing "works," Paul has in view the commandments of Torah, particularly circumcision, not moral action broadly conceived (cf. Rom 4:2).

266 M. Klein. *"Ein Vollkommenes Werk": Vollkommenheit, Gesetz und Gericht als theologische Themen des Jakobusbriefes.* BWANT, 7th ser., 19 (139). Stuttgart: W. Kohlhammer, 1995. [See pp. 199–203.]

The Letter of James is a pseudepigraphon, written against the Pauline understanding of justification by faith alone, a polemic which arises from a different understanding of the object of faith.

267   T. Laato. "Justification according to James: A Comparison with Paul." *TJ* 18 (1997): 43–84.

According to James, salvation is monergistic, arising from the creative word of God (James 1:18, 1:21), which fulfills the promise of the new covenant. The faith by which Abraham was justified was by nature living faith and brought forth works. Terminologically, James and Paul differ. Theologically they agree.

268   K. Haacker. "Justification, Salut et Foi: Etude sur les Rapports Entre Paul, Jacques et Pierre." *ETR* 73 (1998): 177–88.

James does not direct his argument against the innovative Pauline understanding of justification, but develops his thought within Jewish tradition. Here he might be correcting Peter (cf. Acts 3:16; 4:12).

269   P. Stuhlmacher. "Der Jacobusbrief." *Biblische Theologie des Neuen Testaments.* Vol. 2. Göttingen: Vandenhoeck & Ruprecht, 1999. [See pp. 59–70.]

James cannot come to grips with Paul conceptually, and cannot accept justification "by faith alone." In accord with Jewish tradition, James understands Abraham to have been justified by his faithfulness.

270   M. Bockmuehl. *Jewish Law in Gentile Churches: Halakhah and the Beginning of Christian Public Ethics.* Edinburgh: T. & T. Clark, 2000. [See pp. 49–83.]

Through his emissaries to Antioch, James requested stricter observance of *halakhah* on the part of Jewish believers, especially with regard to their contact with Gentiles. He did not dismiss the agreements of the Apostolic Decree, which applied to Gentiles, not Jews. He was motivated by the desire to avoid persecution in Judea and (possibly) by the view that the (ideal) land of Israel included Antioch.

10

Paul's Influence on Early Christian Tradition

The extent to which the second-century church understood Paul's writings and accepted their authority has been a matter of debate for some time, as may be seen from the entries below. The current view that the apostle's influence was large, even in the middle of the second century, appears to be justified. At the same time, Franz Overbeck's much-cited hyperbolism (taken up by von Harnack) retains its truth: "Marcion was the only one in the second century to understand Paul, and he misunderstood him." Anti-Pauline Jewish Christian writings as well as various legendary materials related to Paul may be found in E. Hennecke, *New Testament Apocrypha*, ed. W. Schneemelcher, trans. and ed. R. McL. Wilson, rev. ed., vol. 2 (Louisville: Westminster John Knox; Cambridge, England: J. Clarke, 1991). It is to the legendary *Acts of Paul and Thecla* that we owe the well-known description of Paul as "a man of small stature, with a bald head and crooked legs, in a good state of body, with eyebrows meeting and nose somewhat hooked, full of friendliness; for now he appeared like a man, and now he had the face of an angel." In addition to the studies listed below, see Kuss (#88).

271 W. Bauer, R. A. Kraft, and G. Krodel. *Orthodoxy and Heresy in Earliest Christianity.* Edited by R. A. Kraft. Philadelphia: Fortress; London: SCM, 1971. [See pp. 212–28.] German edition: *Rechtgläubigkeit und Ketzerei im ältesten Christentum.* 2d. ed. BHT 10. Tübingen: Mohr (Siebeck), 1964.

Influential but now dated discussion of the use of Paul in the middle to late second century.

272 H. Campenhausen. *The Formation of the Christian Bible.* Philadelphia: Fortress; London: A. & C. Black, 1972. [See pp. 143–46.] German edition: *Die Entstehung der christlichen Bibel.* Tübingen: Mohr (Siebeck), 1968.

Although Paul's authority was recognized, he lost esteem in the mid–second century due to heretical use of him. See the refutals by Lindemann (#276) and Dassmann (#275).

273 E. H. Pagels. *The Gnostic Paul: Gnostic Exegesis of the Pauline Letters.* Philadelphia: Fortress, 1975.

Examination of the Gnostic use of Paul, the theses of which have largely been answered by Lindemann and Dassmann.

274 J. D. G. Dunn. *Unity and Diversity in the New Testament: An Inquiry into the Character of Earliest Christianity.* 2d ed. Philadelphia: Trinity Press International; London: SCM, 1990. [See pp. 235–366.] Original edition: Philadelphia: Westminster, 1977.

The work of W. Bauer carried back into the New Testament. There is continuity between Jewish Christianity as it appears in the New Testament and that of the second and third centuries. Gnostic or at least pre-Gnostic influence may be traced back to Corinth. The church was characterized by increasing institutionalization and set forms of faith.

275 E. Dassmann. *Der Stachel im Fleisch: Paulus in der frühchristlichen Literatur bis Irenäus.* Münster: Aschendorff, 1979.

Critical investigation of the reception of Paul, beginning with the disputed Pauline letters. There was wide knowledge of Paul, even if his theology was not fully appreciated. Anti-Paulinism does not appear until the pseudo-Clementine writings.

276 A. Lindemann. *Paulus im Ältesten Christentum: Das Bild des Apostels und die Rezeption der paulinischen Theologie in der frühchristlichen Literatur bis Marcion.* BHT 58. Tübingen: Mohr (Siebeck), 1979.

A thorough reexamination of the thesis that the Paul tradition was rescued from its life in the shadows due to the controversy with Marcion. Despite the oft-cited word of Tertullian, that Paul was the *haereticorum apostolus,* reservation over against Paul on the part of second-century Christianity is not discernible. Paul was not the motor or measure of theological thinking, but he and his letters were an integral part of churchly tradition, and their formal authority was never in question (aside from James and Law-faithful Jewish Christianity).

277   G. Lohfink and K. Kertelge. *Paulus in den neutestamentlichen Spätschriften zur Paulusrezeption im Neuen Testament.* Quaestiones Disputatae 89. Freiburg: Herder, 1981.
The reception of Paul in the NT writings.

278   D. R. MacDonald. *The Legend and the Apostle: The Battle for Paul in Story and Canon.* Philadelphia: Westminster, 1983.
The (pseudonymous) Pastoral Epistles triumphed over the legendary Paul of the *Acts of Paul* and the story of Thecla, commissioned by Paul to teach the word of God.

279   W. S. Babcock, ed. *Paul and the Legacies of Paul.* Dallas: Southern Methodist University Press, 1990.
Significant collection of essays, including treatments of Origen, Augustine, and Chrysostom.

280   J. C. Beker. *Heirs of Paul Paul's Legacy in the New Testament and in the Church Today.* Minneapolis: Fortress, 1991.
Survey of the disputed letters within the New Testament, with (diffuse) reflections on how Paul is to be appropriated today.

281   D. L. Balás. "The Use and Interpretation of Paul in Irenaeus's Five Books *Adversus Haereses.*" *Second Century* 9 (1992): 27–39.
Response to the R. Norris essay in Babcock volume (#279). Irenaeus does not perceive the teaching of the Gnostics as being based on Paul in any particular way. He reads Paul in the context of the whole of Scripture, according to his "rule of faith," while the heretics rearrange the mosaic of Scripture.

282   P. Gorday. "Paul in Eusebius and Other Early Christian Literature." Pp 139–65 in *Eusebius, Christianity, and Judaism.* Edited by H. W. Attridge and G. Hata. Studia Post-Biblica 42. Leiden: Brill, 1992.
Paul becomes the means by which Eusebius shows that the Christian dispensation is the fulfillment of the ancient wisdom of the Hebrews.

283   R. Bauckham. "The *Acts of Paul* as a Sequel to Acts." Pp. 105–52 in *The Book of Acts in Its First-Century Setting,* vol. 1: *Ancient Literary Setting.* Edited by B. W. Winter and A. D. Clarke. Grand Rapids: Eerdmans; Carlisle, England: Paternoster, 1993.
An examination of the sources and genre of the *Acts of Paul.*

284   J. C. Paget. "Paul and the Epistle of Barnabas." *NovT* 38 (1996): 359–81.
Against the current trend of supposing that Paul had large in-

fluence on the noncanonical writings of the second century, it
is difficult to demonstrate any direct influence on Barnabas.

285 S. S. Taylor. "Paul and the Aphrahat's Use of the Pauline
Corpus." Pp. 312–31 in *The Function of Scripture in Early
Jewish and Christian Tradition*. Edited by C. A. Evans and
J. A. Sanders. JSNTSup 154. Studies in Scripture in Early
Judaism and Christianity 6. Sheffield: Sheffield Academic
Press, 1998.

Survey of recent debate and examination of the fourth-century
Syriac writings of Aphrahat, which (although Taylor seems un-
willing to accept it) confirm the Overbeck/von Harnack
dictum.

286 R. Werline. "The Transformation of Pauline Arguments in
Justin Martyr's Dialogue with Trypho." *HTR* 92 (1999):
79–93.

Justin turns Paul's argument for the inclusion of the Gentiles
into one which excludes the Jews.

287 M. M. Mitchell. *The Heavenly Trumpet: John Chrysostom
and the Art of Pauline Interpretation*. HUT 28. Tübingen:
Mohr (Siebeck), 2000.

Chrysostom (d. 407), who out of love of Paul created a portrait
of him, stands in the "large space between 'biographical posi-
tivism' and the negation of the author." Since every interpreter
works from an implicit "portrait" of the apostle, Chrysostom
remains instructive for (post)moderns.

11

The Letters of Paul

11.1 Literary Studies

A helpful identifying mark of forms of literary criticism is that their center of authority is the text as text. From this perspective, one may group new criticism/formalism, reader-oriented criticism, postmodernism, poststructuralism, and deconstruction as forms of literary criticism. The overwhelming concentration of such studies has been on narrative. Therefore, there are few noteworthy literary studies in the Pauline Epistles. Since rhetorical criticism (§11.3), epistolography (§11.4), literary style and forms (§11.3.4), and narrative framework (§13.2) are treated separately, only two items that provide helpful bibliography are listed below.

288 M. Minor. *Literary-Critical Approaches to the Bible: An Annotated Bibliography.* West Cornwall, Conn.: Locust Hill, 1992.
Includes rhetorical criticism, epistolography, structuralism, and various studies relating to writing style, under the label "literary-critical approaches." Even with this broader definition, the relatively few entries in its Pauline section makes manifest the paucity of literary analyses on the Pauline letters.

289 S. E. Porter. "Literary Approaches to the New Testament: From Formalism to Deconstruction and Back." Pp. 77–128 in *Approaches to New Testament Study.* Edited by S. E. Porter and D. Tombs. JSNTSup 120. Sheffield: Sheffield Academic Press, 1995.

An insightful, wide-ranging discussion of the theory and practice of various literary criticisms in the New Testament. Porter excludes structuralism and rhetorical criticism, but includes new criticism/formalism, reader-oriented criticism, postmodernism, poststructuralism, and deconstruction under the heading of literary approaches.

11.2 Linguistics and Discourse Analysis

The potential contributions of linguistics and its practical subfield of discourse analysis are still largely unmined. At least four schools of thought may be identified: (1) The North America Summer Institute of Linguistics (SIL) model, which works on the principle of levels and layers of language, with particular focus on issues of Bible translation (see esp. #292); (2) the English and Australian Hallidaian model, which examines interconnected groupings of choices that make up the meaningful components of language (i.e., experiential, interpersonal, logical, and textual; see esp. #297); (3) the continental European model, which divides its analysis into syntax, semantics, and pragmatics and incorporates Greco-Roman rhetorical analysis (see esp. #290); and (4) the South African school, which isolates colons (composed of a nominative and predicate structure) and then establishes their interconnections in diagram form (see esp. #291). On these schools, see further Porter's "Discourse Analysis and New Testament Studies" in #294. The study of linguistics contributes to our understanding of what language is and how it works. Discourse analysis is a reasoned and methodologically explicit way of giving account for how one is understanding the syntax (both micro and macro structures) and semantics of a text. Insofar as Pauline interpretation is an interpretation of texts and thus requires an analysis of the text's lexico-grammatical structure, linguistics and discourse analysis offer substantial help in establishing clarity and rigor in method and necessary controls in quantitative analysis. The newly initiated OpenText.org project, which aims to extend the kinds and levels of annotation available in computer-readable texts of the New Testament, should substantially enrich the resources available for biblical interpretation in the future (see www.opentext.org). For further bibliography, see #295.

290 B. C. Johanson. *To All the Brethren: A Text-Linguistic and*

Rhetorical Approach to 1 Thessalonians. ConBNT 16. Stockholm: Almqvist & Wiksell, 1987.

Perhaps the most developed application of the continental European model, with an attempt to integrate the contributions from the North American and South African models.

291 J. P. Louw. *A Semantic Discourse Analysis of Romans.* 2 vols. Pretoria, South Africa: Department of Greek, University of Pretoria, 1987.

A good demonstration of Louw's method of colon analysis on the entire Book of Romans. Volume 1 represents the linkages between cola and increasingly larger units. Volume 2 contains Louw's commentary and defense of his diagram.

292 D. A. Black, ed. *Linguistics and New Testament Interpretation: Essays on Discourse Analysis.* Nashville: Broadman, 1992.

A diverse collection of useful essays by linguists, Bible scholars, and Bible translators from a symposium sponsored by Wycliffe Bible Translators at the Summer Institute of Linguistics Center in 1991. Note especially J. P. Louw's "Reading a Text as Discourse," which demonstrates the indispensability of discourse analysis for accountable reading, and H. Parunak's "Dimensions of Discourse Structure," which sheds much light on the transition function of Gal. 2:15–21 and on the structure of Galatians.

293 S. E. Porter and D. A. Carson, eds. *Biblical Greek Language and Linguistics: Open Questions in Current Research.* JSNTSup 80. Sheffield: JSOT Press, 1993.

The first half of this volume contains helpful essays on the Porter-Fanning debate on verbal aspect (an essay each by Porter and B. Fanning, with responses from D. Schmidt and M. Silva). In the second half, Reed's essay, "To Timothy or Not? A Discourse Analysis of 1 Timothy," is an excellent example of the application of a Hallidaian model of discourse analysis on a Pauline letter. Demonstrates that Timothy is the letter's intended recipient.

294 S. E. Porter and D. A. Carson, eds. *Discourse Analysis and Other Topics in Biblical Greek.* JSNTSup 113. Sheffield: JSOT Press, 1995.

Contains helpful essays on cohesion shifts (G. Guthrie), constituent order (S. Levinsohn), and how to identify theme (J. Reed), together with penetrating responses from M. Silva and S. Porter. But note especially Porter's introductory essay, "Discourse Analysis and New Testament Studies."

295 J. T. Reed. "Modern Linguistics and the New Testament: A
Basic Guide to Theory, Terminology, and Literature." Pp.
222–65 in *Approaches to New Testament Study*. Edited by
S. E. Porter and D. Tombs. JSNTSup 120. Sheffield: Sheffield Academic Press, 1995.
An indispensable guide to the use and usefulness of modern linguistics in New Testament interpretation. One aspect of this
usefulness is demonstrated in Reed's application of information
flow to Philippians. On discourse analysis, see J. T. Reed, "Discourse Analysis as New Testament Hermeneutic: A Retrospective and Prospective Appraisal," *JETS* 39 (1996): 223–40.

296 J. Holmstrand. *Markers and Meaning in Paul: An Analysis
of 1 Thessalonians, Philippians, and Galatians*. ConBNT
26. Stockholm: Almqvist & Wiksell, 1997.
Examines transition markers in 1 Thessalonians, Philippians,
and Galatians to discern their structure and line of thought.
Highlights some of the linguistic patterns in these three letters.

297 J. T. Reed. *A Discourse Analysis of Philippians: Method
and Rhetoric in the Debate over Literary Integrity*.
JSNTSup 136. Sheffield: Sheffield Academic Press, 1997.
Part 1 explicates a functional (Hallidaian) framework for doing
discourse analysis of New Testament texts. Part 2 applies this
model to Philippians. Finds Philippians to be a hortatory personal letter and demonstrates the viability of reading it as a
single letter. A model for future work on entire books. See also
Reed's essay in #299.

298 S. E. Porter and J. T. Reed, eds. *Discourse Analysis and the
New Testament: Approaches and Results*. JSNTSup 170.
Sheffield: Sheffield Academic Press, 1999.
An invaluable volume providing "state of the art" essays by
leading scholars on method and particular applications of dis-
course analysis. For Pauline interpretation, see especially J. T.
Reed, "The Cohesiveness of Discourse"; R. Erickson, "The
Damned and the Justified in Romans 5.12–21"; J. P. Louw, "A
Discourse Reading of Ephesians 1.3–14"; and S. Levinsohn on
"Some Constraints on Discourse Development."

299 S. E. Porter and D. A. Carson, eds. *Linguistics and the New
Testament: Critical Junctures*. JSNTSup 168. Sheffield:
Sheffield Academic Press, 1999.
These essays show various aspects of the linguistic inadequa-
cies of previous work in NT studies and the tremendous po-
tential contributions of linguistically informed studies in the
future. See D. A. Carson, "An Introduction to Introduction";
G. Guthrie, "Boats in the Bay: Reflections on the Use of Lin-

guistics and Literary Analysis in Biblical Studies"; J. T. Reed, "Modern Linguistics and Historical Criticism: Using the Former for Doing the Latter"; S. E. Porter, "Linguistics and Rhetorical Criticism"; C. Davis, "Oral Biblical Criticism: Raw Data in Philippians"; P. Danove, "Verbs of Experience: Towards a Lexicon Detailing the Argument Structures Assigned by Verbs"; and M. O'Donnell, "Linguistic Fingerprints or Style by Numbers? The Use of Statistics in the Discussion of Authorship of New Testament Documents."

11.3 Rhetorical Criticism

Many proponents of rhetorical criticism claim a long, illustrious history for the application of the method to New Testament interpretation (see, e.g., Watson's "Notes on History and Method" in #303, and Mack, #300). Nevertheless, "[M]uch of this history of rhetorical criticism centered on an analysis of the literary and rhetorical devices that can be isolated in the New Testament as a form of style or ornamentation" (Stamps, #304, p. 131). As such, this history does not provide blanket support for the historical viability of all forms of rhetorical criticism. Several forms of rhetorical criticism are currently being espoused and practiced. At one end of the spectrum is the historical form popularized by H. D. Betz and G. A. Kennedy. (Betz and Kennedy differ in that Betz concentrates on arrangement [thus focusing on structure], whereas Kennedy looks at invention, arrangement, and style.) At the other end of the spectrum are the New Rhetoricians, who use modern categories of rhetoric and concentrate on invention (i.e., the manner of argumentation). From the discipline's inception, most have held to different combinations of these two approaches. If the papers from the international conferences on rhetorical criticism are an accurate reflection, the trend is toward increasing use of modern rhetorical categories and focus on invention. (The papers from the fifth conference came out in March 2002, too late for incorporation into this bibliography.) Until recently, the historical approach had largely failed to satisfy in that it had (1) prescribed Greco-Roman rhetorical structures meant for oral rhetoric on written epistles in a rigid fashion, which seems to be an invalid imposition of an alien genre and an arbitrary and unquantifiable method (see also #342, pp. 69–86); and (2) fallen short on its promise of reconstructing the rhetorical situation. Concurrently, many New Rhetoricians tended to adopt quasi-postmodern assumptions and radicalized ideological suspicions (see esp. #321 and many essays from the international conferences). Promising work that addresses methodological weaknesses and applies the insights of ancient rhetoric (primarily as a heuristic tool on invention) in a thoughtful manner is appearing, however (e.g., #315; #316; and #317). Only a few representative studies are listed under §11.3.2, "Greco-Roman," and §11.3.3, "New Rhetoric." Many more examples may be found in chapter 12, "Special Studies on Individual Pauline Letters" (as well as essays in the collections under §11.3.1, "General Orientation"). See also B. Winter's "Rhetoric" and G. Hansen's "Rhetorical Criticism," *DPL* 820–22 and 822–25. Works limited to studying rhetorical style, devices, and forms are listed in §11.3.4, "Style and Forms."

11.3.1 General Orientation

300 B. L. Mack. *Rhetoric and the New Testament*. Minneapolis: Augsburg, 1990.

> Useful introduction to Greco-Roman rhetoric and the history and development of rhetorical criticism up to the 1980s. In the section on rhetoric in the New Testament and the concluding section, however, Mack appears more like a radical form critic applying rhetorical categories in pursuit of form-critical goals (labeling passages as myths or inventions, reconstructing the alleged social context, criticizing perceived inadequacies of the text, etc.).

301 S. E. Porter and T. H. Olbricht, eds. *Rhetoric and the New Testament: Essays from the 1992 Heidelberg Conference*. JSNTSup 90. Sheffield: JSOT Press, 1993.

> A diverse collection of papers from the first international conference on rhetorical criticism. Four essays are particularly noteworthy: (1) Porter's demonstration that the Greco-Roman rhetorical handbooks give no precedent for systematically analyzing epistles in formal rhetorical categories and call for renewed focus on style (i.e., how rhetorical devices enhance communication and affect the persuasiveness of argumentation); (2) Stamps's important distinction between the historical situation prompting the writing of the text and the portrayal of that situation in the text; (3) Classen's effective juxtaposition of Melanchthon's and Betz's rhetorical criticism to show the usefulness of analyzing the line and structure of argumentation (using both ancient and contemporary understandings of rhetoric) and the incongruity of the wholesale imposition of ancient rhetorical structure onto the different genre of epistology;

and (4) Reed's demonstration of the fallacy of identifying functional similarity with formal dependence, and recommendation of a descriptive, rather than prescriptive, approach.

302 D. Litfin. *St. Paul's Theology of Proclamation: 1 Corinthians 1–4 and Greco-Roman Rhetoric.* SNTSMS 79. Cambridge: Cambridge University Press, 1994.

Excellent survey of the development of rhetoric from Socrates to the Greco-Roman period and comparison with Paul. "The essential difference between proclamation and the approach of the rhetors focuses upon the process of adaptation. Whereas the genius of the rhetorical dynamic was its emphasis upon adaptation with a view to engineering πίστις, the emphasis of proclamation was precisely the opposite. The herald was one who carried the message of another. It was not the herald's task to persuade, but to announce" (247–48).

303 D. F. Watson and A. J. Hauser, eds. *Rhetorical Criticism of the Bible: A Comprehensive Bibliography with Notes on History and Method.* Leiden: Brill, 1994.

Hauser compiled the Old Testament section while Watson did the New Testament. Besides a comprehensive subject bibliography, Watson's "Notes on History and Method" (101–25) provides a helpful orientation to the field.

304 D. L. Stamps. "Rhetorical Criticism of the New Testament: Ancient and Modern Evaluations of Argumentation." Pp. 129–69 in *Approaches to New Testament Study.* JSNTSup 120. Edited by S. E. Porter and D. Tombs. Sheffield: Sheffield Academic Press, 1995.

Perhaps the most helpful introduction to rhetorical criticism of the New Testament. Advocates seeing rhetorical criticism as generally "defined by its attempt to identify the textually-embedded strategies that seek to persuade the reader, to assess the effectiveness of these strategies, and then to evaluate the ideological positions to which the reader(s) is being moved" (167). See also Stamps, "Rhetoric," *DNTB* 953–59.

305 S. E. Porter and T. H. Olbricht, eds. *Rhetoric, Scripture, and Theology: Essays from the 1994 Pretoria Conference.* JSNTSup 131. Sheffield: Sheffield Academic Press, 1996.

A collection of papers from the second international conference on rhetorical criticism, which exhibits a decidedly more postmodern approach to language and reality. Three essays stand out. Malina's essay on social-scientific criticism advances provocative criticisms against "literary rhetorical criticism" (whose roots he traces to Romanticism) and argues for studying patterns of persuasion as rooted in patterns of social interaction. E. Mouton's and Olbricht's descriptive essays shed some light on the communicative intent of Ephesians and Colossians, respectively.

306 S. E. Porter, ed. *Handbook of Classical Rhetoric in the Hellenistic Period, 330 B.C.–A.D. 400.* Leiden: Brill, 1997.

Offers "a comprehensive and wide-ranging introduction to the field of classical rhetoric in the Hellenistic period" (xiv). Part 1 contains six articles defining rhetoric: (1) historical survey; (2) types and genre; (3) arrangement; (4) invention; (5) style; (6) delivery and memory. Part 2 treats rhetorical practice in different types of literary genres: (1) epistles; (2) philosophical prose; (3) historical prose; (4) poetry; (5) biography; (6) oratory and declamation; (7) homily and panegyrical sermon; (8) romance; (9) apocalyptic and prophetic literature; and (10) drama. Part 3 covers (1) the Gospels and Acts; (2) Paul; (3) the general New Testament writings; (4) the Johannine writings; (5) the Greek Christian writers; (6) the Latin church fathers; (7) Philo of Alexandria; (8) Plutarch; (9) Josephus; (10) Cynics; (11) translations of the Old Testament; (12) the Christian Apocrypha; and (13) inscriptions.

307 S. E. Porter and T. H. Olbricht, eds. *The Rhetorical Analysis of Scripture: Essays from the 1995 London Conference.* JSNTSup 146. Sheffield: Sheffield Academic Press, 1997.

As at the second conference, a decidedly postmodern bent is evident. In addition, the New Rhetoric and ideological approaches appear to be ascendant. Porter's critique of uncritical attempts to integrate discourse analysis and ancient rhetoric is very helpful. (See Porter's essay for the bibliographic items.) Also helpful is G. S. Holland's analysis of Paul's use of irony as a rhetorical technique. Classen's essay is a good example of examining Paul's rhetoric in terms of style. Watson's attempt to justify the demarcation of rhetorical units by incorporating epistolary analysis, while suggestive, needs further elucidation in quantifiable terms.

308 R. D. Anderson, Jr. *Ancient Rhetorical Theory and Paul.* Rev. ed. CBET 18. Kampen: Kok Pharos, 1999. Original edition: Louvain: Peeters, 1996.

Carefully evaluates a broad range of possible rhetorical sources and examines Gal. 1:1–5:12, Rom. 1–11, and 1 Corinthians for evidence of ancient rhetorical arrangement and invention. Concludes that Paul did not arrange his letters in the formal structures of Greek speech, but allows that Paul's argumentation may be analyzed via modern rhetoric.

309 P. H. Kern. *Rhetoric and Galatians: Assessing an Ap-*

proach to Paul's Epistle. SNTSMS 101. Cambridge: Cambridge University Press, 1998.

> A formidable marshaling of the evidence against analyzing Galatians according to the conventions of Greco-Roman rhetoric (esp. in terms of structure and species).

310 S. E. Porter and D. L. Stamps, eds. *The Rhetorical Interpretation of Scripture: Essays from the 1996 Malibu Conference.* JSNTSup 180. Sheffield: Sheffield Academic Press, 1999.

> Papers from the fourth international conference. D. Patrick and A. Scult aptly criticize ideological forms of rhetorical criticism as "hermeneutics of suspicion." Provocatively, G. Martín-Asensio advocates M. Halliday's functional grammar as a more suitable method for achieving the aims of rhetorical criticism. Olbricht criticizes classical rhetorical criticism's failure in delivering on promised reconstructions of audience situations. Porter develops his trenchant criticisms in "Paul as Epistolographer and Rhetorician?" Stamps reinforces Porter's critiques and argues for investigating content, form, and persuasion together. See also Porter's essay, "Linguistics and Rhetorical Criticism," in #299.

311 C. J. Classen. *Rhetorical Criticism of the New Testament.* WUNT 128. Tübingen: Mohr Siebeck, 2000.

> Chapters 1 and 3 are revised versions of Classen's papers from the first and third international conferences on rhetorical criticism. Chapters 2 and 5 are revisions of articles translated from German. Chapter 4 is a new essay that analyzes the narrative structure and argumentation of the four Gospels.

11.3.2 Greco-Roman/Historical Model

312 G. A. Kennedy. *New Testament Interpretation through Rhetorical Criticism.* Chapel Hill: University of North Carolina Press, 1984.

> Pioneers an easily applicable method for analyzing textual units in the whole range of New Testament literature according to ancient rhetorical theory. The numerous studies spawned are well represented in #313.

313 D. F. Watson, ed. *Persuasive Artistry: Studies in New Testament Rhetoric in Honor of George A. Kennedy.* JSNTSup 50. Sheffield: JSOT Press, 1991.

> A compilation of essays by Kennedy's students and other scholars consciously adopting and adapting his work.

314 M. M. Mitchell. *Paul and the Rhetoric of Reconciliation:*

An Exegetical Investigation of the Language and Composition of 1 Corinthians. HUT 28. Tübingen: Mohr (Siebeck), 1991.

> First Corinthians is a unified letter in which Paul employs deliberative rhetoric urging concord.

315 A. Ericksson. *Traditions as Rhetorical Proof.* ConBNT 29. Stockholm: Almqvist & Wiksell, 1998.

> Shows how Paul uses eight traditions in 1 Corinthians as part of his rhetorical strategy (argumentation or invention). Helpful clarifications on method in chapters 1–2.

316 J. D. Kim. *God, Israel, and the Gentiles: Rhetoric and Situation in Romans 9–11.* SBLDS 176. Atlanta: Society of Biblical Literature, 2000.

> Clarifies the rhetorical theory of *stasis* (four species of conjecture, definition, quality, and objection) and the relationship between the rhetorical situation and the historical situation. The differentiation of these different stases brings out the flow of Paul's argumentation in Rom. 9–11 well (see the summary on p. 147) and demonstrates that Paul's focus is to prevent the misconception that God's word has failed and that God, therefore, is not faithful.

317 K. J. O'Mahony. *Pauline Persuasion: A Sounding in 2 Corinthians 8–9.* JSNTSup 199. Sheffield: Sheffield Academic Press, 2000.

> Helpful methodological proposal to reverse the stages for constructing a speech in the task of analysis and to work first with the surface phenomena. Chapter 6, in which comparison is made with Betz's work, accounts for the data of 2 Cor. 8–9 better than Betz.

11.3.3 Modern Rhetoric

318 C. Perelman and L. Olbrechts-Tyteca. *The New Rhetoric: A Treatise on Argumentation.* Translated by J. Wilkinson and P. Weaver. Kampen: Kok Pharos, 1969. Original title: *La Nouvelle Rhétorique: Traité l'argumentation.* Paris: Presses Universitaires de France, 1958.

> Stresses that all speech is rhetorical (rhetoric = argumentation and persuasion, not just style). A standard handbook for the so-called "New Rhetoricians," who have followed and developed Perelman and Olbrechts-Tyteca's conception that all discourse functions as a form of persuasive argumentation.

319 A. C. Wire. *The Corinthian Women Prophets: A Recon-*

struction through Paul's Rhetoric. Minneapolis: Fortress, 1990.

Applies modern rhetoric to 1 Corinthians to reconstruct the lives and status of the Corinthian women prophets (on the premise that Paul's goals and the counterarguments he anticipates give access to this information).

320 J. A. Crafton. *The Agency of the Apostle: A Dramatistic Analysis of Paul's Responses to Conflict in 2 Corinthians.* JSNTSup 51. Sheffield: JSOT Press, 1991.

Analyzes Paul's response to conflict in 2 Corinthians by means of K. Burke's dramatist model (i.e., dividing a rhetorical event into act, scene, agent, agency, and purpose). Sees composite letters: 2:14–6:13 + 7:2–4 as a letter of initial response; 10:1–13:13 as a letter of attack; 1:3–2:13 + 7:5–16 as a letter of reconciliation; and chapters 8 and 9 as two letters of collection.

321 E. A. Castelli. *Imitating Paul: A Discourse of Power.* Louisville: Westminster John Knox, 1991.

Subjects Paul's letters to ideological rhetorical analysis (dependent on M. Foucalt), arguing that the notion of imitation functions as a strategy of power (i.e., Paul uses ideological power to secure unity and suppress deviancy).

11.3.4 Style and Forms

322 S. K. Stowers. *The Diatribe and Paul's Letter to the Romans.* SBLDS 57. Chico, Calif.: Scholars Press, 1981.

Major work on diatribe as a dialogical teaching style, especially in connection with Paul's apparent use of it in Romans, with extensive bibliography (to which the reader is referred for more works on diatribe). See also Stowers's essay (in #335) summarizing his work.

323 I. H. Thomson. *Chiasmus in the Pauline Letters.* JSNTSup 111. Sheffield: Sheffield Academic Press, 1995.

Contributes helpful methodological reflections and a useful treatment of five test-case passages (Eph. 1:3–14; 2:11–22; Gal. 5:13–6:2; Col. 2:6–19; Rom. 5:12–21) in the identification of possible intermediate-level chiasmus in Paul's letters. Chapter 1 contains ample citations to prior work on chiasmus.

324 E. W. Güting and D. L. Mealand. *Asyndeton in Paul: A Text-Critical and Statistical Enquiry into Pauline Style.* Studies in the Bible and Early Christianity. Lewiston, N.Y.: Mellen, 1998.

Studies the extent of asyndeton (lack of connectives between members of a series and between sentences) in Romans and the Corinthian correspondence. Valuable for deciding text-critical and stylistic issues in which asyndeton is found in that corpus (the list in section 3 is a ready reference). Adopts a thorough eclecticism and differs from the standard NA^{27} text approximately sixty times.

325 J. D. Harvey. *Listening to the Text: Oral Patterning in Paul's Letters.* ETS Studies. Grand Rapids: Baker; Leicester, England: Apollos, 1998.

Illuminating survey of Paul's use of eight rhetorical devices—chiasmus, inversion, alternation, inclusion, ring-composition, word-chain, refrain, and concentric symmetry. Also includes a helpful survey of recent work in oral speech patterns, rhetorical criticism, and epistolography.

11.4 Epistolography

While rhetorical criticism has overshadowed epistolary studies in recent years, studies on different parts of the epistolary structure have steadily flourished since the 1970s. The picture of the Pauline Epistles that has emerged thus far is that they consist of four major sections: "(1) the Opening (sender, recipient, salutation); (2) the Thanksgiving; (3) the Body (transitional formulae, autobiographical statements, concluding paraenesis, apostolic parousia); and (4) the Closing (peace benediction, hortatory section, greeting, autograph, grace benediction" (#341, p. 11). Nevertheless, the picture is clouded by the presence of different forms of epistolary analysis that have divergent goals and often produce conflicting results: (1) form literary analysis examines structure and formulas; (2) thematic analysis attempts to identify epistolary themes, such as friendship, consolation, or exhortation; and (3) form-critical analysis attempts to isolate oral forms, like liturgy and paraenetic formulas, that are embedded in existing letters (see further C. A. Wanamaker, "Epistolary and Rhetorical Analysis," in #504, pp. 255–86). Recent studies demonstrate the exegetical benefits of careful analysis of the opening, thanksgiving, and closing sections of the Pauline letters. They also show that Paul's writings are genuine letters, thus casting suspicion on forms of rhetorical criticism that ignore or downplay their epistolary character. On the other hand, the inability of such studies to shed much light on the content and function of the body of Paul's letters (beyond the identification of certain transitional formulas and some embedded subforms) shows that careful, exhaustive exegesis of the entirety of Paul's letters remains indispensable. See also #504.

326 A. Deissmann. *Light from the Ancient East: The New Testament Illustrated by Recently Discovered Texts of the Graeco-Roman World.* Translated by L. R. M. Strachan. 2d ed. New York: Doran, 1927. Reprint, Peabody, Mass.: Hendrickson, 1995. [See esp. pp. 146–251.] Original edition: New York: Harper & Row; London: Hodder and Stoughton, 1910. German edition: *Licht vom Osten.* Tübingen: Mohr, 1908; 2d–3d ed., 1909; 4th ed., 1923.

> The two English translations are from the second–third edition and fourth edition of the German, respectively. Deissmann popularized the use of papyri for comparative analysis of Paul's letters, but mischaracterized Paul's letters as haphazardly thrown together and so discouraged careful study of the form and function of these epistles for many decades. (For more historical details, see chapter 1 of #341.) See also his *Bible Studies,* translated by A. Grieve, 2d ed. (1901; Edinburgh: T. & T. Clark, 1903), 3–59. German titles: *Bibelstudien* (Marburg: Elwert, 1895), and *Neue Bibelstudien* (Marburg: Elwert, 1897).

327 R. W. Funk. "The Letter: Form and Style." Pp. 250–74 in *Language, Hermeneutic, and Word of God.* New York: Harper & Row, 1966.

> A useful review of work on the form and style of the Pauline Epistles up to the mid-1960s that contradicts Deissmann's mischaracterization. See also Funk's "The Apostolic *Parousia,*" in *Christian History and Interpretation: Studies Presented to John Knox,* ed. W. R. Farmer, C. F. D. Moule, and R. R. Niebuhr (Cambridge: Cambridge University Press, 1967), 249–68, in which Funk isolates an "apostolic parousia" section (where Paul makes his presence felt by reference to his writing of the letter, the sending of an emissary, or a hoped-for visit) at the end of the body of Paul's letters.

328 T. Y. Mullins. "Formulas in New Testament Epistles." *JBL* 91 (1972): 380–90.

> Against White, Doty, and Funk, who restrict them to the opening formula, Mullins provides concrete examples that show that such features as greeting, thanksgiving, and prayer of supplication may occur anywhere in an ancient letter. Though they often cluster in the opening and closing sections, their essential function is to punctuate a break in thought.

329 J. L. White. *The Form and Function of the Body of the Greek Letter: A Study of the Letter-Body in the Non-liter-*

ary Papyri and in Paul the Apostle. Missoula, Mont.: Scholars Press, 1972.

> Compares the body of the seven undisputed letters of Paul with that of non-literary Greek letters and finds three parts—opening, middle, and closing—separated by certain formulaic and quasi-formulaic transitional constructions. But see also White's essay "Apostolic Mission and Apostolic Message," in *Origins and Method: Towards a New Understanding of Judaism and Christianity,* ed. B. H. McLean, JSNTSup 86 (Sheffield: JSOT Press, 1993), 145–61, in which he acknowledges the need to study the stylistic devices and argumentative rhetoric in the letter's body.

330 P. T. O'Brien. *Introductory Thanksgivings in the Letters of Paul.* Leiden: Brill, 1977.

> Paul's introductory thanksgivings serve various functions (in some cases, one purpose predominates): (1) epistolary (introduce theme[s] of the letter); (2) didactic (by recalling previous teaching); (3) paraenetic; and (4) manifestation of Paul's pastoral concern. See also O'Brien's "Letters, Letter Forms," *DPL* 550–53; the classic study of P. Schubert, *Form and Function of the Pauline Thanksgiving* (Berlin: Töpelmann, 1939); and the recent defense of the epistolary function of Paul's thanksgivings in J. T. Reed's "Are Paul's Thanksgivings 'Epistolary'?" *JSNT* 61 (1996): 87–99.

331 G. P. Wiles. *Paul's Intercessory Prayers: The Significance of Intercessory Prayer Passages in the Letters of Paul.* London: Cambridge University Press, 1978.

> Groups the intercessory material in the seven undisputed Pauline letters into (1) intercessory wish-prayers; (2) intercessory prayer-reports; (3) requests for intercessory prayer; and (4) teaching about intercessory prayer. Argues that these prayers reflect the pastoral situations addressed.

332 S. K. Stowers. *Letter Writing in Greco-Roman Antiquity.* LEC 5. Philadelphia: Westminster, 1986.

> Very brief history of research; discusses social and practical dimensions of letter-writing; and gives examples of various types of letters. See also W. G. Doty, *Letters in Primitive Christianity,* GBS (Philadelphia: Fortress, 1973).

333 D. E. Aune. *The New Testament in Its Literary Environment.* LEC 8. Philadelphia: Westminster, 1987.

> Compares the literary genres and forms in the NT with those of Hellenism. On Paul, see chapters 5 and 6. Valuable for Aune's citation of much useful material and provision of a helpful bibliography.

334 A. J. Malherbe. *Ancient Epistolary Theorists*. SBLSBS 19. Atlanta: Scholars Press, 1988.

A handy collation and translation of statements from ancient rhetorical and literary handbooks concerning the idea of the letter. See now also Malherbe, #439, for a good example of interpretation in light of epistolary conventions.

335 J. L. White. "Ancient Greek Letters." Pp. 85–105 in *Greco-Roman Literature and the New Testament: Selected Forms and Genre*. Edited by D. E. Aune. SBLSBS 21. Atlanta: Scholars Press, 1988.

Many Greek letters fall into four basic types: letters of introduction/recommendation, petition, familial communication, or royal correspondence. Most are less specific, but broadly (1) convey information; (2) make requests or command/instruct; and (3) enhance or maintain personal contact. Christian letters display a combination of genres and a greater diversity of content and function.

336 L. A. Jervis. *The Purpose of Romans: A Comparative Letter Structure Investigation*. JSNTSup 55. Sheffield: JSOT Press, 1991.

After comparing the opening formula, thanksgiving, apostolic parousia, and conclusion of Romans with seven other letters (the other six undisputed ones plus 2 Thessalonians), Jervis concludes that the purpose of Romans was "to preach the gospel by letter to the Christian converts at Rome" (164).

337 E. R. Richards. *The Secretary in the Letters of Paul*. WUNT 2/42. Tübingen: Mohr (Siebeck), 1991.

Detailed examination of the various possible secretarial roles in Greco-Roman antiquity. Suggests the need to take into account the possible influence of a secretary on the organization, contents, and manner of expression in any given Pauline letter. Also suggests that Paul kept personal copies of most of his letters (perhaps hinted at in 2 Tim. 4:13), from which came the first collection of his letters (see esp. pp. 6–8, 165, and 191).

338 I. Taartz. *Frühjüdische Briefe: Die paulinische Briefe im Rahmen der offiziellen religiösen Briefe des Frühjudentums*. Freiburg, Switzerland: Universitätsverlag Freiburg Schweiz; Göttingen: Vandenhoeck & Ruprecht, 1991.

Argues for interpreting Paul's letters in connection with the Jewish official epistolary tradition rather than with the Hellenistic private letter tradition. Five bodies of Jewish letters are examined: (1) Two introductory letters in 2 Maccabees (1:1–9 and 1:10–2:18); (2) the Jeremiah-Baruch epistolary tradition; (3) rabbinic tradition; (4) correspondence from the Elephantine colony in Egypt; and (5) the Bar Kokhba letters. Paul follows the Jewish precedent in appealing both to the collective character of his authority (by listing co-senders) and to divine authority in prophetic fashion.

339 R. N. Longenecker. "On the Form, Function, and Authority of the New Testament Letters." Pp. 101–14 in *Scripture and Truth*. Edited by D. A. Carson and J. D. Woodbridge. Grand Rapids: Zondervan; Leicester, England: Apollos/InterVarsity, 1983. Reprint, Grand Rapids: Baker, 1992; Exeter, England: Apollos, 1995.

Concise, clear discussion of the form of letters in antiquity and the New Testament letters, as well as an excellent treatment of the use of amanueses and of the issues at stake over anonymity and pseudonymity. With respect to form, Longenecker groups the NT and Pauline letters under the two categories of pastoral (modeled after Jewish pastoral letters) and tractate letters.

340 M. L. Stirewalt, Jr. *Studies in Ancient Greek Epistolography*. SBLRBS 27. Atlanta: Scholars Press, 1993.

Contains four essays, "The Uses and Development of Greek Letter-Writing through the Second Century C.E."; "Forgery and Greek Epistolography"; "Chreia and Epistole"; and "Greek Terms for Letter and Letter-Writing from Homer through the Second Century C.E." Some of the conclusions and distinctions appear forced.

341 J. A. D. Weima. *Neglected Endings: The Significance of the Pauline Letter Closings*. JSNTSup 101. Sheffield: JSOT Press, 1994.

Focuses on the seven undisputed letters. Demonstrates that the closing conventions in Paul's letters echo or recapitulate the main themes of each letter to differing extents and thus aid interpretation of the whole. For a brief summary of ancient epistolary theory, see also Weima's "Epistolary Theory," *DNTB* 327–30.

342 J. Murphy-O'Connor. *Paul the Letter Writer: His World, His Options, His Skills*. Collegeville, Minn.: Liturgical Press, 1995.

Useful introduction to Paul as a letter writer. Provides good coverage of the state of research on epistolography, and helpful treatments of rhetorical criticism (65–86) and the Pauline corpus (114–30).

343 M. Müller. *Vom Schluss zum Ganzen: Zur Bedeutung des paulinischen Briefkorpusabschlusses*. FRLANT 172. Göttingen: Vandenhoeck & Ruprecht, 1997.

Explores the endings of the bodies in 1 Thessalonians (5:23–24;
functions as conductive address to God), Philippians (4:19–20;
functions as in 1 Thessalonians), and Romans (15:7–13; summarizes 14:1–15:6 and, indirectly, the whole epistle).

11.5 Pseudonymity

Although the view that pseudepigrapha are present in the
New Testament canon was not seriously entertained until the
mid–nineteenth century, the majority of critical scholarship now
routinely regards certain writings of the New Testament as
pseudepigraphal (falsely ascribed) or pseudonymous (falsely
named). (On this history, see further #351.) In the Pauline corpus,
the Pastoral Epistles are almost unanimously so regarded, with
some debate over 2 Thessalonians, Colossians, and Ephesians.
The debated issues are both historical-literary and historical-psy-
chological. On the one hand, there is dispute over what kind of
literature counts as pseudonymous (1) in the Greco-Roman
world; (2) in Judaism; (3) in the apostolic and immediate postapostolic church; and (4) in the early church (second to fourth century b.c.e.). On the other hand, there is dispute over the attitude
and reception of (1) the Greco-Roman world; (2) Judaism; (3) the
apostolic and immediate postapostolic church; and (4) the early
church toward pseudonymous writings. A significant minority
(e.g., Carson, #354; Ellis, #351; Guthrie, #345; and Porter, #352)
see sufficient reasons to maintain Pauline authorship of the disputed letters. (For a recent forceful defense of Pauline authorship
of the Pastorals, see L. T. Johnson's *The Writings of the New Testament*, rev. ed. [Minneapolis: Fortress, 1999], 423–52; and #446,
pp. 55–97. For the statistical and linguistic inadequacies of studies that use statistics as evidence against Pauline authorship, see
esp. M. O'Donnell's essay in #299.) They further argue that any
writing should be removed from the canon if proven to be pseudonymous. Many of those who reject Pauline authorship advance various theories to vindicate the pseudonymous author
from the charge of deceit and to allow some semblance of continuity with Paul and of canonical authority to remain (see esp.
#348 and #346 for discredited proposals not covered here). Oth-
ers (esp. Donelson, #347) admit the charge of deceit and examine
the pseudonymous author's work in its own right. D. Meade's
work (#348), which defends pseudonymity as part of the accepted
phenomenon of living tradition in Judaism and in apostolic and

immediate postapostolic Christianity, is achieving widespread reception, especially among moderately conservative scholars who reject Pauline authorship of certain epistles but desire to retain these epistles' canonical authority. This thesis is often combined with the supposition of a Pauline school that carries on the legacy of Paul and actualizes his teaching for a later generation (see esp. Dunn, #349; cf. chapter 10, "Paul's Influence on Early Christian Tradition"). See also #337 and the commentaries and special studies on the Pastorals.

344 K. Aland. "The Problem of Anonymity and Pseudonymity in Christian Literature of the First Two Centuries." *JTS* 12 (1961): 39–49. Reprinted in *The Authorship and Integrity of the New Testament*, Theological Collections 4 (London: SPCK, 1965), 1–13.
> Posits two kinds of pseudonymous writings. The first (of the early period) stemmed from inspired, prophetic utterance from the Holy Spirit and was related to anonymity in deference to the Spirit as the true author. The second (of the later period, after the abatement of the spirit of revelation and the emergence of the individuality of the Christian author) told "a fantastic story" in order to claim the authority of the apostles to address contemporary issues. The Pastorals possibly belong to this second kind.

345 D. Guthrie. "The Development of the Idea of Canonical Pseudepigrapha in New Testament Criticism." Pp. 43–59 in *VE* 1. Edited by R. Martin. London: Epworth, 1962. Reprinted in *The Authorship and Integrity of the New Testament*, Theological Collections 4 (London: SPCK, 1965), 14–39.
> Subjects F. C. Baur's and his successors' principles for determining canonical pseudepigrapha (as well as K. Aland's proposal [#344]) to searching criticism.

346 B. M. Metzger. "Literary Forgeries and Canonical Pseudepigrapha." *JBL* 91 (1972): 3–24.
> Surveys a wide range of literary forgeries in antiquity, the motives behind them, and the range of ancient and modern evaluations of pseudepigrapha as well as various attempts to address the ethical, psychological, and theological issues involved. Includes ample citations to older works in the footnotes and bibliography.

347 L. R. Donelson. *Pseudepigraphy and Ethical Argument in the Pastoral Epistles*. Tübingen: Mohr (Siebeck), 1986.
> Chapter 1 surveys scholarly discussion on pseudepigraphy as

well as pseudepigraphical letters in the Greco-Roman world and early Christianity. Concludes that the Pastorals fit well into the pseudepigraphal-letter genre—an intentional deception stemming from doctrinal debates among competing factions. Chapter 2 explains the forms of argument in the Pastorals in terms of the categories of *enthymeme* and *paradigm* from Aristotle's *Rhetoric*. Chapter 3 elucidates the consistent system of theology and ethics found in the Pastorals.

348 D. G. Meade. *Pseudonymity and Canon: An Investigation into the Relationship of Authorship and Authority in Jewish and Earliest Christian Tradition*. WUNT 39. Tübingen: Mohr (Siebeck), 1986.

Claims that there is a pattern of a growing tradition in the New Testament that parallels an alleged, similar pattern in the prophetic, wisdom, and apocalyptic traditions of Judaism. This tradition may grow in the form of anonymous or pseudonymous expansion or contextualization. Thus, the attribution of the Pastorals and Ephesians to Paul and 1 and 2 Peter to Peter is analogous to the attribution of the entire book of Isaiah to Isaiah the prophet.

349 J. D. G. Dunn. *The Living Word*. London: SCM, 1987; Philadelphia: Fortress, 1988. [See esp. pp. 65–85.]

Justifies pseudonymity on the basis of living tradition, drawing on Meade's work (#348). See also Dunn's "Pauline Legacy and School" and "Pseudepigraphy," *DLNT* 887–93 and 977–84.

350 R. Bauckham. "Pseudo-Apostolic Letters." *JBL* 107 (1988): 469–94.

Starts from the premise that pseudepigraphal writers must find a way to address their real audiences, even though they can only directly address the supposed addressees contemporary with the supposed author. Possible solutions, as seen from Jewish pseudepigraphal letters and noncanonical pseudo-apostolic letters, are to address a general readership in general terms (either by a real letter or a letter essay), to impose the situation of the real audience back onto the supposed addressees (either as direct similarity or as a type), or to write a testament. By comparison with those letters, Bauckham ranks the likehood of the pseudonymous origins of 2 Peter and the Pastorals (likely); Ephesians, James, and 2 Thessalonians (possible); and Colossians, 1 Peter, and Jude (unlikely).

351 E. E. Ellis. "Pseudonymity and Canonicity." Pp. 212–24 in *Worship, Theology, and Ministry in the Early Church: Essays in Honor of Ralph P. Martin*. Edited by M. J. Wilkins and T. Paige. JSNTSup 87. Sheffield: JSOT Press, 1992.

Given the apostles' unique authority, Ephesians, the Pastorals, and 1–2 Peter exhibit "clear and sufficient evidence of a deceptive intention," if they are pseudepigrapha (223). Thus, those convinced of these letters' pseudonymous nature cannot sidestep the need to eliminate them from the church's canon.

352   S. E. Porter. "Pauline Authorship and the Pastoral Epistles: Implications for Canon." *BBR* 5 (1995): 105–23.

Contains a useful discussion, with ample bibliographic citations, of why chronology, epistolary format, style, and content are not sufficient reasons for ruling out Pauline authorship of the Pastoral Epistles. Also argues forcefully that pseudonymous authorship and the possibility of deception radically affects the concept of canon and the evaluation of its formation.

353   R. W. Wall. "Pauline Authorship and the Pastoral Epistles: A Response to S. E. Porter." *BBR* 5 (1995): 125–28.

Asserts over against Porter that the faith community's later acceptance of the Pastorals as authoritative tradition renders the issue of historical authorship irrelevant. Apparently relocates the locus of authority to the readers. For a compelling rejoinder, see S. E. Porter, "Pauline Authorship and the Pastoral Epistles: A Response to R. W. Wall's Response." *BBR* 6 (1996): 133–38.

354   D. A. Carson. "Pseudonymity and Pseudepigraphy." Pp. 857–64 in *Dictionary of New Testament Background*. Edited by C. A. Evans and S. E. Porter. Downers Grove, Ill., and Leicester, England: InterVarsity, 2000.

The most up-to-date summary and evaluation of the debate. Concludes that the real choice is between the recognition that certain New Testament documents are pseudonymous and thus intentionally deceptive or that there are no pseudonymous writings in the canon.

11.6 The Pauline Corpus

While varying greatly in detail, theories about the collection of Paul's letters may be divided into two basic categories: (1) theories of a sudden collection; and (2) theories of a gradual growth. Usually, the former category presupposes that Paul's letters fell into relative neglect and that a follower (or a school of followers) gathered and edited the corpus we now possess. Theories of a gradual growth usually presuppose that individual letters of Paul were treasured by the churches that received them and gradually gained wider circulation among churches.

These different theories about the origin, purpose, and dating of the collection of Paul's letters are inextricably linked to different theories about the origin, nature, and dating of different letters in the Pauline corpus and of other books in the New Testament. Supporting arguments are usually ingenious suggestions, based only on slender, circumstantial evidence. (For more detail on these theories and further bibliography, see Gamble, #360; Murphy-O'Connor, #342; and Patzia, #363.) Unlike previous attempts that gave extensive or even primary consideration to secondary attestations from the church fathers, Trobisch (#361) begins with a thorough examination of the manuscript evidence and suggests that Paul personally edited part of the corpus. The exegetical basis for this suggestion (Paul's alleged theological rift with the Jerusalem church) and the overall formulation of his theory, however, depends on ingenious speculation. Gamble (#362) argues from historical evidence for an early corpus collected from Paul's own copies (building in part on Richards, #337).

355 T. Zahn. *Geschichte des neutestamentlichen Kanons.* Erlangen, Germany: Deichert, 1888, 1892. Reprint, New York: G. Olms, 1975. [See 1:811–39.]
   While allowing for early smaller collections, on the basis of the probable witness of Clement, Ignatius, and Polycarp to the Pastoral Epistles and a majority of the other letters, an original collection of all thirteen letters was already in existence prior to 95 C.E. (the writing of the *First Epistle of Clement*).

356 E. J. Goodspeed. *Introduction to the New Testament.* Chicago: University of Chicago Press, 1937. [See pp. 210–39.]
   Goodspeed's mature summary of his own work. Consult also, among others, his *Meaning of Ephesians* (Chicago: University of Chicago Press, 1933).

357 C. L. Mitton. *The New Testament in Its Literary Environment.* London: Epworth, 1955.
   Provides a helpful juxtaposition of the conventional theory (i.e., a gradual-growth theory, with the Pastorals added later) with the alternative proposed by E. J. Goodspeed and J. Knox (i.e., a sudden collection, published around 90 C.E.).

358 D. A. Hagner. *The Use of the Old and New Testaments in Clement of Rome.* Leiden: Brill, 1973. [See esp. pp. 314–31.]
   A detailed study of the quotations and allusions of the Old and New Testaments in Clement of Rome. Since Clement shows knowledge of a majority of epistles originally sent to different geographical regions, he most probably knew a Pauline corpus of at least ten epistles (the Pastorals are also attested, but Hag-

ner allows for the possibility that they were still circulated separately) prior to 95 c.e.

359 K. Aland. "Die Entstehung des Corpus Paulinum." Pp. 302–
50 in *Neutestamentliche Entwürfe*. Munich: Kaiser, 1979.

On the basis of great diversity in textual character shown from
collations of 634 minuscule manuscripts in 256 selected passages, and variance in sequence of Paul's epistles among the
manuscripts, concludes that no uniform "Ur-Corpus" of Pauline Epistles stands behind all later witnesses. On the basis of
statistical data of variant readings, also suggests that several collections of Paul's letters were already in circulation by 90 c.e.

360 H. Y. Gamble. *The New Testament Canon: Its Making and
Meaning*. Philadelphia: Fortress, 1985.

The section on Paul's letters (pp. 35–46) exposes problems with
existing variants of the two basic theories mentioned in the introduction above. Attributes the writing of Colossians, Ephesians, 2 Thessalonians, and the Pastoral Epistles as well as the
gathering of the final corpus of thirteen letters to a Pauline
school. See also Gamble's "Canonical Formation of the New
Testament," *DNTB* 183–95.

361 D. Trobisch. *Paul's Letter Collection: Tracing the Origins*.
Minneapolis: Fortress, 1994. Original title: *Die Entstehung
der Paulusbriefsammlung*. NTOA 10. Freiburg, Switzerland: Universitätsverlag; Göttingen: Vandenhoeck & Ruprecht, 1989.

Argues that all extant manuscripts testify to an early edition of
the Letters of Paul with the uniform sequence Romans, 1–2 Corinthians, Galatians, Ephesians, Philippians, Colossians, 1–2
Thessalonians, 1–2 Timothy, Titus, and Philemon (with Hebrews added at a later stage). Also, Romans, 1–2 Corinthians,
and Galatians formed an original collection (with Rom. 16 as
the cover letter) edited by Paul, with Ephesians–Philemon a
later appendix to the original collection. Finds evidence of edi-
torial reworking for publication. Also, infers from the importance of the collection for Jerusalem throughout Romans–Galatians that Paul published these letters to present his side of the
argument in his conflict with the Jerusalem church. See also
Trobisch's *First Edition of the New Testament* (Oxford: Oxford
University Press, 2000). Original title: *Endredaktion des Neuen
Testaments* (Freiburg, Switzerland: Universitätsverlag; Göttingen: Vandenhoeck & Ruprecht, 1996).

362 H. Y. Gamble. *Books and Readers in the Early Church: A
History of Early Christian Texts*. New Haven: Yale University Press, 1995. [See esp. pp. 59–63, 95–101.]

Argues from the existence of two distinct editions of the Pauline letters in the second century (Marcion's collection and a collection lying behind P[46] and most early Greek manuscripts) that an earlier letter-to-seven-churches edition (1–2 Corinthians, Romans, Ephesians, Thessalonians, Galatians, Philippians, and Colossians [combined with Philemon?]), arranged in decreasing length, stood behind them. Also suggests that this seven-churches edition led to the use of the codex and that the earliest collections came from Paul's own copies. See also Gamble's "The Pauline Corpus and the Early Christian Book," in *Paul and the Legacies of Paul*, ed. W. S. Babcock (Dallas: Southern Methodist University Press, 1990), 265–80.

363 A. G. Patzia. *The Making of the New Testament: Origin, Collection, Text, and Canon.* Leicester, England: Apollos, 1995.

An unusually lucid presentation of the origin, collection, text, and canon of the New Testament. An excellent survey of the issue of the collection of Paul's letters is found on pp. 79–88.

11.7 Paul and the Old Testament

The study of Paul's use of Scripture has focused on at least three matters: (1) the text(s) of Scripture available to Paul and the significance of his own wording of it; (2) early Jewish interpretation of Scripture and Paul's relation to it; (3) Paul's hermeneutic and its theological significance. In addition, recent study in various ways has employed current theories concerning "intertextuality." It is not possible to catalog here the burgeoning list of works on particular texts within Paul's letters. We have attempted rather to indicate the more important general works on the topic, and even here we have had to omit some worthy titles (which may be found in the bibliographies of the works cited). Lists of Pauline citations of the Scriptures beyond those provided in the indices of UBS[4] and NA[27] may be found in Hübner's update of W. Dittmar's collection (*Vetus Testamentum in Novo*, vol. 2 [Göttingen: Vandenhoeck & Ruprecht, 1997]) or in G. L. Archer and G. Chirichigno, *Old Testament Quotations in the New Testament* (Chicago: Moody Press, 1983). In addition to the works cited below, more serious students might consult the classic works of Dodd (*The Old Testament in the New* [1963]), J. Bonsirven (*Exégèse rabbinic et exégèse paulinienne* [1939]), and O. Michel (*Paulus und seine Bibel* [1929]). See also #457, #469, #480, #482, #487, and #832. On Jewish interpretation of Scripture, see now D. Instone Brewer, *Techniques and Assumptions in Jewish Exegesis Before 70 CE*, TSAJ 30 (Tübingen: Mohr [Siebeck], 1992).

364   A. T. Hanson. *Studies in Paul's Technique and Theology.* Grand Rapids: Eerdmans; London: SPCK, 1974.

Discussion of the relation between the Testaments from a modernist perspective. Over against early Jewish interpretation of Scripture, the New Testament displays "christocentric" rather than a "Torah-centric" perspective. The connection between the OT and the NT is found in the "revelation of God's character." Extensive and informative interaction with twentieth-century scholarship.

365   E. E. Ellis. *Paul's Use of the Old Testament.* Reprint, Grand Rapids: Baker, 1981. Original edition: Grand Rapids: Eerdmans, 1957.

One of the classic twentieth-century studies of Paul's methods and hermeneutic, discussing early Jewish exegesis, the interpretive practices of the early church, Paul's topical emphases and his use of typology. See now also Ellis, *The Old Testament in Early Christianity: Canon and Interpretation in the Light of Modern Research* (Grand Rapids: Baker, 1992).

366   L. Goppelt. *Typos: The Typological Interpretation of the Old Testament in the New.* Grand Rapids: Eerdmans, 1982. German edition: *Typos: Die typologische Deutung des Alten Testaments im Neuen* (with a supplement, "Apokalyptik und Typologie bei Paulus"). Darmstadt: Wissenschaftliche Buchgesellschaft, 1969 (reprint of the author's 1939 Erlangen dissertation).

In common with the other NT writers, Paul understands and interprets the OT in terms of historical correspondence and heightening of OT realities *which have to do with the human-divine relation* (and not mere external conditions), a relation fulfilled in Christ. The only typological relation that Paul draws between the coming of Christ into the world is "Adam" typology. Otherwise Christ is presented in terms of a "congregation-typology," in relationship to the salvific ordinances of the OT.

367   R. N. Longenecker. *Biblical Exegesis in the Apostolic Period.* 2d ed. Grand Rapids: Eerdmans; Vancouver: Regent College, 1999. Original edition: Grand Rapids: Eerdmans, 1975.

Paul's use of Scripture explained on the basis of contemporary Jewish practices.

368   D. Koch. *Die Schrift als Zeuge des Evangeliums: Untersuchungen zur Verwendung und zum Verständnis der
Schrift bei Paulus.* BHT 69. Tübingen: Mohr (Siebeck),
1986.
   Thorough study, with examination of Septuagintal usage and
   early Jewish approaches to Scripture. According to Paul, the
   gospel is necessary to the interpretation of Scripture (2 Cor.
   3:13–18). Correspondingly, the Scripture serves as a *present*
   witness to the gospel. Paul, therefore, uses Scripture in a decidedly selective manner, with sometimes considerable alteration
   of the original wording, and a repeatedly "immediate" application of the text.

369   D. Juel. *Messianic Exegesis: Christological Interpretation
of the Old Testament in Early Christianity.* Philadelphia:
Fortress, 1988.
   Early Christian interpretation proceeded not from the conviction that the kingdom had come, but from the conviction that
   the crucified Jesus was the risen Messiah. The plot of Ps. 22 and
   Isa. 53 became the model for understanding Jesus' career.

370   D. M. Smith. "The Pauline Literature." Pp. 265–91 in *It Is
Written: Scripture Citing Scripture (Essays in Honour of
Barnabas Lindars, S.S.F).* Edited by D. A. Carson and
H. G. M. Williamson. Cambridge: Cambridge University
Press, 1988.
   Brief survey and analysis of Pauline usage of the Old Testa-
   ment, with a useful bibliography.

371   R. B. Hays. *Echoes of Scripture in the Letters of Paul.* New
Haven: Yale University Press, 1989.
   A suggestive and fruitful application of a form of intertextual
   interpretation to Paul's use of Scripture, namely, the exploration of the rhetorical and semantic effects of allusion. This
   book is essential reading, particularly since it deftly exposes
   the inadequacies of historicizing Paul's interpretive techniques.
   It may be questioned, however, whether Paul's hermeneutic is
   "ecclesiocentric" and whether the interpretive authority Hays
   allows the community is valid, given the authority over the
   community that Paul understands the apostolic interpretation
   of Scripture to bear.

372   C. D. Stanley. *Paul and the Language of Scripture: Cita-
tion Technique in the Pauline Epistles and Contemporary
Literature.* Cambridge: Cambridge University Press, 1992.
   Study of Paul's citation of Scripture against the background of
   Greco-Roman use of Homer and contemporary Jewish usage.
   Against this background, there is nothing unique or notewor-

thy about the manner in which Paul handles the wording of his biblical quotations.

373   J. W. Aageson. *Written Also for Our Sake: Paul and the Art of Biblical Interpretation.* Louisville: Westminster John Knox, 1993.
Generalized, topical survey.

374   C. A. Evans and J. A. Sanders, eds. *Paul and the Scriptures of Israel.* JSNTSup 83. Sheffield: JSOT Press, 1993.
Discussion of Hays's *Echoes of Scripture in the Letters of Paul* (including a response by Hays), followed by studies of selected passages from Paul.

375   M. Silva. "Old Testament in Paul." Pp. 630–42 in *Dictionary of Paul and His Letters.* Downers Grove, Ill., and Leicester, England: InterVarsity, 1993.
Thorough discussion of questions surrounding Pauline citations of the Scriptures, the relation of allusion to citation, contemporary Jewish exegesis, and Paul's interpretive stance.

376   K. D. Litwak. "Echoes of Scripture? A Critical Survey of Recent Works on Paul's Use of the Old Testament." *Currents in Research: Biblical Studies* 6 (1998): 260–88.
Thoughtful survey of recent works on intertextuality in Paul and Paul's hermeneutics, much of it given to interaction with Hays.

377   F. Wilk. *Die Bedeutung des Jesajabuches für Paulus.* FRLANT 179. Göttingen: Vandenhoeck & Ruprecht, 1998.
A close analysis of Paul's allusions and citations of Isaiah. Paul employs the text in a theologically unified way but not in a linear manner, an observation which, if it holds, calls for revision of many attempts to find a narrative subplot to Paul's use of the OT. Paul's faith in Christ and his interpretation of Isaiah inform one another. Only in the light of the Christ-event is the meaning of the prophet's words revealed. At the same time, only through the Book of Isaiah do certain aspects and consequences of faith in Christ come to light.

378   M. C. Albl. *"And Scripture Cannot Be Broken": The Form and Function of the Early Christian Testimonia Collections.* NovTSup 96. Leiden and Boston: Brill, 1999.
Authoritative collections of excerpts from the OT Scriptures (*testimonia*) were used by early Christians, including the apostle Paul, who (contra Koch and Stanley) makes use of a previously existing collection. Argued from 1 Cor. 15:3–4; Rom. 1:3–4; 3:24–26; 4:25; 11:25–27; 15:12; the parenesis in Rom. 12:19; 13:9; and 2 Cor. 13:1; 6:16–7:1.

11.8 The Paul of the Letters and the Paul of Acts

Redaction criticism of the Gospels brought with it increased attention to the theological character and purpose of Acts. Works such as those by Vielhauer and Haenchen stirred up debate in the 1970s and '80s by arguing that Luke's picture of Paul represents a decline from the theology of the apostle himself. Luke replaces a theology of the cross with a theology of glory, creates continuity between Christian faith and the Law where Paul sees disjunction, adopts a theology of natural revelation that the apostle could not accept, and so on. The debate has quieted considerably in the last decade or so, without any clear resolution. A number of scholars now focus on Luke's picture of Paul, under the assumption that the author of Acts stands in a later generation and did not know the apostle. Aside from a sample or two, we have omitted listing these studies, a number of which may be found in the 1983, 1988, and 1993 collections of the *Society of Biblical Literature Seminar Papers*, and in Charles H. Talbert, ed., *Luke-Acts: New Perspectives from the Society of Biblical Literature Seminar* (New York: Crossroad, 1984). The Book of Acts is thereby often placed into the *Wirkungsgeschichte* of the apostle (see chapter 10, "Paul's Influence on Christian Tradition"). The relationship between Acts and Paul also obviously entails Pauline chronology (on which see chapter 4, "History and Chronology of Paul's Ministry").

379 P. Vielhauer. "The Paulinisms of Acts." Pp. 33–50 in *Studies in Luke-Acts*. Nashville: Abingdon, 1966.

Seminal essay positing fundamental theological differences between Paul and Luke's presentation of Paul. Originally published as "Zum 'Paulinismus' der Apostelgeschichte," *EvT* 10 (1950–51): 1–15.

380 U. Wilckens. "Interpreting Luke-Acts in a Period of Existential Theology." Pp. 60–83 in *Studies in Luke-Acts*. Nashville: Abingdon, 1966.

Important, moderate response to the reading of Acts offered by Vielhauer and others.

381 E. Haenchen. "Luke and Paul." Pp. 112–16 in *The Acts of the Apostles: A Commentary*. Philadelphia: Westminster; London: Blackwell, 1971. German edition: *Die Apostelgeschichte*. 14th ed. KEK. Göttingen: Vandenhoeck & Ruprecht, 1965.

Like Vielhauer's essay, Haenchen's is seminal to subsequent discussion.

382 C. K. Barrett. "The Acts—of Paul." Pp. 86–100 in *New Testament Essays*. London: SPCK, 1972.
   Moderate response to Vielhauer.

383 F. F. Bruce. "Is the Paul of Acts the Real Paul?" *BJRL* 58 (1976): 282–305.
   Examination of "undesigned coincidences" and parallels, followed by examination of three Pauline speeches in Acts.

384 A. J. Mattill, Jr. "The Value of Acts as a Source for the Study of Paul." Pp. 76–98 in *Perspectives on Luke-Acts*. Edited by C. H. Talbert. Edinburgh: T. & T. Clark, 1978.
   Classification of scholarship in this area into four types of treatment.

385 J. Jervell. "Paul in the Acts of the Apostles: Tradition, History, and Theology." Pp. 68–76 in *The Unknown Paul: Essays on Luke-Acts and Early Christianity*. Minneapolis: Augsburg, 1984.
   The Lukan portrait of Paul complements the image obtained from his letters. See also Jervell's chapter "The Signs of the Apostle: Paul's Miracles" (77–95).

386 R. I. Pervo. *Luke's Story of Paul*. Minneapolis: Fortress, 1990.
   Popular presentation of Acts as "story," with the assumption that "Luke" is a third-generation Christian.

387 J. Lentz. *Luke's Portrait of Paul*. SNTSMS 77. Cambridge: Cambridge University Press, 1993.
   Against the background of Greco-Roman concern about social status, Luke characterizes Paul as having the highest social and religious credentials (which is judged to be highly improbable), and a person of the highest moral virtue.

388 S. Schreiber. *Paulus als Wundertäter: Redaktionsgeschichtliche Untersuchungen zur Apostelgeschichte und den Authentischen Paulusbriefen*. Berlin and New York: de Gruyter, 1996.
   The Lukan portrait of Paul as miracle worker cannot be reconciled with Paul's own statements. It presents Paul as a "Christian hero."

389 S. Fowl. "Paul and Paulinisms in Acts." Pp. 883–87 in *Dictionary of the Later New Testament and Its Developments*. Edited by R. Martin and P. Davids. Downers Grove, Ill.: InterVarsity, 1997.
   General description of the Lukan presentation, with important bibliography.

390 S. E. Porter. *The Paul of Acts: Essays in Literary Criticism,*

Rhetoric, and Theology. WUNT 115. Tübingen: Mohr Siebeck, 1999.

> Thorough assessment of the charges that Haenchen and Vielhauer make against the presentation of Paul in the Book of Acts.

391 S. Walton. *Leadership and Lifestyle: The Portrait of Paul in the Miletus Speech and 1 Thessalonians.* SNTSMS 108. Cambridge: Cambridge University Press, 2000.

> Luke seeks to pass on and commend Pauline tradition, which he knows, and knows independently of the epistles. At the same time, the Lukan portrait of Paul as pastor corresponds to that which we find in 1 Thessalonians.

11.9 Commentaries

Because of space constraints, only a representative sample of the most useful commentaries in English were annotated below. Preference was generally given to Greek-based, technical, and up-to-date commentaries (which would themselves provide useful select bibliographies of previous commentaries and other works). An additional number of notable commentaries, by no means exhaustive, are also listed at the head of each subsection by author and date. The annotations usually attempt to highlight the framework of understanding and strengths reflected in each commentary, because interpretive decisions should be influenced primarily by the reasons that informed each commentator's interpretive process rather than by an individual commentator's prestige or by majority opinion. On the proper use of commentaries, see especially Silva (#478), pp. 15–39.

11.9.1 Romans

See also the commentaries by Barrett (1991); Bruce (1985); Byrne (1996); Cottrell (1996); Morgan (NTG; 1995); Morris (1988); Murray (1968); Schlatter (1995); Stott (1994); Stuhlmacher (1994); Wilckens (3 vols.; 1978–81); and Ziesler (1986).

392 E. Käsemann. *Commentary on Romans.* Translated by G. W. Bromiley. Grand Rapids: Eerdmans; London: SCM, 1980. German title: *An die Römer.* 2d ed. HNT 8a. Tübingen: Mohr, 1974. Fourth German edition: 1980.

> Emphasizes theological over historical questions. Aims at both systematic clarity and concrete specificity open to critical testing and correction. Sees the central concern of the text as the

righteousness of God and traces the inner logic of that concern in Käsemann's division of the letter into integrated sections.

393 C. E. B. Cranfield. *A Critical and Exegetical Commentary on the Epistle to the Romans.* 2 vols. ICC. Edinburgh: T. & T. Clark, 1975, 1979.

Gives sustained attention to the history of interpretation and provides two helpful essays at the end of volume 2 on Paul's purposes in writing Romans and on some aspects of Paul's theology (though Cranfield warns that reading these essays without wading through the entire commentary will necessarily lead to misunderstanding). Emphasizes the unity of thought from 1:1 to 16:23 (excluding 16:25–27 as secondary) and pays close attention to the flow of Paul's argument. See also Cranfield's *Romans: A Shorter Commentary* (Grand Rapids: Eerdmans, 1985).

394 J. D. G. Dunn. *Romans.* 2 vols. WBC 38A, 38B. Dallas: Word, 1988.

Comes from the standpoint of the "new perspective on Paul" associated with E. P. Sanders, namely that Paul and his readers are concerned primarily with the inclusion or exclusion of Gentiles and the signs of membership in the people of God.

395 J. A. Fitzmyer. *Romans.* AB 33. New York: Doubleday, 1993.

A very detailed, informative discussion of introductory issues. Helpful summary of Paul's teaching in Romans under the five headings of (1) God; (2) Christ; (3) the Holy Spirit; (4) human beings; and (5) Christian conduct.

396 D. J. Moo. *The Epistle to the Romans.* NICNT. Grand Rapids: Eerdmans, 1996.

Sees the theological starting point of Romans as Christology, the conceptual framework as salvation history, and the theme as the gospel. Reflects thoughtfully on basic issues of Christian theology and practice. Provides extensive treatment and refutation of the "new perspective on Paul" such as found in Dunn, #394. See also Moo's *Romans,* NIV Application Commentary (Grand Rapids: Zondervan, 2000).

397 T. R. Schreiner. *Romans.* BECNT. Grand Rapids: Baker, 1998.

Traces the flow of Paul's thought, wrestles with the theological meaning and implications of that thought, and argues inductively that the glory of God is the central theme of Romans. Sees a threefold purpose in Paul having written the letter: (1) to unify the believers in Rome; (2) to rally support for the mission to Spain; and (3) to bring glory to God's name.

11.9.2 1 Corinthians

See also the commentaries by Blomberg (1994); Collins (1999); Dunn (NTG; 1995); Furnish (1999); Hays (1997); Morris (1985); Oster (1995); Schrage (4 vols.; 1991–2001); Soards (1999); and Witherington (#166).

398 A. Robertson and A. Plummer. *A Critical and Exegetical Commentary on the First Epistle of St. Paul to the Corinthians.* ICC. Edinburgh: T. & T. Clark, 1929.

Its comprehensive introduction still provides much of value (e.g., the discussion of text-critical matters, though in need of updating). Often helpful on particular details of language, but weak on tracking the larger flow of the letter. Sees the Corinthian church splitting into parties of their own accord, without any encouragement from their chosen leaders.

399 C. K. Barrett. *A Commentary on the First Epistle to the Corinthians.* BNTC. Reprint, Peabody, Mass.: Hendrickson, 1993. Original edition: New York: Harper & Row; London: A. & C. Black, 1968.

Useful introduction. Barrett sees the church divided into Paul-, Apollos-, Cephas-, and Christ-groups. Background material and interpretive alternatives are judiciously presented and weighed.

400 H. Conzelmann. *1 Corinthians.* Translated by J. W. Leitch. Hermeneia. Philadelphia: Fortress, 1975. German title: *Der erste Briefe an die Korinth.* KEK. Göttingen: Vandenhoeck & Ruprecht, 1969.

Treats the letter as a unity. Sees no need to posit a Gnostic background (though finds traces of popular ideas of Jewish and Greek origin that later converged in Gnosticism). A distortion of faith from its focus on the word into spiritual experience of the self sufficiently accounts for the ideas and practices Paul confronts.

401 F. F. Bruce. *1 and 2 Corinthians.* NCB. Grand Rapids: Eerdmans, 1980.

Proposes that apparent discrepancies resulted from Paul having dictated the letter in stages (first chapters 1–4, then chapters 5–6 in response to the oral report of bearers of a letter from the Corinthians and chapters 7–16 in response to the letter itself). Sees Paul confronting both libertine incipient Gnostics (with over-realized eschatology and Spirit enthusiasm) and reactionaries against libertinism (ascetics and those trying to impose Jewish observances).

402 G. D. Fee. *The First Epistle to the Corinthians.* NICNT. Grand Rapids: Eerdmans, 1987.

Besides a sustained treatment of the historical background and the flow of Paul's argument, gives considerable attention to contemporary application and all significant textual variants. Proposes that the primary conflict was between Paul and the Corinthian church, without denying the presence of internal strife.

403   A. C. Thiselton. *The First Epistle to the Corinthians: A Commentary on the Greek Text.* NIGTC. Grand Rapids: Eerdmans; Carlisle, England: Paternoster, 2000.
A model of thoroughness of research and clarity of thought and expression. Critically incorporates insights from recent work in social-scientific and rhetorical criticism.

11.9.3 2 Corinthians

See also the commentaries by Baker (1999); Belleville (1996); Best (1987); Bruce (#401); Danker (1989); Garland (1999); Hafemann (2000); Hughes (1966); Kreitzer (NTG; 1996); Kruse (1987); Lambrecht (1999); Murphy-O'Connor (1991); Scott (1998); and Witherington (1995).

404   C. K. Barrett. *A Commentary on the Second Epistle to the Corinthians.* BNTC. New York: Harper & Row; London: A. & C. Black, 1973. Reprint, Peabody, Mass.: Hendrickson, 1993.
Useful introduction. Proposes a two-letter partition of chapters 1–9 and 10–13. Finds the letter's central content and motivation to be to remind the Corinthians that the apostle's legitimacy lies in mirroring the life and preaching of his crucified Lord. Model of conciseness and clarity.

405   V. P. Furnish. *II Corinthians.* AB 32A. Garden City, N.Y.: Doubleday, 1984.
Offers sound methodological reflections on the reconstruction of Paul's opponents in 2 Corinthians. Includes extensive notes that are often informative, particularly on lexical and grammatical matters. The "Comments" section offers well-written, coherent explanation.

406   H. D. Betz. *2 Corinthians 8 and 9.* Hermeneia. Philadelphia: Fortress, 1985.
Sees two letters in 2 Cor. 8–9 (a letter to the Corinthians in chapter 8 and a letter to the Achaians in chapter 9) on the basis of their supposedly self-contained rhetorical structure. Rich in detail and background, but rather arbitrary in its treatment of the text.

407 R. P. Martin. *2 Corinthians*. WBC 40. Waco, Tex.: Word, 1986.

   Extensive bibliography and able summaries of the state of scholarship. The section on "Form/Structure/Setting" often showcases the literary features of a passage well. Makes a special effort to highlight the pastoral dimension in the "Explanation" section.

408 M. E. Thrall. *A Critical and Exegetical Commentary on the Second Epistle to the Corinthians*. 2 vols. ICC. Edinburgh: T. & T. Clark, 1994, 2000.

   Sees chapters 1–8 with 13:11–13; chapter 9; and 10:1–13:10 as originally three separate letters by Paul. Presents a wealth of linguistic, textual, historical, and literary information (but sometimes the long series of arguments with counterarguments leaves the reader confused). Ill-founded divergences at points from scholarly consensus (e.g., the identification of Paul's opponents as non-Christian Jews).

409 P. Barnett. *The Second Epistle to the Corinthians*. NICNT. Grand Rapids: Eerdmans, 1997.

   Excellent introduction, especially the sections defending the unity of the letter and outlining its theology. Sees three interlocking objectives in the letter: (1) to explain and defend Paul's recent actions; (2) to exhort the Corinthians to set certain matters in order before Paul's impending visit; and (3) to teach various doctrines while addressing (1) and (2). Proposes three key themes, with theological background in Isaiah 40–55: (1) the eschatological centrality of Christ; (2) the apostolic ministry in the new covenant; and (3) the hope of glory.

11.9.4 Galatians

See also the commentaries by Coles (1989); Esler (1998); George (1994); Guthrie (1973); Hansen (1994); Lightfoot (1890; reprint, 1993); Lührmann (1992); Jervis (1999); Matera (1992); McKnight (1995); Morris (1996); Mussner (1988); and Ridderbos (1953).

410 E. D. W. Burton. *A Critical and Exegetical Commentary on the Epistle to the Galatians*. ICC. Edinburgh: T. & T. Clark, 1921.

   Though dated, the extensive grammatical and lexical notes are often informative. Defends the South Galatia theory in detail, but considers Acts 15 and Gal. 2:1–10 as relating the same event. Sees Paul rejecting the authority of Old Testament

statutes on the basis of his own interpretation of human experience (on the basis that each generation is the arbiter of its
own religion). Also sees Paul rejecting any authoritative book
or centralized ecclesiastical authority.

411 H. D. Betz. *Galatians: A Commentary on Paul's Letter to
the Churches in Galatia.* Hermeneia. Philadelphia: Fortress, 1979.

Skeptical about the reliability of the Book of Acts, labels the arguments for both the North and South Galatia theories as speculative, yet asserts North Galatia as the destination without
argumentation. Analyzes the letter in terms of Greco-Roman
rhetoric and epistolography (identifying it as an apologetic letter), but largely ignores Jewish backgrounds. Sees ethics as let-
ting the fruit of the Spirit happen (with corresponding complete
freedom from the Torah).

412 F. F. Bruce. *The Epistle of Paul to the Galatians.* NIGTC.
Grand Rapids: Eerdmans; Exeter, England: Paternoster,
1982.

Argues for the South Galatia theory and an early date in part in
reliance on Acts (i.e., identifies the visit in Gal. 2 with the
famine visit of Acts 11:30). Often fails to make explicit the
structure of the argument. Gives balanced consideration to
both Greco-Roman and Jewish backgrounds. Sees the nature of
law radically transformed when interpreted in terms of love
and freedom of the Spirit (e.g., neither enforced by penal sanctions nor produced by laws).

413 R. Y. K. Fung. *The Epistle to the Galatians.* NICNT. Grand
Rapids: Eerdmans, 1988.

Holds to the South Galatia theory and an early date. Maintains
that justification by faith is the heart of the letter and of Paul's
understanding of the gospel. Minimal attention given to literary and text-critical matters. Proposes that believers are free
from obligation to the law's statutes but fulfill the law (which
remains a valid expression of God's will) by the new way of
love.

414 R. N. Longenecker. *Galatians.* WBC 41. Dallas: Word,
1990.

Comprehensive introduction and bibliographies. Detailed defense of the South Galatia theory and an early date. Differs
from Betz's rhetorical and epistolary analysis in proposing a
basic rebuke-request structure and in being more flexible in applying this structural analysis (on the premise that Paul was
using common Greco-Roman conventions rather than carefully
following the rhetorical handbooks). Also considers Jewish exegetical procedures. Sees Paul fighting both an external Jewish

Christian nomistic threat and an internal threat of libertinism. Argues that Christians fulfill the law by love but are not obligated to the law.

415 J. D. G. Dunn. *A Commentary on the Epistle to the Galatians.* BNTC. London: A. & C. Black, 1993.

Opts for South Galatia and late date (Gal. 2:1–10 = Jerusalem Council of Acts 15). Comes from the standpoint of the "new perspective on Paul," that is, Paul is concerned with inclusion or exclusion of Gentiles, opposing the requirement that Gentiles must conform to the law (as a set of Jewish distinctives) to be saved. Despite its questionable slant, valuable for its stimulating exegesis and lucid argumentation. See also Dunn's *The Theology of Paul's Letter to the Galatians* (Cambridge: Cambridge University Press, 1993).

416 J. L. Martyn. *Galatians.* AB 33A. Garden City, N.Y.: Doubleday, 1997.

Opts for North Galatia and late date. Strong apocalyptic perspective: "A basic part of [Paul's] message . . . is the announcement of the death of that shared cosmos with its legal elements, and the emergence of the new cosmos with its new elements" (22).

11.9.5 Ephesians

See also the commentaries by Best (NTG; 1993); Caird (1976); Foulkes (1989); Kitchen (1994); Liefeld (1997); Lincoln and Wedderburn (1993); MacDonald (2000); Mitton (1981); Robinson (1920); Schnackenburg (1991); Snodgrass (1996); Westcott (1906); and Witherington (1998).

417 M. Barth. *Ephesians.* 2 vols. AB 34A, 34B. New York: Doubleday, 1974.

A wealth of information. Defends Pauline authorship, arguing that Ephesians represents a development and summary of Paul's thought. Frequently points out similarities in thought to the Old Testament and the teachings of Jesus.

418 F. F. Bruce. *The Epistles to the Colossians, to Philemon, and to the Ephesians.* NICNT. Grand Rapids: Eerdmans, 1984.

Considers Ephesians a general letter from Paul to Gentile Christians in the province of Asia whom he did not personally know. Argues that it carries the train of thought in Colossians on the role of Christ as cosmic Lord and applies its implications to the church as the body of Christ. Careful exegesis, useful interaction with scholarship, clear and succinct.

419   A. T. Lincoln. *Ephesians*. WBC 42. Dallas: Word, 1990.
            Analyzes the letter's structure in terms of Greco-Roman rheto-
            ric (but see O'Brien's criticism). Rejects Pauline authorship, but
            sees Ephesians as part of the authoritative canon of the church
            (because it was written in continuity with Paul's thought and
            was openly known to be pseudonymous). Sees the emphasis on
            resurrection and exaltation as complementary to Paul's empha-
            sis on the crucified and risen Christ.
420   E. Best. *A Critical and Exegetical Commentary on Eph-
            esians*. ICC. Edinburgh: T. & T. Clark, 1998.
            Believes that two different authors in the Pauline school wrote
            Ephesians and Colossians, without literary dependence. Help-
            ful comments on establishing the purpose of the letter. Argues
            that the author of Ephesians wrote to ensure the corporate ma-
            turity of Christians by means of emphasizing the nature of the
            church and the behavior that would promote true growth. Gen-
            erally lucid writing and clear presentation of alternative views.
            See also Best's *Essays on Ephesians* (Edinburgh: T. & T. Clark,
            1997).
421   P. T. O'Brien. *The Letter to the Ephesians*. PNTC. Grand
            Rapids: Eerdmans, 1999.
            Good defense of Pauline authorship. Concludes that Paul wrote
            Colossians first and Ephesians soon after with a more general
            application of his ideas. Also provides a helpful critique of the
            use of Greco-Roman rules for speech in analyzing Paul's letters.
            Sees the central message of the letter as cosmic reconciliation
            and unity in Christ. Contains careful exegesis and thoughtful
            interaction with other viewpoints.

11.9.6 Philippians

See also the commentaries by Bruce (1989); Caird (1976);
Donfried and Marshall (1993); Lightfoot (1881; reprint, 1993);
Martin (1980 and 1987); Thielman (1995); Vincent (1897); and
Witherington (1994).

422   G. Hawthorne. *Philippians*. WBC 43. Waco, Tex.: Word,
            1983.
            Useful for its extensive bibliography and interaction with vari-
            ous views. On linguistics, textual criticism, flow of thought,
            and interpretation, Silva (#424), Fee (#425) and O'Brien (#423)
            are preferable, but Hawthorne's fresh interpretive suggestions
            should not be ignored. Argues for Caesarea as the place of writ-
            ing and the presence of non-Christian Jewish opponents. Sees
            Philippians as akin to an informal conversation with various
            purposes and thus following no logical progression.

423   P. T. O'Brien. *The Epistle to the Philippians.* NIGTC. Grand Rapids: Eerdmans; Exeter, England: Paternoster, 1991.

Valuable for its extensive bibliography and interaction with alternative views. Meticulous exegesis and careful weighing of arguments. Holds to Rome as the place of writing and Paul's opponents as Judaizers (while the persecutors in 1:27–28 are pagans in Philippi). Contains valuable appendices on "to be with Christ," the meaning of 2:5–11 in context, the Adam-Christ parallel and Christ's preexistence, and the background of the Servant of the Lord of Isa. 53 behind Phil. 2:7. Finds various purposes behind the letter, but especially to call the Philippians to stand firm in the gospel and to be united in Christian love.

424   M. Silva. *Philippians.* WEC. Chicago: Moody, 1988. Reprint, BECNT. Grand Rapids: Eerdmans, 1992.

Sees the occasion as the need to exhort the Philippians to stand fast in the face of great adversity. Finds the presence of heterodox Jewish Christian opponents. Combines a useful paraphrase that summarizes the results of Silva's exegesis, exegetical essays that expound on the units of thought involved, and helpful additional notes. Invaluable comments (both in the introduction and in the commentary proper) on language and style, literary structure, and text-critical matters. A model of lucid writing and brevity.

425   G. D. Fee. *Paul's Letter to the Philippians.* NICNT. Grand Rapids: Eerdmans, 1995.

Proposes that Philippians is a hortatory letter of friendship and that Paul's overarching concern is with the Philippian Christians' progress in the faith. Criticizes the analysis of Paul's letters in terms of Greco-Roman rhetoric (i.e., Paul's use of rhetorical devices is fully explicable in terms of common usage in an oral culture), the tendency to interpret 2:5–11 as a pre-Pauline hymn (i.e., it is Paul's own exalted prose), the attempt to reconstruct various opponents (i.e., external opposition and internal disunity are present but not internal opponents), and speculations on Paul's place of imprisonment as somewhere other than Rome. Valuable treatment of vocabulary, textual criticism, and theological contributions in the introduction. See also Fee's *Philippians,* InterVarsity Press New Testament Commentary (Downers Grove, Ill., and Leicester, England: InterVarsity, 1999).

426   M. Bockmuehl. *The Epistle to the Philippians.* BNTC. London: A. & C. Black, 1997.

Up-to-date introduction that interacts well with the best of previous literature on Philippians. Helpfully evaluates the benefits and limits of sociological and rhetorical analyses. Argues for Roman provenance. Sees the presence of pagan persecution and only the warning of the danger (rather than the presence) of Judaizers. Paul's purpose is progress-oriented rather than problem-solving: to commend Epaphroditus, to acknowledge the Philippians' gift, to give an update on his situation, and to encourage the Philippians.

11.9.7 Colossians and Philemon

See also the commentaries by Abbott (1897); Barclay (NTG; 1997); Caird (1976); Donfried and Marshall (1993; on Philemon only); Garland (1998); Harris (1991); Lightfoot (1875; reprint, 1993); Lincoln and Wedderburn (1993); Martin (1973); Moule (1957); Pokorný (1991); Schweizer (1982); Wall (1993); and Wright (1986).

427   E. Lohse. *Colossians and Philemon*. Hermeneia. Philadelphia: Fortress, 1971. Original title: *Die Briefe an die Kolosser und an Philemon*. 14th ed. KEK. Göttingen: Vandenhoeck & Ruprecht, 1968.
Thin introduction designed to reserve detailed discussion until the body of the commentary. Rejects Pauline authorship (clearly stated only in discussing 4:7–18). Argues that the false teaching threatening to engulf the Colossian Christians was a syncretistic combination of Jewish tradition, pre-Gnostic dualism, and mystery-cultism. Provides convenient reference to texts both in the original and in English translation.

428   P. T. O'Brien. *Colossians, Philemon*. WBC 44. Waco, Tex.: Word, 1982.
Useful bibliographies and introduction. The section on form/structure/setting illuminates the structure of passages. Defends Pauline authorship and inclines toward Roman provenance. Reasons that Epaphras went to Paul to seek advice on how to deal with the false teaching and that Colossians was written in response. Sees Onesimus as a runaway slave whom Paul sent back to Philemon after Onesimus's conversion, asking that Onesimus be accepted as a brother in Christ. Careful and dependable exegesis.

429   F. F. Bruce. *The Epistles to the Colossians, to Philemon, and to the Ephesians*. NICNT. Grand Rapids: Eerdmans, 1984.
Adopts Roman provenance for both Colossians and Philemon. Defends Pauline authorship of Colossians. Accounts for differences in vocabulary and style by suggesting that Paul adapted some of the language and concepts of his opponents to set forth the gospel in contrast to their false teaching. Identifies the false teaching as a form of Jewish mysticism, perhaps *merkabah*

mysticism. Emphasizes Paul's diplomacy in requesting that Philemon receive Onesimus as a brother in Christ and send Onesimus back to serve Paul.

430 M. Barth and H. Blanke. *Colossians*. AB 34B. New York: Doubleday, 1994.

Massive introduction with much useful information, including an illuminating discussion of textual matters (a rare commodity in modern critical commentaries, but sorely needed). Exhaustive discussion of various arguments on the identity of the opponents in Colossians, on the relation or lack thereof between Ephesians and Colossians, and on the authorship of Colossians. Argues that Pauline authorship of both Ephesians and Colossians is still the least problematic solution.

431 J. D. G. Dunn. *The Epistle to the Colossians and to Philemon*. NIGTC. Grand Rapids: Eerdmans; Exeter, England: Paternoster, 1996.

Finds Pauline authorship problematic on the basis of perceived differences from the undisputed Pauline letters in flow of thought, rhetorical strategy, Colossians' more developed Christology, ecclesiology, realized eschatology, and its use of "household rules." Ultimately speculates that Colossians is the final letter with Paul's personal imprimatur, with Timothy as the actual author (linked to Dunn's view that Colossians and Philemon were written at the same time). Sees Colossians warning against a synagogue apologetic rather than errorists of any kind. In Philemon, Dunn sees Paul acting as a friend of the master (*amicus domini*) in interceding for Onesimus over an unknown wrong against his master.

432 M. Barth and H. Blanke. *The Letter to Philemon*. ECC. Grand Rapids: Eerdmans, 2000.

Massive commentary (more than 500 pp.) on Philemon. Includes detailed treatment of the social background of slavery at Paul's time (1–102).

433 J. A. Fitzmyer. *The Letter to Philemon*. AB 34C. New York: Doubleday, 2000.

Sees Paul acting as a friend of the master in interceding for Onesimus, who is in domestic trouble but is not a runaway slave. Clear and succinct (the commentary proper covers only pp. 81–127), yet inclusive in coverage.

11.9.8 1 and 2 Thessalonians

See also the commentaries by Donfried and Marshall (1993); Frame (1912); Holmes (1998); Menken (1994); Richard (1995); and Weatherly (1996).

434   E. Best. *A Commentary on the First and Second Epistles to the Thessalonians.* BNTC. London: A. & C. Black, 1972.

More substantial in size and pays more attention to grammatical and linguistic matters than is usually the case with commentaries in the BNTC series. Finds Luke's account in Acts 17 inaccurate, but upholds Pauline authorship of both 1 and 2 Thessalonians. Sees Paul in 1 Thessalonians addressing a number of ideas stemming from the Hellenistic background of Paul's readers rather than defending himself against any internal group of opponents. Holds that Paul wrote 2 Thessalonians to confront a new development (i.e., misunderstanding of eschatology and worsening of idleness).

435   F. F. Bruce. *1 and 2 Thessalonians.* WBC 45. Waco, Tex.: Word, 1982.

While holding that Paul certainly approved of the entirety of both letters, suggests that the naming of Paul, Silvanus, and Timothy as joint authors could explain differences from other Pauline letters (i.e., Silvanus played a major part in the composition). Helpful introduction. Careful exegesis and evaluation of arguments.

436   I. H. Marshall. *1 and 2 Thessalonians.* NCB. Grand Rapids: Eerdmans, 1983.

Able to be briefer than Best (#434) by referring readers to Best for more detailed treatment of earlier literature and views. Concentrates on research appearing after Best's work, including a detailed analysis and refutation of W. Trilling's arguments against the authenticity of 2 Thessalonians. Agrees with Best that Paul is not refuting any internal group of opponents. Succinct yet cogent exposition.

437   C. A. Wanamaker. *The Epistles to the Thessalonians.* NIGTC. Grand Rapids: Eerdmans; Exeter, England: Paternoster, 1990.

Full introduction with extensive interaction with scholarship. Good at finding weaknesses in alternative viewpoints. Presents a plausible case for the chronological priority of 2 Thessalonians (but see Morris, #438), which defuses arguments against its authenticity and offers an attractive historical reconstruction. Makes some helpful observations from a sociological perspective. Analyzes 1 Thessalonians as a demonstrative letter devoted to praise and 2 Thessalonians as a deliberative letter seeking to persuade and secure a change of mind and behavior.

438   L. Morris. *The First and Second Epistles to the Thessalonians.* Rev. ed. NICNT. Grand Rapids: Eerdmans, 1991. Original edition: 1973.

Good defense of the authenticity of 2 Thessalonians and of the traditional chronological priority of 1 Thessalonians (though Wanamaker [#437] apparently appeared too late for Morris to address directly). Clear writing and generally sound exegesis. See also Morris's *Epistles of Paul to the Thessalonians*, rev. ed., TNTC 13 (Downers Grove, Ill., and Leicester, England: Inter-Varsity, 1984).

439 A. J. Malherbe. *The Letters to the Thessalonians*. AB 32B. New York: Doubleday, 2000.

Identifies both 1 and 2 Thessalonians as pastoral and hortatory and defends Pauline authorship of 2 Thessalonians. Incorporates insights from Greco-Roman epistolary conventions and demonstrates sound use of the writings of moral philosophers and other letters as illumining parallels. Also provides an excellent bibliography.

11.9.9 The Pastoral Epistles

See also the commentaries by Davies (NTG; 1996); Fee (1988); Guthrie (1990); Hanson (1982); Houlden (1989); Kelly (1963); Liefeld (1999); Lock (1928); Scott (1936); Towner (1994); and Young (1994).

440 M. Dibelius and H. Conzelmann. *The Pastoral Epistles*. Translated by P. Buttolph and A. Yarboro. Hermeneia. Philadelphia: Fortress, 1972. Original title: *Die Pastoralbriefe*. 4th ed. Tübingen: Mohr (Siebeck), 1955.

Regards all three letters as pseudonymous. Finds the overall coherence and link in the theme of the apostle as example and in the constant emphasis on the meaning of salvation in the present. Sees opponents espousing a form of Judaizing Gnosticism. Rich compendium of historical and grammatical notes, but the exegesis is often too speculative.

441 J. D. Quinn. *The Letter to Titus*. AB 35. New York: Doubleday, 1990.

Holds that Titus originally stood at the head of the pseudonymous collection now known as the Pastoral Epistles because it lays out the Pauline policy and program for predominantly Jewish Christian congregations. First and Second Timothy follow Titus because they are written to predominantly Gentile Christian congregations. As a collection, the Pastoral Epistles were written to provide continuity with the apostolic and ecclesial mission to bring all persons to believe in and worship Jesus. Detailed notes on historical background and philology.

442 G. W. Knight, III. *The Pastoral Epistles*. NIGTC. Grand
Rapids: Eerdmans; Exeter, England: Paternoster, 1992.
     Defends Pauline authorship as well as a complementarian view
     of 1 Tim. 2:8–15. Sees Paul's two broad concerns in all three let-
     ters as warning against a false teaching and giving instructions
     to the churches in Ephesus and Crete through Timothy and
     Titus. Concentrates too much on the meaning of words to the
     relative neglect of syntax and the flow of thought.

443 I. H. Marshall. *A Critical and Exegetical Commentary on
the Pastoral Epistles*. ICC. Edinburgh: T. & T. Clark, 1999.
     Thinks the Pastorals were written by someone in Paul's name
     shortly after Paul's death without intent to deceive. Very full
     introduction, with especially useful analysis of the structure of
     each letter. The Epistle to Titus concerns how Titus is to deal
     with a defective church situation in Crete, 1 Timothy revolves
     around the truth of the gospel (defense against heresy, personal
     appropriation, and application to church order), and 2 Timothy
     stands in contrast to the previous two letters' concern for
     church order in focusing on the personal demeanor of a church
     leader in suffering for the gospel. Holds that a combination of
     Jewish, Christian, and ascetic elements defines the opponents.
     Good treatment of syntax, the flow of argument, and theology.

444 W. D. Mounce. *Pastoral Epistles*. WBC 46. Nashville: Nelson, 2000.
     Able defense of Pauline authorship as well as a complementar-
     ian interpretation of 1 Tim. 2:8–15. Full introduction, with
     valuable sections on the specific historical reasons accounting
     for most of the *hapax legomena,* on the themes of "faith" and
     "savior, salvation, and good works," and on the various ele-
     ments of the heresy. Good balance of clarity and inclusion of
     technical details.

445 J. D. Quinn and W. C. Wacker. *The First and Second Letters to Timothy*. ECC. Grand Rapids: Eerdmans, 2000.
     Companion volume to #441, brought to completion by W. Wacker
     after Quinn's death. First Timothy is an epistolary commission
     for Timothy. Second Timothy assumes the form of an episto-
     lary testament to Timothy as Paul's child and heir. In both
     cases, predominantly Gentile Christian congregations are ad-
     dressed, over against predominantly Jewish Christian congrega-
     tions in Titus. Rich in notes on historical background and
     philology.

446 L. T. Johnson. *The First and Second Letters to Timothy*. AB
35A. New York: Doubleday, 2001.
     Includes a helpful review of the history of interpretation prior

to the nineteenth century and a forceful demolition of the arguments against the authenticity of the Pastoral Epistles. Generally sound interpretation, with due attention to Greco-Roman rhetoric and moral philosophy. See also Johnson's *Letters to Paul's Delegates: 1 Timothy, 2 Timothy, Titus*, The New Testament in Context (Valley Forge, Pa.: Trinity Press International, 1996).

12

Special Studies

The monographs, *Festschriften*, and other collected essays in this section provide important contributions to the interpretation of particular Pauline letters (but often did not fit easily into the other sections). Where works substantially helpful to the interpretation of particular epistles are listed in other sections, an effort (by no means comprehensive) was made to cross-reference them below. For more extensive help, refer to the select bibliographies in the commentaries, especially where bibliographies are supplied for each interpretive unit: A. Thiselton's 1 Corinthians commentary (#403) is unparalleled in excellence in this regard; the WBC series includes this feature in its format, although the bibliographies supplied by individual authors range from moderately useful to outstanding.

12.1 Romans

See also S. K. Soderlund and N. T. Wright, eds., *Romans and the People of God: Essays in Honor of Gordon D. Fee on the Occasion of His Sixty-fifth Birthday* (Grand Rapids: Eerdmans, 1999); #291; #316; #322; #336; #515 (vols. 3 and 4); #739; #747; #751; and #754.

447 K. P. Donfried, ed. *The Romans Debate*. 2d ed. Peabody, Mass.: Hendrickson, 1991. Original edition: 1977.
Besides the original ten essays on the purpose and occasion of Romans, includes thirteen more essays concerning historical and sociological factors relevant to determining the purpose of Romans, its structure and rhetoric, and some key issues of de-

bate over its theology. Note the helpfulness of Donfried's introductions (for the 1977 ed. and 1991 additions) in providing an orientation to the overall debate.

448 H. Y. Gamble. *The Textual History of the Letter to the Romans: A Study in Textual and Literary Criticism.* SD 42. Grand Rapids: Eerdmans, 1977.

A thorough treatment of the original address and extent of Romans and the derivation of its deviant forms that correlates textual and literary criticism closely. Argues for the originality of the sixteen-chapter version (minus the doxology).

449 N. Elliott. *The Rhetoric of Romans: Argumentative Constraint and Strategy and Paul's Dialogue with Judaism.* JSNTSup 45. Sheffield: JSOT Press, 1990.

Useful survey and treatment of the "double character" problem of Romans (i.e., its Jewish subject matter yet Gentile Christian audience, as well as the apparent mismatch between the content of the letter body and the requirements of the concrete situation addressed). The analysis of Paul's use of rhetorical topics (mixing ancient and modern rhetoric indiscriminately) is helpful, even if not always convincing.

450 A. J. M. Wedderburn. *The Reasons for Romans.* Edinburgh: T. & T. Clark, 1988. Reprint, 1991.

Gives sustained attention to various proposals and argues for a network of interlocking factors: the presence of both Judaizing and Law-free Christians in Rome; the circumstances of both Paul and the Roman church; and Paul's planned visit to Rome.

451 H. Boers. *The Justification of the Gentiles: Paul's Letters to the Galatians and Romans.* Peabody, Mass.: Hendrickson, 1994.

A structuralist approach to Paul's thought, attempting to reassert something of Bultmann's existentialism: Paul operates with existential and social "micro-universes."

452 S. Stowers. *A Rereading of Romans: Justice, Jews, and Gentiles.* New Haven: Yale University Press, 1994. Reprint, 1997.

Proposes a new reading of Romans in light of the sociocultural, historical, and rhetorical contexts of Paul's world (arguing that Paul aims to persuade the Roman Christians that the acceptance and self-mastery they sought is found only in what God has done and is doing in Christ, and not in following Jewish teachers who advocate works from the Law).

453 J. D. Moores. *Wrestling with Rationality in Paul: Romans 1–8 in a New Perspective.* SNTSMS 82. Cambridge: Cambridge University Press, 1995.

Uses Umberto Eco's semiotics and Aristotle's notion of *enthymemes* to illumine Paul's logic in Rom. 1–8. The first chapter does not introduce the reader adequately to either concept, but the persistent reader will gain significant insights from this work.

454 M. P. Middendorf. *The "I" in the Storm: A Study of Romans 7*. St. Louis: Concordia Academic Press, 1997.

A useful interaction with the plethora of diverse interpretations of Rom. 7. Concludes that Paul describes the actual effect of the Law upon him as an unbeliever (7:7–11) and its double effect on him as a believer (7:14–25) to affirm that no one can become righteous or maintain a righteous standing before God by observing the Law's commands.

455 R. H. Bell. *No One Seeks for God: An Exegetical and Theological Study of Romans 1.18–3.20*. WUNT 106. Tübingen: Mohr (Siebeck), 1998.

A detailed exegesis of Rom. 1:18–3:20 that argues that this passage sets up an antithetical situation demonstrating the necessity of the revelation of the righteousness of God (Rom. 3:21–31). Rejects common suggestions of the possibility of natural theology and of judgment according to works for believers.

456 M. Reasoner. *The Strong and the Weak: Romans 14.1–15.13 in Context*. SNTSMS 103. Cambridge: Cambridge University Press, 1999.

While identifying part of the division between the strong and the weak along ethnic lines, reads the division primarily in terms of the Roman social background of asceticism (esp. vegetarianism), superstition, and obligation.

457 T. W. Berkley. *From a Broken Covenant to Circumcision of the Heart: Pauline Intertextual Exegesis in Romans 2:17–29*. SBLDS 175. Atlanta: Society of Biblical Literature, 2000.

After a useful survey of previous work on intertextuality, defines a method that isolates intertextual reference (involving conscious exegetical dependence of mutually interpreting OT texts). Applied to Rom. 2:17–29, identifies Jer. 7:2–11; 9:23–26; and Ezek. 36:16–17 interpreting Deut. 29–30 and Gen. 17: on the basis of Jer. 7:2–11 and 9:23–26, Paul charges the Jews with covenant-breaking disobedience (thus dishonoring God's name), so that circumcision becomes valueless. Through Deut. 30:6; Ezek. 36:6; and Jer. 9:26, Paul reinterprets circumcision in Gen. 17 as heart circumcision and through Deut. 29:29 and Ezek. 36:16–27, he redefines a Jew as one inwardly circumcised by the Spirit, so as to undermine Jewish assurance of privilege.

458 J. C. Miller. *The Obedience of Faith, the Eschatological People of God, and the Purpose of Romans.* SBLDS 177. Atlanta: Society of Biblical Literature, 2000.

    Successfully unites Paul's own signals of key themes and intent in the letter-frame with the content of the entire letter: Paul wrote Romans "to shape a community of the new age where Jew and gentile dwelt in unity" (19), to immunize them from criticism of the gospel (Rom. 1–11 thus serves as the salvation-historical basis for unity).

12.2 1 Corinthians

Most of the rhetorical and socio-scientific studies on 1 Corinthians could just as easily have been placed in §13.3, "Rhetoric," and §7.2, "Social Background." See also #129; #154; #157; #171; #174; #302; #314; #315; #515 (vol. 2); #564; #604; #732; #735; #803; #832; J. C. Hurd, *The Origin of 1 Corinthians,* 2d ed. (Macon, Ga.: Mercer University Press, 1983); and R. Bieringer, ed., *The Corinthian Correspondence,* BETL 125 (Louvain: Louvain University Press, 1996).

459 J. K. Chow. *Patronage and Power: A Study of Social Networks in Corinth.* JSNTSup 75. Sheffield: JSOT Press, 1992.

    Examines patron-client ties in the Roman colony and in the church at Corinth and Paul's response to the situation to shed light on the relationships and problems reflected in 1 Corinthians.

460 S. M. Pogoloff. *Logos and Sophia: The Rhetorical Situation of 1 Corinthians.* SBLDS 134. Atlanta: Scholars Press, 1992.

    A helpful reconstruction of the rhetorical situation of 1 Corinthians, arguing that the divisions at Corinth are over rhetoric and status.

461 P. D. Gardner. *The Gifts of God and the Authentication of a Christian: An Exegetical Study of 1 Corinthians 8–11:1.* Lanham, Md.: University Press of America, 1994.

    Makes a strong exegetical case for the hypothesis that the "strong's" mistaken identification of "knowledge" as an authenticator of their secure status in the covenant community underlies Paul's argument in 1 Cor. 8–11:1.

462 C. Forbes. *Prophecy and Inspired Speech in Early Christianity and Its Hellenistic Environment.* WUNT 2/75. Tübingen: Mohr (Siebeck), 1995.

    Investigates the widely held hypothesis that early-Christian inspired speech was closely related to inspired speech in Greco-Roman religions and that this similarity explains Paul's conflict with his Corinthian converts (who imported previously held pagan ideas) in 1 Cor. 12–14. Finds no convincing Greco-Roman religious parallels and suggests a combination of Christian experience, Hellenistic-Jewish popular philosophy, and a misunderstanding of Paul's own teaching as the causes of the conflict.

463 D. B. Martin. *The Corinthian Body.* New Haven: Yale University Press, 1995.

Part 1 deals with hierarchy and part 2 pollution. Pollution and hierarchy are conjoined in Paul's understanding of physiology: the female is "more porous, penetrable, weak, and defenseless" (249) (and thus must be subordinated for the protection of the body). On the other hand, "Paul attempts to undermine the hierarchical ideology of the body prevalent in Greco-Roman culture. . . . He calls on Christians of higher status to please those of lower status" (248).

464 D. G. Horrell. *The Social Ethos of the Corinthian Correspondence: Interests and Ideology from 1 Corinthians to 1 Clement.* Studies of the New Testament and Its World. Edinburgh: T. & T. Clark, 1996.

Operating in the framework of sociologist A. Giddens's "structuration theory," each formulation of teaching in 1 Corinthians is assessed as to the extent it "might support or legitimate the interests of dominant social groups and the hierarchical social order" (282).

465 L. L. Welborn. *Politics and Rhetoric in the Corinthian Epistles.* Macon, Ga.: Mercer University Press, 1997.

Argues that Paul uses the conventions of ancient politics to dissuade the Corinthians from factionalism (1 Cor. 1–4); to counsel concord (1 Cor. 4:6); to effect reconciliation (2 Cor. 1:1–2:13; 7:5–16); and to defend his character (2 Cor. 1:17). (Along the way, 2 Cor. 10–13 is identified as the letter of tears and 2 Cor. 2:14–7:4 as a fragment from an earlier work.)

466 A. T. Cheung. *Idol Food in Corinth: Jewish Background and Pauline Legacy.* JSNTSup 176. Sheffield: Sheffield Academic Press, 1999.

Argues against the prevailing modern consensus that Paul regarded idol food as a matter of indifference and proposes instead that idol food should be avoided if identified. Whether or not one accepts Cheung's thesis, provides useful interaction with modern scholarship and with early Christian documents.

467 J. S. Lamp. *First Corinthians 1–4 in Light of Jewish Wis-*

dom Traditions: Christ, Wisdom, and Spirituality. SBEC 42. Lewiston, N.Y.: Mellen, 2000.

After demonstrating the importance of wisdom in Israelite religion and finding a point of contact in Yahwistic and Hellenistic worldviews in the personification of wisdom, Lamp argues that Paul adapts Jewish wisdom tradition in his confrontation with Corinthian Christians, who were influenced by Greco-Roman rhetoric.

468 J. R. Asher. *Polarity and Change in 1 Corinthians 15.* HUT 42. Tübingen: Mohr (Siebeck), 2001.

Argues that Paul uses a didactic style of accommodation and correction in 15:35–57 to persuade the Corinthians concerning the validity of the resurrection of the dead; that is, the resurrection is compatible with the principle of cosmic polarity, and change solves the problem of polarity and the resurrection.

469 H. H. D. Williams. *The Wisdom of the Wise: The Presence and Function of Scripture within 1 Cor. 1:18–3:23.* Leiden: Brill, 2001.

An impressive study that finds six citations, two allusions, and seven echoes of OT Scripture in 1 Cor. 1:18–3:23. They are used in relationship to their original context, though often interpreted in relation to the new era in Christ and with a view to the Corinthian situation, functioning to support, advance, or supply portions of Paul's argument.

12.3 2 Corinthians

See also #129; #150; #171; #253; #317; #470; #515 (vol. 2); #539; #593; #781; and R. Bieringer and J. Lambrecht, *Studies on 2 Corinthians,* BETL 112 (Louvain: Louvain University Press/ Peeters, 1994).

470 S. J. Hafemann. *Suffering and the Spirit: An Exegetical Study of II Cor. 2:14–3:3 within the Context of the Corinthian Correspondence.* WUNT 2/19. Tübingen: Mohr (Siebeck), 1986. American edition: *Suffering and Ministry in the Spirit: Paul's Defense of His Ministry in II Corinthians 2:14–3:3.* Grand Rapids: Eerdmans, 1990.

The American edition is a further abridgement of the WUNT abridgement of Hafemann's dissertation. An exegetical study of 2 Cor. 2:14–3:3 that finds Paul defending his apostolic ministry in three stages: (1) his suffering as a vehicle for God's glory and power to be revealed; (2) his sufficiency for this ministry as evidenced by his practice of self-support; and (3) the existence of the Corinthians as Christians through his ministry (of mediating the Spirit to them). See also K. Sandnes, *Paul—One of the Prophets? A Contribution to the Apostle's Self-Understanding*, WUNT 2/43 (Tübingen: Mohr [Siebeck], 1991); and W. Lane, "Covenant: The Key to Paul's Conflict with Corinth," *TynBul* 33 (1982): 3–29.

471 L. L. Belleville. *Reflections of Glory: Paul's Polemical Use of the Moses-Doxa Tradition in 2 Corinthians 3.1–18.* JSNTSup 48. Sheffield: JSOT Press, 1991.

Examines the biblical and extrabiblical use of the Moses glory tradition, the epistolary structure and forms of 2 Cor. 1–7, and exegetical techniques from Paul's day to explain Paul's thought in 2 Cor. 3:12–18. Argues that Paul does not interpret Exod. 34:28–35 in a proper sense, but rather uses it (and various traditional interpretations and haggadic expansions) to advance his polemic (the underlying issue being the basis for apostolic credibility).

472 D. A. Renwick. *Paul, the Temple, and the Presence of God.* BJS 224. Atlanta: Scholars Press, 1991.

Argues that the quest for the presence of God was pervasive in ancient Judaism, especially for pre–70 C.E. Pharisees. In 2 Cor. 2:14–3:18, Paul not only defends his apostleship, but also describes the nature of the Christian life in terms of God's presence in Christ by the Spirit (rather than in the Law, the old covenant, and the temple).

473 W. J. Webb. *Returning Home: New Covenant and Second Exodus as the Context for 2 Corinthians 6.14–7.1.* JSNTSup 85. Sheffield: JSOT Press, 1993.

Addresses the apparent lack of contextual compatibility between 2 Cor. 6:14–7:1 and its surrounding context by highlighting Paul's identification of himself with the servant of Yahweh in using new-covenant and exilic-return traditions.

474 M. M. DiCicco. *Paul's Use of Ethos, Pathos, and Logos in 2 Corinthians 10–13.* Lewiston, N.Y.: Mellen, 1995.

Examines the theory and practice of ethos, pathos, and logos in Greco-Roman rhetoric and investigates Paul's use of these techniques in 2 Cor. 10–13. Argues that Paul used them to reestablish his competence and credibility, to refute his critics' accusations, and to regain his converts' allegiance.

475 B. K. Peterson. *Eloquence and the Proclamation of the Gospel in Corinth.* SBLDS 163. Atlanta: Scholars Press, 1998.

Identifies chapters 10–13 as the tearful letter that comes between 1 Corinthians and 2 Cor. 1–9. Traces the *stasis* of Paul's argument and how it changes as he moved his audience along in 2 Cor. 10–13. Argues that Paul sought to persuade his audience to abandon a view of faith, church, and ministry that conformed to their society's values, and to accept, instead, a cruciform model that negated those values.

12.4 Galatians

See also #296; #309; #450; #515 (vol. 1); #663; #734; and #828.

476 G. W. Hansen. *Abraham in Galatians: Epistolary and Rhetorical Contexts*. JSNTSup 29. Sheffield: JSOT Press, 1989.
By means of epistolary conventions (supplemented by chiasm and both ancient and modern categories of rhetoric), isolates 1:6–4:11 as a rebuke section and 4:12–6:10 as a request section. Argues that Paul's overall purpose was to defend his mission to the Gentiles, a purpose achieved by rebuking his Gentile converts for forsaking the gospel preached beforehand to Abraham and by requesting them to be loyal to the gospel like him and to cast out the troublemakers.

477 K. A. Morland. *The Rhetoric of Curse in Galatians: Paul Confronts Another Gospel*. Emory Studies in Early Christianity 5. Atlanta: Scholars Press, 1995.
Illumines Paul's use of curses in Galatians by rhetorical criticism (focusing on common, ancient Greco-Roman patterns of argumentation and style) and a semantic-field analysis of Jewish curse texts. By presenting the situation in Galatia as one of apostasy and seduction and by invoking covenantal curses on his opponents, Paul was challenging his audience to choose between him and the gospel, on the one hand, and his opponents and their "gospel," on the other.

478 M. Silva. *Interpreting Galatians: Explorations in Exegetical Method*. 2d ed. Grand Rapids: Baker, 2001.
Provides lucid and judicious instructions on linguistic, literary, historical, and theological aspects of the exegetical task, while shedding considerable light on Paul's letter.

479 W. B. Russell, III. *The Flesh/Spirit Conflict in Galatians*. Lanham, Md.: University Press of America, 1997.
Against the common interpretation of flesh/spirit as an internal conflict in individual Christians, argues that it contrasts two successive redemptive-historical eras or modes of living.

480 R. E. Ciampa. *The Presence and Function of Scripture in Galatians 1 and 2*. WUNT 102. Tübingen: Mohr Siebeck, 1998.
An ambitious study that seeks to contribute both to the under-

standing of the function of Scripture in Gal. 1 and 2 (and thus also for the whole of Galatians) and to a comprehensive method for a more integrated understanding of the function of Scripture within the semantic and rhetorical structure of Paul's letters.

481 B. W. Longenecker. *The Triumph of Abraham's God: The Transformation of Identity in Galatians.* Nashville: Abingdon, 1998.

Explores Paul's apocalyptic gospel in Galatians in terms of his overall worldview (God's triumph in Christ) along with the gospel's concrete results and application to those in Christ, and its relation to transformed patterns of Christian social behavior, God's covenant with Israel and the Law, and Paul's hermeneutic.

482 W. N. Wilder. *Echoes of the Exodus Narrative in the Context and Background of Galatians 5:18.* Studies in Biblical Literature 23. New York: Peter Lang, 2001.

Provides a useful interaction with the history of interpretation from patristic to modern times. Provocative argument for an implicit second-exodus typology behind Gal. 5:18 ("under the law" = Egypt-like slavery; and "led by the Spirit" = cloudlike guidance), primarily mediated through Ps. 143 (esp. v. 10).

12.5 Ephesians

See also #816 and N. A. Dahl, *Studies in Ephesians: Introductory Questions, Text- and Edition-Critical Issues, Interpretation of Texts and Themes,* ed. D. Hellholm, V. Blomkvist, and T. Fornberg, WUNT 131 (Tübingen: Mohr [Siebeck], 2000).

483 A. Van Roon. *The Authenticity of Ephesians.* NovTSup 39. Leiden: Brill, 1974.

A lengthy defense of Pauline authorship of Ephesians, with particular attention to the character of the epistle, some matters of style, and links between certain words and ideas found in other Pauline epistles.

484 C. E. Arnold. *Ephesians—Power and Magic: The Concept of Power in Ephesians in the Light of Its Historical Setting.* SNTSMS 63. Grand Rapids: Baker; Cambridge: Cambridge University Press, 1989. Paperback edition: Baker, 1992.

Attempts to shed light on the "power" motif in Ephesians by studying the author's development of that theme against the backdrop of the religious climate in Asia Minor in the first century C.E.

485 W. H. Harris. *The Descent of Christ: Ephesians 4:7–11 and Traditional Hebrew Imagery.* Biblical Studies Library.

Grand Rapids: Baker, 1998. Original edition: AGJU 32. Leiden: Brill, 1996.

Careful interpretation of Eph. 4:9–10 with detailed examination of Jewish traditions associating Moses' ascent to heaven with Ps. 68:19 and of the link of this psalm to Pentecost. Argues that Eph. 4:9–10 refers to a descent of Christ (subsequent to his exaltation) associated with the giving of the Spirit and spiritual gifts at Pentecost.

486 W. W. Klein. *The Book of Ephesians: An Annotated Bibliography.* Books of the Bible 8. New York: Garland, 1996.

Besides the more usual arrangement according to themes, also arranges according to chapter-and-verse units of Ephesians. Lacks indices, and a substantial number of entries are not annotated.

487 T. Moritz. *A Profound Mystery: The Use of the Old Testament in Ephesians.* NovTSup 85. Leiden: Brill, 1996.

Highlights the prevalence and the important functions of OT traditions in Ephesians. Also suggests that Ephesians is a rewritten version of Colossians that is enriched with OT traditions, perhaps contextualized for a more Jewish-minded audience.

488 T. R. Yoder Neufeld. *"Put on the Armour of God": The Divine Warrior from Isaiah to Ephesians.* JSNTSup 140. Sheffield: Sheffield Academic Press, 1997.

A tradition-historical study of the Divine-Warrior-in-full-armor motif, with careful exegetical attention to Isa. 59; Wisd. of Sol. 5; 1 Thess. 5; and culminating in Eph. 6.

489 R. R. Jeal. *Integrating Theology and Ethics in Ephesians.* SBEC 43. Lewiston, N.Y.: Mellen, 2000.

Analyzes Ephesians as a "sermon" comprised of a combined *exordium/narratio* (1:3–3:21) followed by an exhortation (4:1–6:9) and conclusion (6:10–20). The link between theology and ethics (the exhortation to Christian maturity in 4:1–6:9) is achieved by reminding the audience of theological concepts and realities (named in 1:3–3:21) in which they personally participate.

12.6 Philippians

See also #161; #296; #297; and #515 (vol. 1).

490 L. G. Bloomquist. *The Function of Suffering in Philippians.* JSNTSup 78. Sheffield: JSOT Press, 1993.

Useful survey of the history of interpretation on suffering in Philippians. Paul uses the theme of suffering in Philippians in four rhetorical ways: to endear himself to the Philippians; to identify with his audience's suffering; to portray their common suffering as a partial fulfillment of the Christ-type; and to engender hope in vindication after suffering.

491 D. Peterlin. *Paul's Letter to the Philippians in the Light of Disunity in the Church.* NovT 79. Leiden: Brill, 1995.

Helpfully highlights Paul's addressing of disunity in Philippians. That the topic of disunity runs through the whole letter is more doubtful. See also T. C. Geoffrion, *The Rhetorical Purpose and the Political and Military Character of Philippians: A Call to Stand Firm* (Lewiston, N.Y.: Mellen, 1993), which highlights the call to unity.

492 G. W. Peterman. *Paul's Gift from Philippi: Conventions of Gift-Exchange and Christian Giving.* SNTSMS 92. Cambridge: Cambridge University Press, 1997.

A study of Greco-Roman social conventions of giving and receiving (as well as the conventions in the OT and extrabiblical Jewish literature) that sheds light on how Paul prioritized the gospel in either rejecting or engaging in such conventions as the situation dictated. Also provides brief treatment of the Corinthian conflict, Rom. 15:25–31; Philem. 17–19; 1 Tim. 5:4; and Rom. 5:7.

493 C. W. Davis. *Oral Biblical Criticism: The Influence of the Principles of Orality on the Literary Structure of Paul's Epistle to the Philippians.* JSNTSup 172. Sheffield: Sheffield Academic Press, 1999.

Attempts to bring modern linguistics, epistolography, and especially rhetorical criticism under the service of oral biblical criticism. Various rhetorical devices are identified to help delineate compositional units, which are then analyzed in terms of their logical and thematic progression. Finds Philippians to be a unitary composition: 1:3–26 and 4:10–20 provide examples of unity; 1:27–2:18 and 3:1–4:9 command the Philippians to be unified; and Timothy and Epaphroditus exemplify unity in the central part of the concentric structure in 2:19–30. See also Davis's essay in #299.

12.7 Colossians

See also J. E. Crouch, *The Origin and Intention of the Colossian Haustafel,* FRLANT 109 (Göttingen: Vandenhoeck & Ruprecht, 1972); and F. O. Francis and W. A. Meeks, eds., *Conflict at Colossae,* 2d ed., SBLSBS 4 (Missoula, Mont.: Scholars Press, 1975).

494 G. E. Cannon. *The Use of Traditional Materials in Colossians.* Macon, Ga.: Mercer University Press, 1983.

Finds a large amount of traditional material in Colossians (which renders lexical and stylistic analysis ineffective) and argues that these materials are used in ways consonant with Paul's unique concerns elsewhere in his undisputed letters, thereby strengthening the case for Pauline authorship. A case against Pauline authorship is made by M. Kiley, *Colossians as Pseudepigraphy* (Sheffield: JSOT Press, 1986).

495 R. DeMaris. *The Colossian Controversy: Wisdom in Dispute at Colossae.* JSNTSup 96. Sheffield: Sheffield Academic Press, 1994.

The Colossian philosophy appears to be a distinctive blend of popular Middle Platonic, Jewish, and Christian elements that cohere around the pursuit of wisdom. Challenged by Arnold (#496).

496 C. Arnold. *The Colossian Syncretism: The Interface between Christianity and Folk Belief at Colossae.* WUNT 2/77. Tübingen: Mohr (Siebeck); Grand Rapids: Baker, 1995.

Using local archaeological evidence and inscriptions, Arnold argues that the Colossian heresy represents "folk religion" in which the veneration of angels served magical, apotropaic purposes. See also his *Ephesians—Power and Magic* (#484).

497 T. J. Sappington. *Revelation and Redemption at Colossae.* JSNTSup 53. Sheffield: JSOT Press, 1991.

Investigates the ascetic-mystical piety of Jewish apocalypticism and argues that the Colossian error is a type of Jewish/Gentile Christianity influenced by it. But see also the different perspectives of R. DeMaris (#495); C. Arnold (#496); and T. Martin, *By Philosophy and Empty Deceit: Colossians as Response to a Cynic Critique,* JSNTSup 118 (Sheffield: Sheffield Academic Press, 1996).

498 W. T. Wilson. *The Hope of Glory: Education and Exhortation in the Epistle to the Colossians.* NovTSup 88. Leiden: Brill, 1997.

Understands Colossians as a pseudonymous document elaborately constructed to exhort its readers in content and manner similar to Hellenistic moral philosophy.

12.8 1 and 2 Thessalonians

See also R. F. Collins, *Studies on the First Letter to the Thessalonians,* BETL 66 (Louvain: Louvain University Press, 1984); R. F. Collins, ed., *The Thessalonian Correspondence,* BETL 87 (Louvain: Louvain University Press, 1990); #290; #296; #515 (vol. 1); #752; and J. T. Reed's "To Timothy or Not? A Discourse Analysis of 1 Timothy," in #293.

499   R. Jewett. *The Thessalonian Correspondence: Pauline Rhetoric and Millenarian Piety.* Foundations and Facets. Philadelphia: Fortress, 1986.
    Combines both rhetorical and social-scientific criticism in reconstructing the proposed underlying problem of "millenarian radicalism" in Thessalonica.

500   A. Malherbe. *Paul and the Thessalonians: The Philosophic Tradition of Pastoral Care.* Philadelphia: Fortress, 1987.
    Attempts to shed light—by comparison with contemporary Greco-Roman moral philosophers—on how Paul converted the Thessalonians, shaped them into a community, and continued to care for them after his departure.

501   G. S. Holland. *The Tradition That You Received from Us: 2 Thessalonians in the Pauline Tradition.* HUT 24. Tübingen: Mohr (Siebeck), 1988.
    Proposes that 2 Thessalonians was written by a thoroughgoing apocalypticist to reinterpret Paul's eschatological instructions in 1 Thessalonians to help a generation faced with the delay of the parousia and to combat advocates of realized eschatology. For a rhetorical study that likewise posits pseudonymity, see F. Hughes, *Early Christian Rhetoric and 2 Thessalonians,* JSNTSup 30 (Sheffield: JSOT Press, 1989).

502   J. A. D. Weima and S. E. Porter. *An Annotated Bibliography of 1 and 2 Thessalonians.* NTTS. Leiden: Brill, 1998.
    Annotations on some 1,200 bibliographic references relevant to the study of 1–2 Thessalonians (almost exhaustive for the twentieth century and good representation of the nineteenth; only materials in section 1 are listed without annotation). Unparalleled resource for the study of these letters.

503   T. D. Still. *Conflict at Thessalonica: A Pauline Church and Its Neighbours.* JSNTSup 183. Sheffield: Sheffield Academic Press, 1999.
    Uses the social-scientific study of deviance and conflict to shed light on conflict between Christians and non-Christians. Argues that Paul was persecuted and driven out by non-Christian Jews because of his Law-free living and teaching, while his converts were harassed by their fellow Gentiles and perceived as exclusive, offensive, and even subversive.

504   K. P. Donfried and J. Beutler, eds. *The Thessalonians Debate: Methodological Discord or Methodological Synthesis?* Grand Rapids: Eerdmans, 2000.

A collection of papers stemming from four annual meetings of the Thessalonians Correspondence Seminar of the Studiorum Novi Testamenti Societas (SNTS). Part 1 focuses on 1 Thess. 2:1–12, allowing different starting points and divergent interpretations to be juxtaposed. Part 2 examines these differences in the context of larger methodological issues.

12.9 Pastoral Epistles

See also #146; #347; #352; #813; #819; and #830.

505 B. Fiore. *The Function of Personal Example in the Socratic and Pastoral Epistles.* AnBib 105. Rome: Biblical Institute Press, 1986.

Examines a long tradition of Greco-Roman exhortation literature to explain the function of the personal examples in the Pastoral Epistles. Concludes that the author (pseudonymous, with a Cynic background) used these examples to set standards for leadership and to encourage the Christian community to adopt high moral standards.

506 M. Prior. *Paul the Letter-Writer and the Second Letter to Timothy.* JSNTSup 23. Sheffield: JSOT Press, 1989.

Adduces contemporaneous parallels in which co-ascription in the opening meant some level of actual coauthorship, and highlights the perceivable difference between Ignatius's private and public correspondence to contend for the possible significance of coauthorship, Paul's use of secretaries, and the distinction between private and public correspondence. Suggests that the Pastorals may be the most authentically Pauline since they may be the only letters written by Paul alone, without a secretary, to individuals.

507 R. M. Kidd. *Wealth and Beneficence in the Pastoral Epistles: A "Bourgeois" Form of Early Christianity?* SBLDS 122. Atlanta: Scholars Press, 1990.

Argues against critical scholarship's reconstruction of the Christianity depicted in the Pastoral Epistles: Christians did not form a bourgeoisie that had accommodated itself to the surrounding culture by adopting a "conservative" ethic incompatible with Paul's vibrant apocalypticism.

508 J. D. Miller. *The Pastoral Letters as Composite Documents.* SNTSMS 93. Cambridge: Cambridge University Press, 1997.

Sees (alleged) lack of organization and development of thought and the presence of different genres of material in the Pastoral Epistles as evidence that they are anthologies of traditional materials (i.e., they are the work of a compiler rather than an author).

509 M. Harding. *Tradition and Rhetoric in the Pastoral Epistles*. Studies in Biblical Literature 3. New York: Peter Lang, 1998.

Assumes pseudonymity and investigates the persuasive techniques of the Pastor (i.e., the use of the epistolary moral exhortation tradition, the rhetoric of persuasive speech, and Pauline tradition).

13

Pauline Theology

13.1 Comprehensive Treatments

There is a paucity of modern, comprehensive treatments of Paul's theology. Many of the significant treatments of Paul's theology are embedded as part of larger New Testament theologies. Only a few of these NT theologies are singled out for mention below (the reader should consult others, e.g., R. Bultmann, #22, 1:185–352, for supplementary treatments of Paul). Of course, both the context of Paul's theology and also the issues surrounding its interpretation can only be properly appreciated within the larger framework of New Testament theology and the history of its interpretation. The reader should refer to Hasel (#512) and chapter 2, "History of Modern Interpretation." Three significant features distinguish all Pauline theologies in varying degrees. First, some scholars accept all thirteen letters traditionally attributed to Paul, while others reject up to six of these letters. The resultant picture of Paul's theology is predictably different, depending on the extent of the corpus regarded as authentically Pauline and thus incorporated in the synthesis. Second, there is an increasing tendency to see Paul's writings as contingent, and hence sometimes inconsistent (radical forms of this view, which see no coherent theology in Paul, may partly account for the dearth of comprehensive syntheses of Paul). Third, some regard the task of doing Pauline theology as purely descriptive, whereas others attempt some form of contemporary application or contextualization.

510   D. E. H. Whiteley. *The Theology of St. Paul.* 2d ed. Oxford: Basil Blackwell, 1974. Original edition: 1964.

Competent, systematic coverage of Paul's theology. Excludes the Pastorals and uses Ephesians in a qualified manner.

511   H. Ridderbos. *Paul: An Outline of His Theology.* Translated by J. R. de Witt. Grand Rapids: Eerdmans, 1997. Original edition: 1975. Dutch title: *Paulus: Ontwerp van zijn theologie.* Kampen, the Netherlands: J. H. Kok, 1966.

A valuable comprehensive outline of Paul's theology that locates the center of his thought within the framework of redemptive history, especially in God's activity in the advent and work of Christ. Paul's eschatology and Christology are intertwined because his eschatology is "Christ-eschatology."

512   G. Hasel. *New Testament Theology: Basic Issues in the Current Debate.* Grand Rapids: Eerdmans, 1978.

Excellent survey of recent debates over the nature, function, method, and scope of New Testament theology as a discipline. See also D. A. Carson's "New Testament Theology," *DLNT* 796–814.

513   J. C. Beker. *Paul the Apostle: The Triumph of God in Life and Thought.* 2d ed. Philadelphia: Fortress, 1984. Original edition: 1980.

Posits that the coherent center of Paul's thought lies in "the triumph of God," that is, in God's victory and redemption of the creation order inaugurated in Christ, and that Paul addresses contingent situations in light of this coherent center (with occasional inconsistencies).

514   P. Stuhlmacher. *Biblische Theologie des Neuen Testaments.* Vol. 1: *Grundlegung von Jesus zu Paulus.* Göttingen: Vandenhoeck & Ruprecht, 1992.

This two-volume biblical theology of the New Testament (vol. 2 came out in 1997) represents the culminating work of an important contemporary, conservative (by German standards) Lutheran scholar. Deals with the proclamation of Paul in eight sections (221–390): (1) sources, chronology, and the particular nature of the Pauline work; (2) the origin and beginning of Pauline theology; (3) the Law with Paul; (4) world, man, and sin; (5) Christ—the end of the Law; (6) gospel, justification, faith; (7) sacrament, Spirit, and church; and (8) life and obedience out of grace—the Pauline exhortation.

515   *Pauline Theology.* Vol. 1: *Thessalonians, Philippians, Galatians, and Philemon.* Edited by J. M. Bassler. Vol. 2: *1 and 2 Corinthians.* Edited by D. M. Hay. Vol. 3: *Romans.* Edited by D. M. Hay and E. E. Johnson. Vol. 4: *Looking*

Back, Pressing On. Edited by E. E. Johnson and D. M. Hay. Minneapolis: Fortress, 1991, 1993, 1995, 1997.

Four volumes of essays originating from the discussions of the SBL Pauline Theology Group between 1986–95. The investigation proceeded one letter at a time (beginning with the shortest letters) to respond to the challenge posed by diversity and historical contingency. The first two volumes contain essays on method, theologies of individual letters, and partial syntheses. The third volume begins with three comprehensive overviews of Romans, followed by essays treating successive sections of Romans (alternating with response essays). Volume 4 treats three distinct but related conversations in the ten-year discussion: part 1 looks back on the discussion of Romans; part 2 covers the debate over faith in or of Jesus Christ; and part 3 evaluates the results of the entire project.

516 G. E. Ladd. *A Theology of the New Testament.* Rev. ed. Grand Rapids: Eerdmans, 1993. Original edition: 1974.

Surveys the discipline of New Testament theology and offers positive solutions to its problems. The revised edition includes a valuable update of the select bibliography. The section on Paul (397–614) illumines Paul's thought by highlighting Christ as the center of redemptive history within a framework involving the mutual interplay of realized and futuristic eschatology.

517 K. Berger. *Theologiegeschichte des Urchristentums Theologie des Neuen Testaments.* 2d ed. Tübingen and Basel: Francke, 1995. Original edition: 1994.

Extensive treatment of Paul and his historical and theological relation to other traditions within earliest Christianity.

518 C. M. Pate. *The End of the Age Has Come: The Theology of Paul.* Grand Rapids: Zondervan, 1995.

A concise volume that highlights the overlapping of two ages (the already–not yet tension brought about by Christ's coming, death, and resurrection) as the key to Paul's thought. Demonstrates this thesis by showing the essential eschatological nature of the major categories of Paul's thought: theology, Christology, soteriology, anthropology, pneumatology, ecclesiology, society, and eschatology.

519 N. T. Wright. *What Saint Paul Really Said: Was Paul of Tarsus the Real Founder of Christianity?* Grand Rapids: Eerdmans, 1997.

Not a complete study of Paul, yet covers what Wright considers key areas of Paul's proclamation and its implications. Wright's response to the thesis that Paul was the real founder of Christianity comes as an afterthought (the last chapter was added after receiving A. N. Wilson's *Paul* [#100]). Until Wright

completes volume 5 on Paul in his projected six-volume series,
Christian Origins and the Question of God, this little volume
provides the best glimpse of Wright's conception of Paul's theology (see also #235).

520 J. D. G. Dunn. *The Theology of Paul the Apostle*. Grand
Rapids: Eerdmans, 1998.

A substantial, up-to-date theology of Paul from a major proponent of the new perspective on Paul. Includes nine letters in
discussion, excluding the Pastoral Epistles and Ephesians. Romans serves as a sort of template for the book's organization.
Contains extensive interaction with scholarship and helpful
bibliographies at the head of each chapter.

521 T. R. Schreiner. *Paul, Apostle of God's Glory in Christ: A
Pauline Theology*. Downers Grove, Ill.: InterVarsity,
2001.

Begins with a helpful discussion on the inadequacy of various
proposed centers for Paul's theology. Then argues inductively
from various texts that the supremacy of God in and through
Jesus Christ underlies and permeates Paul's theology and life
vision. Valuable not only for its forceful synthesis, but also for
its contextually sensitive and exegetically sound treatment of a
full array of Pauline texts.

13.2 Narrative Framework

A new subgenre of "narrative world" is emerging for the description of Paul's theology. The strengths of this approach are
that it recognizes (1) the narrative component in the human experience of reality; and thus (2) the narrative component of Paul's
biblical worldview; and (3) the coherence of Paul's particular
theological beliefs and exhortations within this worldview.
When a narrative approach to the biblical text is combined with
a critical realist epistemology (as in Wright [#522]), the intent of
the author, the embodiment of the author's intent in the text,
the authorially constrained referentiality of the text to the objective world, and the possibility of the audience's approxima-
tion toward the meaning of the text are all properly affirmed
without falling into either naive realism (characteristic of much
modern historical-critical scholarship) or radical skepticism
(characteristic of most poststructuralist, postmodern, reader-response reactions to modern scholarship). Nevertheless, at least
four areas of refinement to the approach are needed: (1) more
thorough, firsthand exegetical treatment of the Old Testament to

refine the picture of the OT story; (2) further critical work on the relationship between the story exhibited in noncanonical Jewish literature and the story exhibited in the OT and NT canon; (3) further work on articulating well-defined criteria and quantifiable methods for identifying and reconstructing the story embedded in various forms of discourse; and (4) a recognition of the unimaginable disruptions and paradoxes in Scripture, by which God alone maintains the continuity of God's saving purposes (see E. Käsemann, "Justification and Salvation History in the Epistle to the Romans," in *Perspectives in Paul* [Philadelphia: Fortress, 1971], 60–78). Besides the works listed below, see also Peterson (#148); Fowl (#234); and Hays (#663).

522 N. T. Wright. *Christian Origins and the Question of God.* Vol. 1: *The New Testament and the People of God.* Philadelphia: Fortress; London: SPCK, 1992.

Articulates an impressive critical realist framework for interpreting worldviews and the particular beliefs and aims that flow from them. Story belongs to the essence of the experience of human life and, in combination with symbol, praxis, and basic questions and answers, forms worldviews. Paul's world of thought is substantially the story of Jesus found in Luke, Matthew, and Mark (see esp. pp. 403–9).

523 B. Witherington, III. *Paul's Narrative Thought World: Tapestry of Tragedy and Triumph.* Louisville: Westminster John Knox, 1994.

Sees all of Paul's theology and ethics as grounded in the grand narrative of the Hebrew Scriptures (and some of the developments after OT times), the Jesus traditions, and Paul's conversion experience. Crises were occasions for Paul to express his Christocentric theology, not catalysts for innovation or ad hoc response.

524 S. C. Keesmaat. *Paul and His Story: (Re)Interpreting the Exodus Tradition.* JSNTSup 181. Sheffield: Sheffield Academic Press, 1999.

Proposes that Paul reinterprets and appropriates Israel's exodus tradition for the Christian community in the same manner that "living traditions" function in human communities in general—that is, traditions are recurrently reinterpreted and actualized (thus transforming them) from generation to generation. Examines this alleged reappropriation in Rom. 8:14–39 and Gal. 4:1–7 through intentional intertextual echoes (building on Hays [#663]).

13.3 God

While treatments of the doctrine of God abound in the fields of systematic theology, philosophy, and Old Testament studies in the twentieth century, the doctrine of God may still aptly be termed "the neglected factor in New Testament Theology" (coined by Dahl [#529] in 1975). Most analyses of Paul's theology in this century (including evangelical Pauline theologies like Ridderbos [#511] and Ladd [#516]) forgo a section on God and provide no extended treatment of theology proper. Monographs and journal articles are few and far between. Moreover, the majority of these explore how Paul's belief in Christ influenced his theology of God (e.g., #309; #527; #528; and #531). Dunn attributes this phenomenon largely to Paul's own lack of exposition of his convictions about God because his audience shared his beliefs (derived from his Jewish heritage). At the same time, Dunn notes that the revelation of Christ affected Paul's beliefs (#520, pp. 28–29; see pp. 27–50 for Dunn's treatment of the doctrine). The existing literature differs significantly on the nature and extent of continuity/discontinuity between Paul's and his Jewish heritage's understanding of God. Future studies need to articulate clear definitions and criteria for comparison and apply a more comprehensive and rigorously controlled method. In the absence of truly comprehensive treatments of Paul's doctrine of God, the best overview is D. Guthrie and R. Martin, "God," *DPL* 354–69. See also §13.4, "Christology." On divine sovereignty, see #680.

525   G. Delling. "Partizipiale Gottesprädikationen in den Briefen des Neuen Testaments." *ST* 17 (1963): 1–59.

   Studies the participial formulas of praise and other types of participial constructions that describe God and Christ. Suggests that they formed part of the early church's missionary preaching and liturgy (though providing insufficient data to reconstruct credal confessions). See also the abbreviated form of this study, "Geprägte partizipiale Gottesaussagen in der urchristlichen Verkündigung," in *Studien zum Neuen Testament und zum hellenistischen Judentum: Gesammelte Aufsätze, 1950–1968*, ed. F. Hahn, T. Holtz, and N. Walter (Göttingen: Vandenhoeck & Ruprecht, 1970), 401–16.

526   L. Morris. "The Theme of Romans." Pp. 249–63 in *Apostolic History and the Gospel: Biblical and Historical Essays Presented to F. F. Bruce on His Sixtieth Birthday.*

Edited by W. W. Gasque and R. P. Martin. Grand Rapids: Eerdmans, 1970.

Begins with the startling statistic that the word "God" occurs most frequently in Romans (once some function words are excluded) and then examines the content of Paul's statements. Argues that Romans is a book about God. See also chapter 1, "God at the Center," in Morris's *New Testament Theology*; and "The Apostle and His God," in *God Who Is Rich in Mercy*, ed. P. T. O'Brien and D. G. Peterson (Homebush West, Australia: Anzea, 1986), 165–78.

527 H. Moxnes. *Theology in Conflict: Studies in Paul's Understanding of God in Romans.* NovTSup 53. Leiden: Brill, 1980.

Part 1 surveys Paul's use of God language in Rom. 1–4 and 9–11, arguing that Paul made historical conflicts over the law, mission, and group identity into controversies over the understanding of God. Part 2 concentrates on Rom. 4:13–22, arguing that Paul interprets and modifies traditional statements about God by making the statement "who gives life to the dead and calls into existence the things that do not exist" (4:17) into a hermeneutical antithesis: law versus faith, wrath versus grace, letter versus Spirit.

528 J. M. Bassler. *Divine Impartiality: Paul and a Theological Axiom.* SBLDS 59. Chico, Calif.: Scholars Press, 1982.

Traces the concept of God's impartiality in the Old Testament, deuterocanonical, rabbinic literature, and Philo before examining Paul's use of the concept in Romans (also briefly Gal. 2, 1 Cor. 1–4, and other NT texts). Argues that the application of divine impartiality to dismantle the Jew-Greek dichotomy is unique to Paul (even as different texts both before and after him applied this concept in diverse ways).

529 N. A. Dahl. "The Neglected Factor in New Testament Theology." Pp. 153–63 in *Jesus the Christ: The Historical Origins of Christological Doctrine.* Edited by D. H. Juel. Minneapolis: Fortress, 1991.

A previously unpublished reflection composed in 1975. Calls attention to the neglect of the doctrine of God in the descriptive task of New Testament theology and provides some helpful proposals and seeds of thought.

530 P. G. Klumbies. *Die Rede von Gott bei Paulus in ihrem zeitgeschichtlichen Kontext.* FRLANT 155. Göttingen: Vandenhoeck & Ruprecht, 1992.

Seeks to understand Paul's use of the word "God" against the background of Jewish writings of the Hellenistic period and supposed pre-Pauline traditions (e.g., Rom. 3:25–26a; 1 Cor. 8:6; and Phil. 2:6–11). Sees Paul's belief in Christ resulting in a "christologically defined God" that is set both against the idols and the God of the Jews.

531 N. Richardson. *Paul's Language about God.* JSNTSup 99. Sheffield: Sheffield Academic Press, 1994.

Examines Paul's language about God in Rom. 9–11; 1 Cor. 1:18–3:23; 2 Cor. 2:14–4:7; Rom. 12:1–15:13; 2 Cor. 5:19; and 1 Cor. 8:6. Concludes that Paul universalizes and radicalizes the OT understanding of God's grace and love through Christ, uses God-language to define Christ, and redefines God's identity by language about Christ.

13.4 Christ

Recent studies in Christology have focused extensively on the question of why and how religious devotion to Jesus arose. While (1) the transferred focus to a Jewish background and (2) the discrediting of the old history-of-religions school's view that early cultic devotion to Jesus is attributable to pagan corruption of the Jewish monotheistic tradition (e.g., Bousset [#18]) are welcome, the revisionary reading of the Jewish evidence on monotheism that narrowly concentrates on alleged semi-divine intermediary figures is questionable. The most nuanced treatment is L. Hurtado's *One God, One Lord* (#536), which partially rejects this revisionary reading of monotheism but accepts that these intermediary figures formed a tradition of divine agency that early Christians reinterpreted in light of their religious experience of Jesus. (For an overview of Hurtado's project for a new history-of-religions school, see his "Christ-Devotion in the First Two Centuries: Reflections and a Proposal," *TJT* 12 [1996]: 17–33. See also his *At the Origins of Christian Worship* [#805]; "First-Century Jewish Monotheism," *JSNT* 71 [1998]: 3–26; and "Jesus' Divine Sonship in Paul's Epistle to the Romans," in *Romans and the People of God* [Grand Rapids: Eerdmans, 1999], 217–33.) The most up-to-date study arguing for a distinctly angelomorphic Christology is C. Grieschen (#548; see pp. 7–48 for a useful survey of research and clarification of terminology and method). R. Bauckham (#547), however, advances an alternative approach by highlighting the unbridgeable gap between Creator and creature in Jewish monotheism and the NT's inclusion of Jesus in the God of Israel's unique identity. Because of the avalanche of literature and space limitations, older literature (e.g., the many studies on christological titles) and other questions will necessarily be slighted. For a useful annotated bibliography covering this earlier literature, see A. Hultgren (#8, esp. pp. 296–321). See also the introductory articles in *DPL:* B. Witherington, "Christ" and "Christology," 95–100 and 100–115; L. Hurtado, "Lord," "Pre-existence," and "Son of God," 560–69, 743–46, and 900–906; A. Luter, "Savior," 867–69; P. O'Brien, "Firstborn," 301–3; L. Kreitzer, "Adam and Christ," 9–15; and D. Clines, "Image of God," 426–28. Dunn (#520, pp. 196–206 and 234–65) and chapters 2–6 in Wright (#235) should not be ignored. On Paul's designation of Jesus as "God" (Rom. 9:5 and Titus 2:13), see M. Harris, *Jesus as God: The New Testament Use of "Theos" in Reference to Jesus* (Grand Rapids: Baker, 1992), 143–85. On Paul's application of OT passages in which *kurios* translates YHWH to Jesus, see D. Capes, *Old Testament Yahweh Texts in Paul's Christology,* WUNT 2/47 (Tübingen: Mohr [Siebeck], 1992). On the close interrelation between Paul's doctrine of God and Christ, see #531 and #728. See also chapter 8, "Paul and Jesus," and especially §9.2, "Hymns and Creeds."

532 M. Hengel. *The Son of God: The Origin of Christology and the History of Jewish-Hellenistic Religion.* Translated by J. Bowden. Philadelphia: Fortress, 1976. Original title: *Der Sohn Gottes: Der Entstehung der Christologie und die jüdisch-hellenistische Religionsgeschichte.* Tübingen: Mohr (Siebeck), 1975.
   Helpful survey demonstrating that Paul's conception of the Son of God predated Paul and that it includes preexistence, mediation at creation, and sending into the world. See also Hengel's *Studies in Early Christology* (Edinburgh: T. & T. Clark, 1995).

533 C. F. D. Moule. *The Origin of Christology.* Cambridge: Cambridge University Press, 1977.
   Defends a "developmental" rather than an "evolutionary" model (which draws on resources from Hellenistic religions) of Christology, first by affirming the origin of "Son of Man," "Son of God," "Christ," and *kurios* from Jesus and then, more extensively, by appeal to early Christian (esp. Pauline) understanding and experience of Christ as a corporate personality.

534 J. D. G. Dunn. *Christology in the Making: A New Testament Inquiry into the Origins of the Doctrine of the Incarnation.* 2d ed. London: SCM, 1989; Grand Rapids: Eerdmans, 1996. Original edition: 1980.

An important challenge to the traditional acceptance of an early doctrine of preexistence and incarnation in the NT (arguing that it is found only in John), based on an evolutionary model defined by "historical context of meaning" and "conceptuality in transition." Inadequate attempts to refute Dunn are surveyed in the foreword to the second edition (xi–xxxix). See also #520, pp. 266–93. But see Bauckham's more convincing model (#547) and the exegetical objections of B. Byrne, "Christ's Pre-existence in Pauline Soteriology," *TS* 58 (1997): 308–30.

535 H. H. Rowdon. *Christ the Lord: Studies in Christology Presented to Donald Guthrie.* Downers Grove, Ill.: InterVarsity, 1982.

See especially I. Marshall, "Incarnational Christology in the New Testament"; R. France, "The Worship of Jesus: A Neglected Factor in Christological Debate"; R. Martin, "Some Reflections on New Testament Hymns"; D. de Lacey, " 'One Lord' in Pauline Christology"; and J. Balchin, "Paul, Wisdom, and Christ."

536 L. W. Hurtado. *One God, One Lord: Early Christian Devotion and Ancient Jewish Monotheism.* 2d ed. Edinburgh: T. & T. Clark, 1998. Original edition: 1988.

Chapter 1 surveys divine-agency speculation in ancient Jewish tradition. Chapters 2–4 examine three types of agents of God in more detail: (1) personified Wisdom and Logos; (2) exalted patriarchs; and (3) principal angels. Chapter 5 interprets Jesus in light of this divine-agency tradition and highlights six features of a "mutation" into a "binatarian" theism: (1) hymnic practices; (2) prayer; (3) use of Christ's name; (4) the Lord's Supper; (5) confession of faith in Christ; and (6) prophetic announcements of the risen Christ. This Christian mutation is explained by religious experience (e.g., Jesus' extraordinary earthly ministry, visions of and prophetic words from the exalted Jesus, and defensive reaction to Jewish concern for the uniqueness of God, leading to reinterpretation of the OT to justify devotion to Jesus). Besides Bauckham's critique (#547), see also P. Rainbow, "Jewish Monotheism as the Matrix for New Testament Christology: A Review Article," *NovT* 33 (1991): 78–91.

537 S. G. Sinclair. *Jesus Christ according to Paul: The Christologies of Paul's Undisputed Epistles and the Christology of Paul.* Berkeley, Calif.: Bibal, 1988.

Using six of the undisputed letters, examines literary units that naturally attract the reader's attention (the introduction, conclusion, etc.) for christological emphases. Argues that Paul's

Christology consists irreducibly of the cross, the resurrection, and the presence of the Spirit, emphasized to differing degrees according to the pastoral situation addressed. For other descriptive approaches, see M. de Jonge (#233); and E. Richard, *Jesus, One and Many: The Christological Concept of New Testament Authors* (Wilmington, Del.: Michael Glazier, 1988).

538 P. M. Casey. *From Jewish Prophet to Gentile God: The Origins and Development of New Testament Christology.* Louisville: Westminster John Knox; Cambridge, England: James Clarke, 1991.

Links perceptions of Jesus' identity with community identity. As the only binding factor of a community of Jews and Gentiles, Jesus increasingly gained significance, but the constraints of monotheism remained until the breach with the synagogue occurred in John's community. See especially chapters 7–9.

539 C. M. Pate. *Adam Christology as the Exegetical and Theological Substructure of 2 Corinthians 4:7–5:21.* Lanham, Md.: University Press of America, 1991.

Paul's belief that the primeval glory lost by Adam has been restored through Christ's (the last Adam's) righteous suffering forms the theological and exegetical foundation of 2 Cor. 4:7–5:21.

540 M. Barker. *The Great Angel: A Study of Israel's Second God.* London: SPCK, 1992.

On Paul and the NT, see pp. 213–32. Sometimes helpful in showing the parallels in Jesus' role as redeemer and savior with Yahweh's role in the OT. The main thesis, however—involving Jewish and Christian belief in Yahweh as a second God (one of the sons of El Elyon)—is not substantiated by the evidence.

541 C. C. Newman. *Paul's Glory-Christology: Tradition and Rhetoric.* NovTSup 69. Leiden: Brill, 1992.

Argues that the Damascus Christophany as a revelation of God's end-time resurrection glory provides the underlying coherence to Paul's theological thought.

542 M. C. de Boer. *From Jesus to John: Essays on Jesus and New Testament Christology in Honour of Marius de Jonge.* JSNTSup 84. Sheffield: JSOT Press, 1993.

See especially J. Dunn, "How Controversial Was Paul's Christology?"; E. Ellis, "Χριστός in 1 Corinthians 10.4, 9"; and L. Keck, "Toward the Renewal of New Testament Christology."

543 A. J. Malherbe and W. A. Meeks, eds. *The Future of Christology: Essays in Honor of Leander E. Keck.* Minneapolis: Fortress, 1993.

See especially J. Fitzmyer, "The Christology of the Epistle to the Romans"; V. Furnish, "'He Gave Himself [Was Given] Up . . .]'"; and J. Dunn, "Christology as an Aspect of Theology."

544 J. B. Green and M. Turner, eds. *Jesus of Nazareth: Lord and Christ*. Grand Rapids: Eerdmans; Exeter, England: Paternoster, 1994.

See especially D. Wenham, "The Story of Jesus Known to Paul"; G. Fee, "Christology and Pneumatology in Romans 8:9–11—and Elsewhere: Some Reflections on Paul as a Trinitarian"; C. Arnold, "Jesus Christ: 'Head' of the Church (Colossians and Ephesians)"; M. Turner, "The Spirit of Christ and 'Divine' Christology"; J. Dunn, "The Making of Christology—Evolution or Unfolding?"; R. Longenecker, "The Foundational Conviction of New Testament Christology: The Obedience/Faithfulness/Sonship of Christ"; and P. Ellingworth, "Christology: Synchronic or Diachronic?"

545 C. J. Davis. *The Name and Way of the Lord: Old Testament Themes, New Testament Christology*. JSNTSup 129. Sheffield: Sheffield Academic Press, 1996.

Searches pre-Christian Jewish texts for parallels on applying a text about God to a possibly divine second figure (including the angel, word, wisdom, and glory of the LORD), but finds that the nature of these figures is unclear (and application to clearly nondivine figures is infrequent). Concludes that pre-Christian parallels are inadequate to account for the NT practice of applying such passages to Jesus. Likewise, Christian usage of Isa. 40:3 and Joel 2:32 is not adequately explained by pre-Christian usage. Other NT evidence provides a salvation-historical interpretive framework, however, that "Jesus is the climax of God's earthly revelation and the object of invocation because he is divine" (178).

546 A. Lau. *Manifest in Flesh: The Epiphany Christology of the Pastoral Epistles*. WUNT 2/86. Tübingen: Mohr (Siebeck), 1996.

Argues that the Pastoral Epistles faithfully articulate and adapt the "apostolic" (Pauline) gospel in a new historical context by means of an "epiphany christology." Traces the background of this epiphany language to the theophanies in Hellenistic-Jewish writings.

547 R. Bauckham. *God Crucified: Monotheism and Christology in the New Testament*. Exeter, England: Paternoster, 1998; Grand Rapids: Eerdmans, 1999.

A concise statement of his argument from the still-in-progress volume *Jesus and the Identity of God: Jewish Monotheism and New Testament Christology* (provisional title). Chapter 1 evaluates the broader Jewish understanding of the uniqueness of

God: the evidence for a standard notion of a heavenly viceroy (which could serve as a precedent for Christology) is lacking, yet the possibility of making distinctions in God's identity is left open (e.g., the personification of God's Word and Wisdom within the unique divine identity). Chapter 2 shows that the NT writers deliberately and comprehensively include Jesus in the unique identity of Israel's God: they include him in the unique divine sovereignty over and creation of all things, identify him by the divine name (YHWH), and worship him in recognition of his unique divine identity. Chapter 3 shows how the NT sheds further light on the identity of the God of Israel as the God who includes the humiliated and the exalted Jesus in his identity.

548 C. A. Grieschen. *Angelomorphic Christology: Antecedents and Early Evidence.* AGJU 42. Leiden: Brill, 1998.

Argues that "angelomorphic traditions, especially those growing from the Angel of the Lord traditions, had a significant impact on the early expressions of Christology to the extent that evidence of an Angelomorphic Christology is discernible in several documents dated between 50 and 150 C.E." (6). On Paul, see pp. 315–46. The strongest part of his case is chapter 3 on the OT Angel of the Lord traditions. Chapter 4 on angelomorphic divine hypostases also yields some useful insights. Needs greater recognition of the possibility that the noncanonical Jewish material represents diverse interpretations of the OT tradition, which may not bear much substantive resemblance to the NT interpretation of them.

549 W. Horbury. *Jewish Messianism and the Cult of Christ.* London: SCM, 1998.

Challenges the consensus that messianic hope in the Second Temple period was diverse and weak, and proposes that the cult of Christ originated from Jewish homage to the messianic king, which formed a counterpart to Gentile ruler-cults.

550 H. Stettler. *Die Christologie der Pastoralbriefe.* WUNT 2/105. Tübingen: Mohr (Siebeck), 1998.

Examines the christological passages in the Pastorals in terms of form and tradition, exegesis, and theological significance. Argues that the author reformulates Christology inherited from Paul (and other early formulations) in new language to safeguard the community from docetic Christology, but in a manner that preserves essential continuity.

551 B. Witherington, III. *The Many Faces of the Christ: The Christologies of the New Testament and Beyond.* New York: Crossroad, 1998.

A useful synthetic study that finds an overall unifying high
Christology in the New Testament going back to Jesus' own
self-presentation as well as experience of the risen Lord.
Rightly questions common assumptions about evolution of
Christology. See especially pp. 73–126. See also Witherington's
Jesus the Sage: The Pilgrimage of Wisdom (Minneapolis:
Fortress, 1994), 249–333.

552   D. D. Hannah. *Michael and Christ: Michael Traditions
and Angel Christology in Early Christianity.* WUNT 2/
109. Tübingen: Mohr (Siebeck), 1999.

Examines a broad range of Jewish (both pre- and post-NT) and
Christian literature (up to the early third century) for Michael
traditions. Finds three kinds: (1) theophanic angel Christology;
(2) angel Christologies; and (3) angelic Christology. On the NT,
see pp. 122–62.

553   F. J. Matera. *New Testament Christology.* Louisville: Westminster John Knox, 1999.

A useful descriptive approach to Christology that interprets
Jesus' relationship to God and humanity, the significance of his
life, death, and resurrection, and the christological titles in the
framework of the explicit and implicit stories of Jesus in each
book. On Paul, see pp. 83–172.

554   C. C. Newman, J. R. Davila, and G. S. Lewis, eds. *The Jew-
ish Roots of Christological Monotheism: Papers from the
St. Andrews Conference on the Historical Origins of the
Worship of Jesus.* JSJSup 63. Leiden: Brill, 1999.

A collection of papers that makes clear the range of differences
on the appropriate background/evidence and the evaluation of
the evidence. See especially R. Bauckham, "The Throne of God
and the Worship of Jesus"; L. Hurtado, "The Binatarian Shape
of Early Christian Worship"; and P. Casey, "Monotheism, Worship, and Christological Developments in the Pauline Churches."

555   D. G. Horrell and C. M. Tuckett. *Christology, Controversy,
and Community: New Testament Essays in Honour of
David R. Catchpole.* NovTSup 99. Leiden: Brill, 2000.

See E. Ellis, "Preformed Traditions and Their Implications for
Pauline Christology," who argues for a deity Christology in the
preformed traditions before Paul. His argument forms part of a
new reconstruction of the history of early Christianity found in
his *Making of the New Testament Documents* (#244). See also
D. Horrell, " 'No Longer Jew or Greek': Paul's Corporate Christology and the Construction of Christian Community," and
P. Borgen, "Openly Portrayed as Crucified: Some Observations
on Gal 3:1–14."

13.5 The Spirit

The study of the Holy Spirit properly includes the Spirit's personhood, redemptive work, and manifestations/gifts. Most modern research centers on the experience of the Spirit and his gifts, spurred in part to support or respond to the Pentecostal and charismatic movements. The bulk of the scholarly literature has focused mainly on Luke-Acts, with important exceptions. (On the other hand, in the popular and semipopular literature, a strong appeal to Paul had always characterized the position of Reformed and other cessationist evangelicals.) G. Fee's monumental *God's Empowering Presence* (#567) fills a notable void in expounding the range of Paul's understanding of the Holy Spirit, with attention to his personhood, empowering work, and gifts within an eschatological framework (though emphasizing experience and with conclusions largely amenable to Pentecostal/charismatic views). Within the evangelical camp, the increasing commitment to study the Scriptures afresh and to engage in irenic dialogue over the cessation/continuance of miraculous gifts is an encouraging sign of the Spirit's present work in the church. See also Thiselton (#403, pp. 900–1168); Dunn (#520, pp. 413–41, 552–62); Ridderbos (#511, pp. 214–23, 438–67); G. Fee, "Pneuma and Eschatology in 2 Thessalonians 2.1–2: A Proposal about 'Testing the Prophets' and the Purpose of 2 Thessalonians" (in #734, pp. 196–215); idem, "Gifts of the Spirit," *DPL* 339–47; T. Paige, "Holy Spirit," *DPL* 404–13; and J. D. G. Dunn, *The Christ and the Spirit: Collected Essays of James D. G. Dunn*, vol. 2: *Pneumatology* (Grand Rapids: Eerdmans, 1998). For further works (ideally) impinging on a theology of the Holy Spirit, see §13.3, "God"; §13.4, "Christ"; §13.6, "Salvation"; §13.7, "Eschatology"; §13.9, "The Church"; and §13.10, "Ethics."

556 G. Vos. "The Eschatological Aspect of the Pauline Conception of the Spirit." Pp. 91–125 in *Redemptive History and Biblical Interpretation: The Shorter Writings of Geerhardus Vos*. Edited by R. B. Gaffin, Jr. Phillipsburg, N.J.: P & R, 1980. Original edition: Pp. 209–59 in *Biblical and Theological Studies*. New York: Scribner's Sons, 1912.

   Examines the connection between Paul's conception of the Spirit and eschatology. Demonstrates that (1) the eschatological significance of the Spirit explains Paul's conception of the Christian life as thoroughly from and by the Spirit in its mode of existence and quality; (2) Christ's messianic role as life-giving Spirit stems from postresurrection, eschatological-soteriological realities and does not refer to his preexistent state; and (3) life in the Spirit is thoroughly supernatural and eschatological.

557   R. B. Hoyle. *The Holy Spirit in St. Paul.* Garden City, N.Y.: Doubleday, 1929.

Part 1 surveys Paul's experiences of the Spirit in vision, revelation, spiritual gifts, transformation, and so on. Part 2 considers Paul's expressions of these experiences in light of the Old Testament, Judaism, Greco-Roman philosophy, and the mystery religions. Dated, but informative on scholarship at the beginning of the twentieth century.

558   N. Q. Hamilton. *The Holy Spirit and Eschatology in Paul.* Edinburgh and London: Oliver & Boyd, 1957.

Chapters 1 and 2 show that Paul's pneumatology is based on his Christology and eschatology, respectively. Chapter 3 relates the christological and eschatological aspects of Paul's doctrine of the Spirit so as to illumine the nature of the Christian life between Christ's resurrection and second coming. Chapters 4–6 critique Schweitzer's consistent eschatology, Dodd's realized eschatology, and Bultmann's reinterpreted eschatology.

559   J. D. G. Dunn. *Baptism in the Holy Spirit: A Re-examination of the New Testament Teaching on the Gift of the Spirit in Relation to Pentacostalism Today.* SBT, 2d ser., 15. London: SCM, 1970.

Responds primarily to the Pentecostal teaching on baptism in the Spirit as distinct and subsequent to conversion (though appreciating the emphasis on the dynamic experience of the Spirit), but also argues against the straightforward identification of baptism in the Spirit with water baptism and other distinctions of two gifts of the Spirit (e.g., conversion and confirmation). See especially pp. 103–52 on Paul. See also G. Fee, "Baptism in the Holy Spirit: The Issue of Separability and Subsequence," in *Gospel and Spirit: Issues in New Testament Hermeneutics* (Peabody, Mass.: Hendrickson, 1991), 105–19, who defends the Pentecostal experience as necessitated by the loss in church history of much of the experiential dimension of life in the Spirit. Cf. F. D. Bruner, *A Theology of the Holy Spirit: The Pentecostal Experience and the New Testament Witness* (Grand Rapids: Eerdmans, 1970).

560   J. D. G. Dunn. *Jesus and the Spirit: A Study of the Religious and Charismatic Experience of Jesus and the First Christians as Reflected in the New Testament.* Reprint, Grand Rapids: Eerdmans, 1997. Original edition: London: SCM, 1975.

Examines the New Testament's portrayal of the religious experience of Jesus and first-generation Christianity. See especially part 3, "The Religious Experience of Paul and the Pauline Churches."

561 R. B. Gaffin, Jr. *Perspectives on Pentecost: Studies in New Testament Teaching on the Gifts of the Holy Spirit.* Grand Rapids: Baker, 1979.

A careful exegetical and biblical-theological reflection on the redemptive historical significance of the coming of the Spirit at Pentecost. Stresses the revelatory nature of prophecy and tongues and thus their temporary nature based on the temporary and foundational nature of the apostles and prophets (Eph. 2:20). See also W. Grudem, ed., *Are Miraculous Gifts for Today? Four Views* (Grand Rapids: Zondervan, 1996), in which the four essays by R. Gaffin, R. Saucy, C. S. Storms, and D. Oss (representing the cessationist; open, but cautious; third wave; and Pentecostal/charismatic positions, respectively) exhibit a laudable focus on Scripture and an irenic tone.

562 D. J. Lull. *The Spirit in Galatia: Paul's Interpretation of Pneuma as Divine Power.* Chico, Calif.: Scholars Press, 1980.

Examines Paul's statements about the Spirit in Galatians in terms of their origin in Christian experience (received at the hearing of the gospel rather than at baptism) and in Paul's polemic against his opponents. Uses categories from process theology to criticize the shortcomings of interpretations of Paul's pneumatology in terms of an existentialist understanding of existence or a universal creative Spirit.

563 W. A. Grudem. *The Gift of Prophecy in 1 Corinthians.* Washington, D.C.: University Press of America, 1982.

Examines the gift of prophecy in 1 Cor. 12–14, with brief comparisons to elsewhere in the NT, and finds that it is different from the verbally inspired, canonically written prophecies of the OT prophets. It is a form of divine guidance that is fallible and not strictly binding (with only general content given and requiring evaluation).

564 D. A. Carson. *Showing the Spirit: A Theological Exposition of 1 Corinthians 12–14.* Grand Rapids: Baker, 1987.

A careful exegetical study of 1 Cor. 12–14 with strong theological reflection and interaction with both scholarly and popular views. In the last chapter, Carson incorporates Acts and the rest of the NT in a wide-ranging reflection on the biblical evidence. Refines, but basically upholds, the views of Grudem on NT prophecy and the continuance of miraculous gifts such as tongues.

565 S. S. Schatzmann. *A Pauline Theology of Charismata.* Peabody, Mass.: Hendrickson, 1987.
Exegetical investigation of Paul's concept of "charismata" in all thirteen letters. Concludes that (1) charismata express the diversity of the Spirit's gifts; (2) every Christian is charismatic as a member of Christ's body; (3) charismata are intended for service; (4) all the gifts are equally valuable and are not hierarchically arranged; (5) charismata are not correlated with authority; and (6) all ministry stems from charismata.

566 F. W. Horn. *Das Angeld des Geistes: Studien zur paulinischen Pneumatologie.* FRLANT 154. Göttingen: Vandenhoeck & Ruprecht, 1992.
Part 1 deals with the presuppositions of Pauline pneumatology. Part 2 traces its developments: early Pauline preaching in 1 Thessalonians, confrontation with pneumatic enthusiasm in 1 Corinthians, and confrontation with Jewish Christian countermissions in 2 Corinthians, Galatians, and Philippians. Part 3 covers the Spirit as pledge, its activities, and the Spirit as both eschatological function and substance. See also Horn's "Holy Spirit," *ABD* 3:260–80, esp. 269–76.

567 G. D. Fee. *God's Empowering Presence: The Holy Spirit in the Letters of Paul.* Peabody, Mass.: Hendrickson, 1994.
Part 1 presents a systematic, detailed exegesis of all Pauline passages in the thirteen letters that relate to the Holy Spirit. Part 2 depends on the exegesis of part 1 while offering a theological and practical elaboration of Fee's article, "Pauline Literature," in *Dictionary of Pentecostal and Charismatic Movements* (Grand Rapids: Zondervan, 1988), 665–83. Seeks not only to inform, but to persuade the contemporary church to recover a biblical perspective on the Spirit's role in Paul's eschatology, theology proper, soteriology, and ecclesiology. See also Fee's *Paul, the Spirit, and the People of God* (Peabody, Mass.: Hendrickson, 1996), in which his persuasive aim is laid out more clearly: to recapture Paul's perspective of the Christian life as a dynamically experienced and eschatologically oriented life in the Spirit.

568 G. D. Fee. "Towards a Pauline Theology of Glossolalia." Pp. 24–37 in *Pentecostalism in Context: Essays in Honor of William W. Menzies.* Edited by W. Ma and R. P. Menzies. Journal of Pentecostal Theology Supplement Series 11. Sheffield: Sheffield Academic Press, 1997. Original publication: *Crux* 31 (March 1995): 22–23, 26–31.
Briefly reviews (1) the theme of power and weakness in Paul; (2) the data on glossolalia from 1 Corinthians; (3) the corre-

spondence to praying in the Spirit in Rom. 8:26–27; and (4) concludes that Paul sees glossolalia as both the manifestation of the new eschatological age's power and of human weakness, so that God's power is perfected in the midst of our weakness. See also J. D. G. Dunn, "Spirit Speech: Reflections on Romans 8:12–17," in *Romans and the People of God*, 82–91, who argues that Rom. 8:12–27 shows the existence of kinds of Spirit speech other than inspired or charismatic glossolalia.

569 M. Turner. *The Holy Spirit and Spiritual Gifts in the New Testament Church and Today*. Rev. ed. Peabody, Mass.: Hendrickson, 1998. Original title: *The Holy Spirit and Spiritual Gifts, Then and Now*. Carlisle, England: Paternoster: 1996.

A wide-ranging book exploring the significance of the gift of the Spirit in the New Testament. See especially chapters 7 (method of establishing a Pauline pneumatology), 8 (characteristic themes of the Spirit in Paul), and 15 (God's gifts and the Spirit of life in the Pauline churches).

13.6 Salvation

Paul's understanding of salvation is inseparable from any other aspect of his thought. Persons investigating themes that appear in this section should be aware of the need to cross-check the bibliography in other sections. Furthermore, while one must avoid the tendency to become slavishly attached to the study of Pauline terms, those exploring topics in this area *must* check the appropriate entries in the following lexical sources, since we have not listed the numerous useful articles found there: *Theological Dictionary of the New Testament*, ed. G. Kittel, trans. G. Bromiley (Grand Rapids: Eerdmans, 1964–76); *New International Dictionary of New Testament Theology*, ed. C. Brown (Grand Rapids: Zondervan, 1975–78); *Exegetical Dictionary of the New Testament*, ed. H. Balz and G. Schneider (Grand Rapids: Eerdmans, 1990–93) (= *Exegetisches Wörterbuch zum Neuen Testament* [Kohlhammer: Stuttgart, 1978–80]); and C. Spicq, *Theological Lexicon of the New Testament*, translated and edited by J. Ernest (Peabody, Mass.: Hendrickson, 1994) (= *Notes de lexicographie néo-testamentaire*, Orbis biblicus et orientalis [Fribourg, Switzerland: Éditions universitaires; Göttingen: Vandenhoeck & Ruprecht, 1978]). Likewise, all overviews and theologies of Paul treat the following themes in some fashion or another. The student should refer to the bibliographies in those sections.

13.6.1 Promise

570   J. D. Hester. *Paul's Concept of Inheritance: A Contribution to the Understanding of "Heilsgeschichte."* Scottish Journal of Theology. Occasional Papers. Edinburgh: Oliver & Boyd, 1968.

> The concept of *inheritance* is promissory by nature. When Paul speaks of it he always introduces the paradox of salvation "already fulfilled, but not yet." An "heir" is one who must depend on promise. The promise to Abraham of land and seed has been fulfilled in Christ and the new creation.

571   G. Sass. *Leben aus den Verheißungen: Traditionsgeschichtliche und biblisch-theologische Untersuchungen zur Rede von Gottes Verheißungen im Frühjudentum und beim Apostel Paulus.* FRLANT 164. Vandenhoeck & Ruprecht, 1995.

> Extensive study of Paul's usage against its background in early Judaism and in the Scriptures, with thorough (and rich) theological reflections on the results. The concept of the *promise* of God has a history in early Judaism: Paul was saying nothing new in using this term. In a number of instances, however, he displaces the usual appeal to *covenant* with *promise* (e.g., Gal. 3:18), thereby replacing the usual tension between the divine pledge of grace (*promise*) and human response (*Law*) with an affirmation of the sovereignty of the merciful, electing God. The antithesis between the *Law* and *promise* is to be understood in this way. Better than *covenant, promise* expresses the fellowship of Jews and Gentiles chosen by God. It likewise corresponds better to the Pauline tension between the "already" and "not yet" of salvation. Over against *gospel,* which is proclaimed by humans, a *promise* for Paul is spoken directly by God, and contains a broader content (2 Cor. 1:20). *Promise* for Paul has central theological significance and provides the horizon in which the text of Scripture is to be understood.

13.6.2 The Law

Interpreters have long varied in their understanding of such expressions as "law," "works of the law," and "legalism." The meaning of the terms continues to be a matter of debate. Furthermore, the interpretive categories that scholars adopt may themselves be misleading: it is questionable, for example, whether it makes sense to say that Paul sometimes speaks "positively" of the Law and sometimes "negatively." The term *covenant* likewise is now frequently used to signify Israel's election, without any consideration of Paul's own usage of the term. We have attempted to select representative works, but again have been forced to omit a considerable number of significant studies. The following surveys provide additional bibliography and good introductions to the developing discussion: D. J. Moo, "Paul and the Law in the Last Ten Years," *SJT* 40 (1987): 287–307; C. Roetzel, "Paul and the Law: Whence and Whither?" *Currents in Research: Biblical Studies* 3 (1995): 249–75; and V. Koperski, *What Are They Saying about Paul and the Law?* (New York and Mahwah, N.J.: Paulist, 2001). Further discussion may be found in the commentaries on Romans and Galatians (esp. Dunn [#394 and #415]; Moo [#396]; and Schreiner [#397]), and in works listed in chapter 6, "Paul and First-Century Judaism." A treatment of Paul's understanding of the Law also appears in Seifrid (#688, pp. 95–127). For traditional debates about the place of the Law in the life of the Christian, see G. Bahnsen et al., *Five Views on Law and Gospel* (Grand Rapids: Zondervan, 1996) (formerly titled *The Law, the Gospel, and the Modern Christian* [1993]).

572   A. J. Bandstra. *The Law and the Elements of the World: An Exegetical Study in Aspects of Paul's Teaching.* Kampen, the Netherlands: Kok, 1964.
      The term στοιχεῖα in Gal. 4:3, 9 and Col. 2:8, 20 refers to the fundamental forces inherent in the world, by which Paul specifically means the Law and the flesh as operative in the world of humanity before and outside of Christ.

573   C. E. B. Cranfield. "St. Paul and the Law." Pp. 148–72 in *New Testament Issues.* Edited by R. Batey. New York: Harper & Row, 1970. Original publication: *SJT* 17 (1964): 43–68.
      Paul regards faith to be opposed to "legalism," not to the Law itself.

574   A. van Dülmen. *Die Theologie des Gesetzes bei Paulus.* SBM 5. Stuttgart: Katholisches Bibelwerk, 1968.
      The old aeon of the Law prepares for the new by intensifying, or by totalizing, judgment. It thus brings the old to its nadir and so prepares for the new. The spiritual Law, that is, Law of Christ, is the old Law in the aeon of the Spirit.

575   R. Bring. *Christus und das Gesetz: Die Bedeutung des Gesetzes des Alten Testaments nach Paulus und sein Glauben an Christus.* Leiden: Brill, 1969.

Christ fulfills the entire Scripture, both the promise and the demand of the Law, in bearing the curse of the Law on the cross. Doing the Law now means to be conformed to Christ's righteousness. Bring, the author, attributes only a positive function to the Law: it is a perversion of the Law, that is, legalism, which Paul rejects.

576 U. Wilckens. "Was heißt bei Paulus: 'Aus Werken des Gesetzes wird kein Mensch gerecht'?" Pp. 51–108 in *Evangelisch-Katholischer Kommentar zum Neuen Testament: Vorarbeiten.* Neukirchener: Neukirchen-Vlyun, 1969.

Important response to Bultmann: Paul does not regard the attempt to keep the Law as a sin, but the failure to keep it. Yet Wilckens here misconstrues the issue. Paul indeed does not condemn the attempt to keep the Law, but he does reject the attempt to find one's righteousness in it. And that is another matter entirely.

577 H. Hübner. *Law in Paul's Thought.* Translated by J. Greig. Edinburgh: T. & T. Clark, 1984. German title: *Das Gesetz bei Paulus.* 2d ed. FRLANT 119. Göttingen: Vandenhoeck & Ruprecht, 1982. Original German edition: 1978.

Paul's understanding of the Law develops between the writing of Galatians and Romans. Whereas in the former he regards the Law in a "quantitative" manner as a body of demands, in the latter he regards it "qualitatively," as the cause of legalism. In this way Paul integrates his understanding of Law into justification.

578 R. Heiligenthal. *Werke als Zeichen: Untersuchungen zur Bedeutung der menschlichen Taten im Frühjudentum, Neuen Testament und Frühchristentum.* WUNT 2/9. Tübingen: Mohr (Siebeck), 1983.

Paul uses the expression "works" only in relation to the promise of justification in the final judgment, in characterization of the fulfillment of the Law as the only possible criterion of the final judgment. In Romans he draws upon the Alexandrian-Jewish creation theology (Philo), according to which the proper response to God is found in "faith" or, respectively, in "the fear of God," not in deeds. Paul's innovation over against this traditional separation of grace and works is the separation of the grace of God from the Law. "Works" are not "accomplishments," but actions subject to judgment, which therefore are soteriologically ambivalent.

579 D. J. Moo. "Law, 'Works of the Law,' and Legalism in Paul." *WTJ* 45 (1983): 73–100.

Linguistic study of Paul's terminology, which argues that

"Law" does not signify "legalism" for Paul and that "works of the Law" signifies "works done in obedience to the Law."

580 H. Räisänen. *Paul and the Law.* WUNT 29. Tübingen: Mohr (Siebeck), 1983; Philadelphia: Fortress, 1986.

Paul's views concerning the Law developed over time, not immediately at his conversion. They were crystallized by the challenge to the status of Gentile believers at Antioch, and display various inconsistencies: (1) the Law is indivisible—it has been reduced in Christ; (2) Christ ends the Law—Christ establishes it; (3) the Law can be fulfilled—it cannot be fulfilled; (4) the Law was intended to generate sin—it was intended to give life; (5) Israel still elect—Israel has been rejected. While the thesis will not stand, Räisänen sets out the problems of understanding Paul's language with admirable clarity. See also his *Torah and Christ: Essays in German and English on the Problem of the Law in Early Christianity,* ed. A.-M. Enroth, Suomen Eksegeettisen Seuran Julkaisuja 45 (Helsinki: Finnish Exegetical Society, 1986); and *Jesus, Paul, and Torah: Collected Essays,* JSNTSup 43 (Sheffield: JSOT Press, 1992).

581 R. Badenas. *Christ the End of the Law: Romans 10.4 in Pauline Perspective.* JSNTSup 10. Sheffield: JSOT Press, 1985.

Argues that τέλος signifies "goal." His survey of interpretation of Rom. 10.4 sheds considerable light on trends in the modern period (pp. 5–37).

582 J. M. Espy. "Paul's 'Robust Conscience' Re-examined." *NTS* 31 (1985): 161–88.

Rejects Stendahl's thesis that Paul reacted to a perceived failure of Israel as a whole. The Law, according to Paul, serves to charge all individuals with sin. Before his conversion, Paul inwardly suppressed the knowledge that he was a sinner and transgressor.

583 R. Gundry. "Grace, Works, and Staying Saved in Paul." *Bib* 66 (1985): 1–38.

Important response to E. P. Sanders and the "new perspective."

584 E. Schnabel. *Law and Wisdom from Ben Sira to Paul: A Tradition-Historical Enquiry into the Relation of Law, Wisdom, and Ethics.* WUNT 2/16. Tübingen: Mohr (Siebeck), 1985.

In the realm of soteriology, the Christ is the wisdom of God, who has brought the Law, which condemns, to an end. In the realm of ethics, however, the Torah is no longer *nuda lex* but is located "in Christ," and is still valid for the Christian (along with the words of Christ and apostolic instruction). Paul fur-

ther presupposes the traditional connection between the Law
and wisdom, so that responsibility remains to observe God's revealed will manifest in the orders of creation and in diverse situations that require wisdom. In a certain measure, this study
responds to a Kantian ethic of individual autonomy in a manner that roughly approximates Calvin's understanding of the
Law. Extensive, valuable research on the connection between
wisdom and Law in early Judaism. One may question, nevertheless, whether the presence of the *new* creation (and there-
with Paul's conception of "freedom") is adequately represented
in this scheme, and whether the distinction between redemption and ethics proposed here corresponds to Paul's thought.

585 P. Stuhlmacher. "The Law as a Topic of Biblical Theology."
Pp. 110–33 in *Reconciliation, Law, and Righteousness: Es-
says in Biblical Theology*. Philadelphia: Fortress, 1986.
Outline of a tradition-historical understanding of the Law, in
which the promise of a Zion-Torah for the nations (Isa. 2:2–4;
Mic. 4:1–4; etc.) is fulfilled in Jesus Christ.

586 S. Westerholm. *Israel's Law and the Church's Faith: Paul
and His Recent Interpreters*. Grand Rapids: Eerdmans,
1988.
Thorough and insightful review of the debate. Important, fresh
response to the "new perspective on Paul." Presentation of
"justification apart from the works of the Law" in terms of
grace and "merit."

587 B. Martin. *Christ and the Law in Paul*. NovTSup 62. Leiden: Brill, 1989.
Paul has a coherent understanding of the Law. His "positive"
statements about it concern the way of life for believers. His
"negative" statements about it have to do with Christ bringing
the end to the "death-dealing effects" of the Law.

588 M. Silva. "The Law and Christianity: Dunn's New Synthesis." *WTJ* 53 (1991): 339–53.
Significant review of Dunn and the "new perspective" in general.

589 J. D. G. Dunn. "Yet Once More—'The Works of the Law':
A Response." *JSNT* 46 (1992): 99–117.
The expression "works of the Law" characterizes the whole
mind-set of "covenantal nomism" and expresses the conviction
that status within the covenant (righteousness) is maintained
by doing what the Law requires ("works of the Law"). The soteriological prerequisite that Jews assume is not sinlessness,
but covenant status. It is not that works of the Law will earn
salvation or outweigh sins. They do not involve "any attempt
to earn favour with God," but are marks of a favored-nation sta-

tus. See also Dunn's commentaries on Romans (#394) and Galatians (#415); see also his "4QMMT and Galatians," *NTS* 43 (1997): 147–53. On the topic of "staying in," see Gundry (#583).

590 M. Winger. *By What Law? the Meaning of "Nomos" in the Letters of Paul.* SBLDS 128. Atlanta: Scholars Press, 1992.
Useful treatment of Paul's usage. See also Winger's "Meaning and Law," *JBL* 117 (1998): 105–10.

591 T. R. Schreiner. *The Law and Its Fulfillment: A Pauline Theology of the Law.* Grand Rapids: Baker, 1993.
Presentation of a traditional (substantially Reformed) reading of Paul, in criticism of recent discussion of Paul, with trenchant critiques of the "new perspective" at various points.

592 F. Thielman. *Paul and the Law: A Contextual Approach.* Downers Grove, Ill.: InterVarsity, 1994.
A qualified embrace of the "new perspective" built on the premise that many Jews of Paul's time believed that Israel was still in exile. Paul hopes that, once reminded of the standard Jewish position on the plight of Israel, Judaizing Christians and unbelieving Jews will realize that the period of Israel's restoration has dawned, that the Mosaic covenant is obsolete, and that they should embrace the gospel of God's redemptive work in Christ. See also "Law," *DPL* 529–42.

593 S. Hafemann. *Paul, Moses, and the History of Israel: The Letter/Spirit Contrast and the Argument from Scripture in 2 Corinthians 3.* WUNT 81. Tübingen: Mohr (Siebeck), 1995.
The "letter" signifies the death-dealing function of the Law without the accompanying power of the Spirit. Following the worship of the golden calf and the second inscription of the Law, Moses wears the veil because Israel, whose sinfulness is now manifest, must be protected from the death-dealing effects of the glory of God. The "covenant" cannot be restored completely until the hearts of the people are re-created.

594 J. D. G. Dunn, ed. *Paul and the Mosaic Law.* WUNT 89. Tübingen: Mohr (Siebeck), 1996; Grand Rapids: Eerdmans, 2001.
Important collection of essays from the 1994 Durham-Tübingen Research Symposium on Early Christianity and Judaism. The volume includes essays by H. Lichtenberger, M. Hengel, J. Lambrecht, B. Longenecker, G. Stanton, K. Kertelge, N. T. Wright, R. Hays, O. Hofius, H. Hübner, S. Westerholm, H. Räisänen, P. Tomson, S. Barton, J. Barclay, and J. Dunn.

595 C. Kruse. *Paul, the Law, and Justification.* Leicester, England: Apollos, 1996.

Survey of current research followed by a thorough letter-by-letter discussion of the topic in the Pauline letters. Critical assessment of the "new perspective."

596 K. Kuula. *The Law, the Covenant, and God's Plan.* Helsinki: Finnish Exegetical Society; Göttingen: Vandenhoeck & Ruprecht, 1999.

Thorough interaction with recent interpretation of Paul, in which the author refines and reinforces Räisänen's line of thought. Paul's conception of the Law is fraught with tension between his fundamental christological convictions and his traditional ideals. His apocalyptic dualism lies behind a number of his problematic statements (especially in Galatians). Christ and covenant cannot be reconciled.

597 C. M. Pate. *The Reverse of the Curse: Paul, Wisdom, and the Law.* WUNT 2/114. Tübingen: Mohr (Siebeck), 2000.

Review of current discussion and critique of various proponents of the "new perspective" concerning the place of the Law in Paul's thought. Prior to his conversion, Paul associated the wisdom of God with the Law and thought of salvation as dependent on adherence to it. This "covenantal nomism" espoused in Paul's day was essentially synergistic, and therefore legalistic. At his conversion, Paul came to see Christ as the wisdom of God and the end of the Law.

598 L. Thurén. *Derhetorizing Paul: A Dynamic Perspective on Pauline Theology and the Law.* WUNT 124. Tübingen: Mohr (Siebeck), 2000.

A fresh examination of Paul's treatment of the Law from the perspective of speech-act theory and modern rhetoric. In order to understand Paul's theology we must penetrate his rhetoric (which itself is theology). Useful and sensible discussion of current debate. The approach to Paul is something like that of J. C. Beker, but somewhat more sophisticated.

13.6.3 Sin, Suffering, and Death

The discussion of Paul's understanding of sin and death naturally has focused on Rom. 5:12–21 and 1 Cor. 15. On these passages, see the commentaries, treatments of Paul's theology, as well as E. P. Sanders, "Sin, Sinners (New Testament)," *ABD* 6:40–47; and L. Morris, "Sin, Guilt," and S. Hafemann, "Suffering," *DPL* 877–81, 919–21.

599 E. Brandenburger. *Adam und Christus: Exegetisch-religionsgeschichtliche Untersuchung zu Röm. 5:12–21 (1. Kor. 15).* WMANT 7. Neukirchen: Neukirchener, 1962.

The distinctive purpose of Rom. 5:21–21, which explains 5:1–11 (5:12a: διὰ τοῦτο), is found in its explication of the lordship of sin and the conquest of sin by grace. A fresh unpacking of the saving event is found here: Christ is "Anthropos," whose "deed" effects the change of aeons. Paul corrects this conception, borrowed from Gnostic ideas in Hellenistic Judaism, with his teaching on justification. The section therefore provides an important transition to the ideas of lordship and slavery that Paul employs in Rom. 6–8. Helpful exegetical observations, doubtful history.

600 A. J. M. Wedderburn. "The Theological Structure of Romans 5:12." *NTS* 19 (1972–73): 339–54.

Paul's statement in Rom. 5:12 can be understood against the background of early Judaism (esp. *4 Ezra, 2 Baruch*). Gnostic categories are inadequate. The irreducible tension between the cosmic/universal and individual dimensions of sin must not be diluted.

601 C. Black. "Pauline Perspectives on Death in Romans 5–8." *JBL* 103 (1984): 413–33.

There is no Pauline doctrine of death, only a variety of inherited perspectives (both Hellenistic and Jewish). Yet for Paul, death is an intrusion on the work of God the Creator.

602 D. A. Black. *Paul, Apostle of Weakness: "Astheneia" and Its Cognates in the Pauline Literature.* American University Studies: Series VII, Theology and Religion 3. New York: Peter Lang, 1984.

Paul's conception of weakness is rooted in his Christology.

603 G. Röhser. *Metaphorik und Personifikation der Sünde: Antike Sündenvorstellungen und paulinische Hamartia.* WUNT 2/25. Tübingen: Mohr (Siebeck), 1987.

Paul's personification of "sin" (a particular form of hypostatizing metaphor) is rhetorical, doing nothing other than representing the essence of human failures, which recur with destructive force upon human beings. This conception is derived from the OT tradition of the connection between sin and disaster, not from ideas of demonic powers (against Bultmann, Käsemann).

604 M. de Boer. *The Defeat of Death: Apocalyptic Eschatology in 1 Corinthians 15 and Romans 5.* JSNTSup 22. Sheffield: JSOT Press, 1988.

Paul understands death in cosmological terms derived from Jewish apocalyptic eschatology, as a power. Although there is a dialectical tension between the "already" of Christ's resurrection and the "not yet" of ours, death itself has been defeated in Christ.

605 M. Hooker. "Adam in Romans 1." Pp. 73–84 in *From Adam to Christ: Essays on Paul.* Cambridge: Cambridge University Press, 1990.

> Paul deliberately casts his description of human idolatry and wickedness in terms that recall Adam's fall.

606 C. M. Pate. *The Glory of Adam and the Afflictions of the Righteous: Pauline Suffering in Context.* Lewiston, N.Y.: Mellen, 1993.

> The Pauline conception of suffering involves the understanding that Adamic glory that had been lost is restored by Christ and his suffering, in which believers participate.

607 H. Blocher. *Original Sin: Illuminating the Riddle.* New SBT. Grand Rapids: Eerdmans, 1999.

> Fresh examination of the doctrine of original sin, from the *locus classicus*, Rom. 5:12–14. Adam appears in Rom. 5:12 as the means by which human sins are treated judicially. On the basis of their actual sinning (ἐφ' ᾧ), death reached all persons, because they had Adam as head. The text is a sort of parallel to Rom. 2, which describes the work of the Law written in the heart. Considerable theological reflection on the forms of the doctrine and their problems.

13.6.4 The Human Being before God (Anthropology)

While Paul's anthropology may be divided into the human relation with God and with the world, as we have done for practical reasons, the two relations are obviously connected (see §13.8, "Israel"; §13.9, "The Church"; and §13.10, "Ethics"). All aspects of anthropology are pressingly in need of review, particularly (in the present section) the relation between individual and community. Just as Rom. 5:12–21 plays a central role in any discussion of Paul's understanding of sin and death, Rom. 7 is fundamental to any treatment of Paul's anthropology. The reader therefore ought to check the commentaries and special studies on this text. In addition to the entries below, see Laato (#113); Middendorf (#454); and L. Kreitzer, "Adam and Christ," and D. J. A. Clines, "Image of God," *DPL* 9–15, 426–28.

608 W. G. Kümmel. "Paul." Pp. 38–71 in *Man in the New Testament.* Translated by J. Vincent. Philadelphia: Westminster; London: Epworth, 1963. German edition: *Das Bild des Menschen im Neuen Testament.* Zürich: Zwingli, 1948.

> Helpful survey of Pauline terminology, with the argument that Rom. 7 refers to the non-Christian. See also Kümmel (#42).

609 J. A. T. Robinson. *The Body: A Study in Pauline Theology.* SBT 5. Chicago: Henry Regnery; London: SCM, 1952.

The distinction between "body" and "flesh" is that of creation and fallen creation. Christ's body in the cross and resurrection embodies the whole of humanity.

610 W. D. Stacey. *The Pauline View of Man.* London: Macmillan, 1956.

Paul's approach was synthetic, aspectual. His terms overlap and reflect OT cquivalents, or at least reflect biblical usage (e.g., σῶμα).

611 J. Jervell. *Imago Dei: Gen. 1, 26f. im Spätjudentum, in der Gnosis und in den paulinischen Briefen.* FRLANT 58. Göttingen: Vandenhoeck & Ruprecht, 1960.

The divine image in the human being consists in Christ. This image is equivalent to God's glory (and God's righteousness), which is restored in the apostolic preaching. It also remains, in a sense, in the fallen human being, since Christ is creator and ruler of the world.

612 A. Sand. *Der Begriff "Fleisch" in den paulinischen Hauptbriefen.* Biblische Untersuchungen 2. Regensburg: Friedrich Pustet, 1967.

Σάρξ carries the following senses: (1) the living material body; (2) the collective sense of all humanity; and (3) the human being enslaved under the power of sin. With the third concept, the ground of the OT and early Judaism is left behind.

613 E. Käsemann. "On Paul's Anthropology." Pp. 1–31 in *Perspectives on Paul.* Translated by M. Kohl. Philadelphia: Fortress, 1971. German edition: *Paulinische Perspektiven.* Tübingen: Mohr (Siebeck) 1969.

Useful as a window to an important debate. Against Bultmann's construction of Paul's theology around the individual, anthropology is concretized cosmology. The world stands under the lordship of the crucified and risen Christ, in whom the new creation has entered the present order.

614 R. Jewett. *Paul's Anthropological Terms: A Study of Their Use in Conflict Settings.* AGJU 10. Leiden: Brill, 1971.

Thorough examination of Pauline terminology in Paul's letters, with the thesis that he borrowed terms from his opponents and that his usage was shaped and developed by particular conflicts.

615 R. H. Gundry. *"Soma" in Biblical Theology with Emphasis on Pauline Anthropology.* Grand Rapids: Academie Books, 1987. Original edition: SNTSMS 29. Cambridge: Cambridge University Press, 1976.

In distinction to Bultmann's "holistic" understanding of σῶμα as the self-conscious person, Gundry maintains that, for Paul, the word retains a solely physical sense. See also J. A. T. Robinson (#609) and W. Stacey (#610), who adopt understandings close to that of Bultmann.

616 H.-J. Eckstein. *Der Begriff Syneidesis bei Paulus.* WUNT 2/10. Tübingen: Mohr (Siebeck), 1983.

Syneidesis ("conscience") for Paul is an authority that judges and makes one conscious of blame or approval on the basis of recognized norms. It therefore does not entail a principial knowledge of good and evil nor a power of moral decision for the good (*synteresis*), nor a moral authority which judges concrete behavior (as in Scholasticism). For Paul it is neutral and not reflective of the human being "turned in upon the self," or it is a divine voice, but a human quality, which has limited capacity.

617 G. Theissen. *Psychological Aspects of Pauline Theology.* Philadelphia: Fortress; Edinburgh: T. & T. Clark, 1987. German edition: *Psychologische Aspekte paulinischer Theologie.* FRLANT 131. Göttingen: Vandenhoeck & Ruprecht, 1983.

Modern psychology applied to Rom. 7 and other texts.

618 P. Perkins. "Pauline Anthropology in Light of Nag Hammadi." *CBQ* 48 (1986): 512–21.

Use of Adam tradition in Rom. 7:7–25 and 1 Cor. 15 suggests that it may not stem from gnosticizing opponents. Nor has Paul borrowed the Adam tradition from Platonic categories. The tradition could not imagine Paul's universal, nondualistic view of humanity.

619 M. Seifrid. "The Subject of Romans 7:14–25." *NovT* 34 (1992): 313–33.

Paul does not here describe either his pre-Christian or Christian experience. He rather speaks, from his perspective as a believer in Christ, of the human being confronted with the Law. Insofar as the Law is concerned, his former person remains with him so long as he remains in his mortal body. Only in Christ has sin been overcome.

620 T. Heckel. *Der innere Mensch: Die paulinische Verarbeitung eines platonischen Motivs.* WUNT 2/53. Tübingen: Mohr (Siebeck), 1993.

Study of Paul's understanding of the "inner person," with a historical review of the concept, particularly in Plato and Philo. Paul's initial use of the expression was occasioned by his opponents in Corinth (2 Cor. 4). He gives the expression a (corrective) temporal dimension. His use of it in Rom. 7:22 is based on

Christian reflection on pre-Christian existence, in which one measures one's person by one's works.

621 U. Schnelle. "Pauline Anthropology." Pp. 37–113 in *The Human Condition: Anthropology in the Teachings of Jesus, Paul, and John*. Translated by O. C. Dean, Jr. Minneapolis: Fortress; Edinburgh: T. & T. Clark, 1996. German edition: *Neutestamentliche Anthropologie: Jesus-Paulus-Johannes*. Biblisch-Theologische Studien 18. Neukirchen-Vluyn: Neukirchener, 1991.

Substantial treatment of Paul's usage and concepts, taking the cross and resurrection of Christ as the starting point and basis. Attention to development in Paul's thought from a critical perspective.

13.6.5 The Cross and Atonement

Although the cross and its work have broad implications for Paul, namely, "the word of the cross" (1 Cor. 1:18), much of the discussion of the cross in Paul's thought has revolved around his understanding of the atonement. One matter of debate has been the origin of his conception of it: whether it is to be found in Jesus and/or earliest Christianity (and therefore in some manner in the sacrificial system of the Old Testament) or in the Greco-Roman world (the former being by far the more likely). In curious relation to this question, it had been argued in an earlier generation that Paul understands the atoning significance of the cross biblically (only) in the destructive human guilt and its effects, and not in the aversion of divine wrath (which was thought to be entirely pagan). Cf. C. H. Dodd, *The Bible and the Greeks* (London: Hodder & Stoughton, 1935), and the response from L. Morris (#628). More recently there has been argument as to whether Jesus' death should be regarded as "representative" or "substitutionary." In addition to the entries below, the reader may usefully consult the following dictionary articles: J. M. Gundry-Volf, "Expiation, Propitiation, Mercy Seat," *DPL* 279–84; and C. M. Tuckett, "Atonement in the New Testament," *ABD* 1:518–22.

622 E. Lohse. *Märtyrer und Gottesknecht: Untersuchungen zur Urchristlichen Verkündigung vom Sühnetod Jesu Christi*. 2d ed. FRLANT 46. Göttingen: Vandenhoeck & Ruprecht, 1963. First edition: 1955.

In Rom. 3:24–26, Christ's death is presented as an atoning sacrifice, just like the death of the martyrs in 4 Macc. 17:21f., which derives from Jewish tradition.

623 E. Käsemann. "The Saving Significance of the Death of Jesus in Paul." Pp. 32–59 in *Perspectives on Paul.* Translated by M. Kohl. Philadelphia: Fortress, 1971. German edition: *Paulinische Perspektiven.* Tübingen: Mohr (Siebeck) 1969.

Käsemann's article depicts the cross as the central theme of Paul's theology, in which God strips the godless human being of all pride and establishes God's lordship. Stuhlmacher (along with others) has corrected Käsemann's treatment of the theme of atonement as a traditional matter with which Paul was not concerned. On this topic, see Zahl (#686).

624 S. Lyonnet and L. Sabourin. *Sin, Redemption, and Sacrifice: A Biblical and Patristic Study.* AnBib 48. Rome: Pontifical Biblical Institute, 1970.

Survey of NT terms for sin and redemption, with a historical survey of the interpretation of 2 Cor. 5:21.

625 S. Williams. *Jesus' Death as Saving Event: The Background and Origin of a Concept.* HDR 2. Missoula, Mont.: Scholars Press, 1975.

The idea of Jesus' death as a saving event had its origin in the tradition of beneficial human death for others, a tradition transmitted to Hellenistic Christianity via Hellenistic Judaism (4 Maccabees, and the story of the Maccabean martyrs). But contrary to the author's argument, the idea of vicarious death appears already in Isa. 53. See M. de Jonge, "Jesus' Death for Others and the Death of the Maccabean Martyrs," in *Text and Testimony: Essays on New Testament and Apocryphal Literature in Honour of A. F. J. Klijn*, ed. T. Baarda et al. (Kampen, the Netherlands: Kok, 1988), 142–51.

626 M. Hengel. "The Atonement." In *The Cross of the Son of God.* Translated by J. Bowden. London: SCM, 1986. Original English publication: *The Atonement.* London: SCM, 1981. Original German publication: "Der stellvertretende Sühnetod Jesu: Ein Beitrag zur Entstehung des urchristlichen Kerygmas." *IKaZ* 9 (1980): 1–25, 135–47.

The interpretation of Jesus' death as an atonement goes back to the earliest believing community, indeed to Jesus himself, and was developed especially among the Hellenists (see §9.1), under the influence of Scripture (especially Isa. 53) and traditions regarding the death of martyrs.

627 P. Stuhlmacher. "Jesus' Resurrection and the View of

Righteousness in the Pre-Pauline Mission Congregations." Pp. 50–67 in *Reconciliation, Law, and Righteousness: Essays in Biblical Theology*. Translated by E. R. Kalin. Philadelphia: Fortress, 1986. German edition: *Versöhnung, Gesetz und Gerechtigkeit: Aufsätze zur biblischen Theologie*. Göttingen: Vandenhoeck & Ruprecht, 1981.

> Rom. 4:25 and especially Rom. 3:25–26 as representative of the theology of the Stephen-circle. See now also chapter 14, "Die Ausbildung des Christusbekenntnisses" (#514, pp. 179–96).

628 L. Morris. *The Atonement, Its Meaning and Significance*. Downers Grove, Ill., and Leicester, England: InterVarsity, 1983.

> Fresh presentation of Christ's death as an objective act of atonement, which is propitiatory and substitutionary. See also Morris's *Apostolic Preaching of the Cross* (Grand Rapids: Eerdmans, 1955); and *The Cross in the New Testament* (Grand Rapids: Eerdmans, 1965).

629 K. Kleinknecht. *Der leidende Gerechtfertigte: Die alttestamentlich-jüdische Tradition vom "leidenden Gerechten" und ihre Rezeption bei Paulus*. WUNT 2/13. Tübingen: Mohr (Siebeck), 1984.

> Paul relates OT/Jewish traditions of the suffering righteous to the death and resurrection of Christ, as did early Christian tradition before him. Jesus Christ is the preexistent Messiah who entered the role of the despised, suffering, and murdered righteous. The righteous who belong to Christ enter with him into the world's enmity.

630 C. Cousar. *A Theology of the Cross: The Death of Jesus in the Pauline Letters*. Overtures to Biblical Theology. Minneapolis: Fortress, 1990.

> Topical treatment of the Pauline texts in conversation with Luther's theology of the cross and the work of Käsemann.

631 K. Grayston. *Dying, We Live: A New Enquiry into the Death of Christ in the New Testament*. New York: Oxford University Press, 1990.

> Christ's death as an "aversion sacrifice," which turns away danger and restores confidence in God. Traditio-historical approach to the topic.

632 D. Seeley. *The Noble Death: Graeco-Roman Martyrology and Paul's Concept of Salvation*. JSNTSup 28. Sheffield: JSOT Press, 1990.

> Paul understood Jesus' vicarious death to operate mimetically, that is, by imaginative reenactment. In this understanding, he

is indebted to Greco-Roman martyrology (esp. 2 and 4 Maccabees) and not the temple cult. Paul differs from Hellenistic tradition in that he understands the imaginative reenactment to have an objective effect.

633 J. D. G. Dunn. "Paul's Understanding of the Death of Jesus as a Sacrifice." Pp. 35–56 in *Sacrifice and Redemption: Durham Essays in Theology.* Edited by S. Sykes. Cambridge: Cambridge University Press, 1991.

For Paul, Jesus is in his life the representative of fallen humanity. In Jesus' death, likewise, he represented humanity. For Paul, this is the meaning of the language and imagery of sacrifice. The idea of substitution is too narrow. Divine wrath destroys sin. Any notion of punishment is only secondary. Dunn's earlier discussions of this matter may be found in the article's bibliography. See also his *Theology of Paul the Apostle* (#520, pp. 207–33).

634 R. Hamerton-Kelly. *Sacred Violence: Paul's Hermeneutic of the Cross.* Minneapolis: Fortress, 1991.

A reading of Paul based on the social theory of the poststructuralist literary critic René Girard: human society is founded on the reciprocal mimesis of the desire of another, which itself is "the hunger for the envy of the other" (23). This mimetic rivalry progresses toward violence in a definite pattern, and issues in the transference of mutually destructive violence to a surrogate victim, to whom society attributes the cause of the "mimetic disorder," as well as the status of the sacred (with prohibition, ritual, and myth). This theory eliminates the transcendent in that it refuses to allow God to act as holy judge, a loss which ironically leads it into the act of scapegoating Judaism on account of its (sacrificial) scapegoating.

635 W. Kraus. *Der Tod Jesu as Heiligtumsweihe: Eine Untersuchung zum Umfeld der Suhnevorstellung in Romer 3, 25–26a.* WMANT 66. Neukirchen-Vluyn: Neukirchener, 1991.

In Rom. 3:25–26a, Paul cites Christian tradition, which interpreted Jesus' death in the context of the Day of Atonement. The term ἱλαστήριον is to be understood as "place of atonement" and not more narrowly as "mercy seat." There is no contrast here between the hiddenness of the "mercy seat" and the openness of Jesus' death. Προτίθημι is rather to be understood in the sense of eschatological announcement. The atoning death of the Maccabean martyrs (4 Macc. 17:21–23) does not play a role here. Rom. 3:25a does not have the general concept of forgiveness in view, but the removal of guilt from the sanctuary.

Πάρεσις is not to be understood as "forgiveness" but as the post-ponement of punishment of former sins, which have finally been atoned by the death of Jesus. The confession thereby implies the inefficacy of the former sacrifices, deriving from the self-definition of the early believing community over against the temple (and not directly from Jesus). Paul's accomplishment is to interpret the formula in terms of the revelation of the righteousness of God. There is a connection between this text and the thought of Hebrews.

636 M. D. Hooker. *Not Ashamed of the Gospel: New Testament Interpretations of the Death of Christ*. Grand Rapids: Eerdmans, 1995.

Christ died not instead of the human race, but as their representative. See also Hooker's "Interchange in Christ," *JTS* 22 (1971): 349–61; "Interchange and Atonement," *BJRL* 60 (1978): 462–81; "Interchange and Suffering," in *Suffering and Martyrdom in the New Testament: Studies Presented to G. M. Styler*, ed. W. Horbury and B. McNeil (Cambridge: Cambridge University Press, 1981), 70–83.

637 B. H. McLean. *The Cursed Christ: Mediterranean Expulsion Rituals and Pauline Soteriology*. JSNTSup 126. Sheffield: Sheffield Academic Press, 1996.

Jewish sacrifice, aside from the scapegoat, had to do with purification of the holy place, not the bearing of personal sins. Paul's soteriology is built on Mediterranean expulsion ("scapegoat") ritual. Although Paul's expectation of salvation first centered on the parousia, by the time he wrote 1 Corinthians the resurrection had come to the forefront. After the affliction in Asia, Paul thought in terms of the present effect of participation in Christ, and therefore only late in his career interpreted Christ's death as "apotropaic," that is, as substitutionary.

638 T. Söding. *Das Wort vom Kreuz: Studien zur paulinischen Theologie*. WUNT 93. Tübingen: Mohr (Siebeck), 1997.

A collection of essays that might have been individually listed under justification, participation (in Christ), and other headings. The central thrust of all of them, however, is the meaning of the cross for Paul's theology. While the Catholic commitments of Söding are unmistakable, at numerous points he is more soundly evangelical than some scholarship that goes by that name.

639 D. P. Bailey. "Concepts of *Stellvertretung* in the Interpretation of Isaiah 53." Pp. 223–51 in *Jesus and the Suffering Servant: Isaiah 53 and Christian Origins*. Edited by W. R. Farmer. Harrisburg, Pa.: Trinity Press International, 1998.

Current discussion of atonement ("representation" versus "substitution," and German terminology) with special attention to Hofius and B. Janowski.

640 D. P. Bailey. "Jesus and the Mercy Seat: The Semantics and Theology of Paul's Use of *Hilasterion* in Romans 3:25." *TynBul* 51 (2000): 155–58.

Summary of the author's Cambridge dissertation, forthcoming in the WUNT (2) series. The term ἱλαστήριον signifies the "mercy seat" (כַּפֹּרֶת) in Rom. 3:25. Paul speaks of Jesus as the center of the new sanctuary established by God. Cf. D. Hill, *Greek Words and Hebrew Meanings: Studies in the Semantics of Soteriological Terms*, SNTSMS 5 (Cambridge: Cambridge University Press, 1967).

13.6.6 Redemption, Adoption (Sonship), Freedom

As our grouping of these terms already indicates, Paul's understanding of "redemption" is typological in nature. Just as God once delivered his people from Egypt, so now, through Christ, God has delivered his people from sin and death. One currently prominent reading of Paul understands him as viewing God's redemptive work in Christ as Israel's return from exile, which the prophetic literature of the OT describes as a second exodus. The question of whether Paul thinks in terms of a historical continuum (as this interpretation supposes) or in terms of recapitulative acts of God has not been fully addressed. Nor is it clear that "return from exile" adequately describes the whole of Paul's soteriology, with its expectations for Israel and its unmistakably individualistic aspect. In any case, this aspect of Paul's soteriology is likely to become a focal point of study.

641 I. H. Marshall. "The Development of the Concept of Redemption in the New Testament." Pp. 239–57 in *Jesus the Saviour: Studies in New Testament Theology*. Downers Grove, Ill.: InterVarsity, 1978. Original publication: Pp. 153–69 in *Reconciliation and Hope: New Testament Essays on Atonement and Eschatology Presented to L. L. Morris on his Sixtieth Birthday*. Edited by R. Banks. Grand Rapids: Eerdmans; Exeter, England: Paternoster, 1975.

The NT concept of redemption, which is associated with biblical, sacrificial imagery, goes back to Jesus' interpretation of his mission (Mark 10:45; Isa. 53).

642 B. Byrne. *"Sons of God"—"Seed of Abraham": A Study of the Idea of the Sonship of God of All Christians in Paul,*

against the Jewish Background. Rome: Biblical Institute Press, 1979.
The title "son" refers to the exalted status of Christ, which, although present in his earthly ministry, has become manifest only with his resurrection. Those who believe in Christ likewise presently participate in "sonship," the glory of which will yet be revealed. Paul has rethought Jewish tradition in the light of the crucified and risen Messiah.

643 W. Haubeck. *Loskauf durch Christus: Herkunft, Gestalt und Bedeutung des paulinischen Loskaufmotivs.* Giessen, Germany: Brunnen, 1985.
The Pauline motif of redemption, which is largely shaped by the idea of atonement, is characterized by the idea that Christ has effected a change of possession or ownership (1 Cor. 6:19; Titus 2:14). This has its analogy in the OT motif of redemption.

644 J. M. Scott. *Adoption as Sons of God: An Exegetical Investigation into the Background of ΥΙΟΘΕΣΙΑ in the Pauline Corpus.* WUNT 2/48. Tübingen: Mohr (Siebeck), 1992.
The term υἱοθεσία bears the sense of "adoption as son(s)" as is usual in Hellenistic Greek. In Gal. 3–4, however, it entails an exodus typology based on the expectation of the Messiah (2 Sam. 7:12–14), namely, that God would redeem his people from exile in a second exodus. The same applies to Rom. 8, which also contains elements of an exodus typology, which is here future-oriented. See also "Adoption, Sonship," *DPL* 15–18.

645 S. Vollenweider. *Freiheit als neue Schöpfung: Eine Untersuchung zur Eleutheria bei Paulus und in seiner Umwelt.* FRLANT 147. Göttingen: Vandenhoeck & Ruprecht, 1989.
Detailed examination of Paul's conception of freedom against the background of Stoicism, Gnosticism, early Judaism, and early Jewish Christianity. The primary *historical* influence on Paul's thought lies in the Greek conception of freedom, which had already informed (Palestinian) Jewish thought and especially earliest Jewish Christianity, which reflected the distinction between written and unwritten law in its ambivalence toward the Law. Paul understands freedom primarily as freedom from the Law, but his thought is distinctive: Christ marks the entrance of eschatological freedom of the new (space-time) creation into the present, not into a timeless reality.

13.6.7 The Gospel, Proclamation, and Mission

Aside from the question of relations between Jews and Gentiles, Paul's theology of mission is often neglected by biblical scholars. Or, more properly stated, the missionary character of

Paul's theology as a whole is overlooked. Scholars have made
Paul into a thinker, a theologian like themselves. Paul describes
his work in other ways: he is a farmer working a field, a builder
engaged in construction, an ambassador making appeal, a soldier
waging war, and so on. Thinking and acting are integrated for
him. We cannot understand Paul unless we understand him as a
missionary. For this reason, contributions such as those listed
below (and those which shall yet appear) are welcome.

646   O. Cullmann. "Eschatology and Missions in the New Testament." Pp. 409–21 in *The Background of the New Testament and Its Eschatology*. Edited by W. D. Davies and
D. Daube. Cambridge: Cambridge University Press, 1956.
   The entire "interim" period until the coming of Christ is to be
   a time of missions.

647   F. Hahn. *Mission in the New Testament*. Translated by
F. Clarke. London: SCM, 1965. [See pp. 95–110.] German
edition: *Das Verständnis der Mission im Neuen Testament*. WMANT 13. Neukirchen-Vlyun: Neukirchener,
1963.
   The worldwide scope of Paul's mission is derived from the
   gospel itself, and is worked out in his understanding of the Law,
   righteousness, and Israel's election.

648   P. Stuhlmacher. *Das paulinische Evangelium*. FRLANT
95. Göttingen: Vandenhoeck & Ruprecht, 1968.
   The root of Paul's understanding of the gospel lay in Hellenistic-Jewish Christianity, which derived the expression not from
   the Caesar cult, but from the promise of salvation found in OT
   and Jewish tradition, which it regarded has having come to fulfillment in Jesus (e.g., Isa. 52:7; 61:1).

649   N. Dahl. "The Missionary Theology in the Epistle to the
Romans." Pp. 70–94 in *Studies in Paul: Theology for the
Early Christian Mission*. Minneapolis: Augsburg, 1977.
   An overview of Romans from the (proper, but generally over-
   looked) perspective of Paul as a missionary, with a theology of
   missions.

650   W.-H. Ollrog. *Paulus und seine Mitarbeiter: Untersuchungen zu Theorie und Praxis der paulinische Mission*.
WMANT 50. Neukirchen-Vluyn: Neukirchener, 1979.
   Paul's coworkers may be seen to consist of three groups:
   (1) those who accompanied Paul and were consistently engaged
   as "supra-congregational" missionaries; (2) those sent by congregations (the largest group); and (3) independent co-coworkers

(e.g., Apollos, Prisca, and Aquila). The sending of missionaries by the Pauline congregations reflects their self-understanding as missionizing communities (facilitated by "body-of-Christ" ecclesiology). This mission resulted in Paul's shift from traveling mission to the development of mission centers. Paul's coworkers were able to develop their own theological positions, so that there was considerable variety and vitality in this circle (e.g., Colossians may be an expression of this independent thought).

651 J. Fitzmyer. "The Gospel in the Theology of Paul." Pp. 149–61 in *To Advance the Gospel: New Testament Studies*. New York: Crossroad, 1981. Original publication: *Interpretation* 33 (1979): 339–50.

In Paul's understanding, the gospel is revelatory, dynamic, promissory, universal, and given for proclamation. It liberates from legalism, while it simultaneously represents a God-given norm. Despite Greco-Roman parallels (especially the calendrial inscription from Priene), Paul depends on the OT in his understanding of gospel (e.g., Isa. 52:7).

652 D. Senior and C. Stuhlmueller. *The Biblical Foundations for Missions*. Maryknoll, N.Y.: Orbis, 1983. [See pp. 161–210.]

There is a Christ-centered focus to Paul's understanding of mission: Jesus Christ is the Savior of the world.

653 D. Bosch. "Mission in Paul: Invitation to Join the Eschatological Community." In *Transforming Mission: Paradigm Shifts in the Theology of Mission*. American Society of Missiology 16. Maryknoll, N.Y.: Orbis, 1991.

The unity of the church above all social differences is non-negotiable, since it is the vanguard of the new creation. A responsible and sensitive witness to Jews is to continue. Christian social responsibility is bound by the recognition that the consummation of the kingdom will take place at God's initiative. Mission has the redemption of the world in its scope.

654 P. Bowers. "Church and Mission in Paul." *JSNT* 44 (1991): 89–111.

Paul did not expect his congregations to engage actively in mission. Only certain believers would be called to this task. O'Brien (#656) has offered an initial response.

655 P. Bowers. "Mission." Pp. 608–19 in *Dictionary of Paul and His Letters*. Downers Grove, Ill.: InterVarsity, 1993.

Brief but weighty survey of Paul's theology of mission against the backdrop of current scholarship.

656 P. T. O'Brien. *Gospel and Mission in the Writings of Paul:*

An Exegetical and Theological Analysis. Grand Rapids:
Baker; Carlisle, England: Paternoster, 1995. Original edi-
tion: Consumed by Passion: Paul and the Dynamic of the
Gospel. Homebush West, Australia: Lancer, 1993.

> Paul's passion for mission stemmed not only from his own con-
> version, but also from his understanding of the fulfillment of
> God's purposes in Jesus Christ. All believers are to be caught up
> in the "powerful advance of the gospel." Each one, according to
> their gifts, was to be active in witness and to be consumed by
> the same passion as Paul.

657 J. M. Scott. Paul and the Nations: The Old Testament and
Jewish Background of Paul's Mission to the Nations with
Special Reference to the Destination of Galatians. WUNT
84. Tübingen: Mohr (Siebeck), 1995.

> In developing his missionary strategy, Paul appropriated the
> "table of the nations" (Gen. 10; 1 Chron. 1:1–2:2), by which Is-
> rael understood its place in the world. Paul understands the
> mission to be territorially circumscribed in this way. Paul re-
> garded "the Galatians" in a Jewish sense as occupying the
> whole of the Roman province. One objection to the "South
> Galatian" hypothesis thereby falls away.

658 P. G. Bolt and M. D. Thompson, eds. The Gospel to the Nations: Perspectives on Paul's Mission in Honor of P. T.
O'Brien. Downers Grove, Ill.: InterVarsity; Leicester, England: Apollos, 2000.

> Collection of exegetical and theological studies centering on
> Paul's mission.

659 A. Köstenberger and P. T. O'Brien. Pp. 161–201 in Salvation to the Ends of the Earth: A Biblical Theology of Mission. New SBT 11. Downers Grove, Ill.: InterVarsity; Leicester, England: Apollos, 2001.

> Paul understood his mission on the basis of the hope of the
> (OT) Scriptures, that the nations would partake in the blessings
> promised to Israel. The gospel of the crucified and risen Christ
> is the power by which God effects his saving purpose. Paul ex-
> pects believers in his congregations to be actively engaged in
> Paul's mission and in evangelism.

13.6.8 Faith

Recent Pauline scholarship has focused especially on the interpretation of the expression "the faith of Christ" in its various
forms. Beyond the entries below, see A. Hultgren, "The Pistis
Christou Formulation in Paul," NovT 22 (1980): 148–63;

S. Williams, "Again *Pistis Christou*," *CBQ* 49 (1987): 431–47;
B. Longenecker, "*Pistis* in Romans 3:25: Neglected Evidence for
the 'Faithfulness of Christ,'" *NTS* 39 (1993): 478–80; R. A. Harrisville, III, "*Pistis Christou*: The Witness of the Fathers," *NovT*
36 (1994): 233–41; and A. Vanhoye, "*Pistis Xristou*: Fede in
Cristo o affidabilità di Cristo?" *Bib* 80 (1999): 1–21 (πίστις Χριστοῦ = trustworthiness of Christ).

660 A. Schlatter. *Der Glaube im Neuen Testament.* 3d ed.
Calw, Germany, and Stuttgart: Vereinsbuchhandlung,
1905. Original edition: 1885.
Comprehensive treatment of faith in the New Testament,
against the background of early Judaism. Schlatter understands
faith for Paul primarily as an act of the will that grasps Christ.
Faith has no power within itself, but receives power through
the work and gift of the one who believes. Obviously dated, but
still worth reading.

661 E. V. N. Goetius. "Pistis Iēsou Christou." Pp. 35–45 in *Lux
in Lumine: Essays to Honor W. Norman Pittenger.* Edited
by R. A. Norris, Jr. New York: Seabury, 1966.
"The faith of Christ" should be rendered as "the trustworthiness of Christ."

662 R. Bultmann. "πιστεύω." Vol. 6, pp. 174–228 in *Theological Dictionary of the New Testament.* Edited by G. Friedrich. Translated by G. Bromiley. Grand Rapids: Eerdmans,
1968.
Important analysis of the Pauline usage in which (nevertheless)
Bultmann's existentialism plays a large role.

663 R. B. Hays. *The Faith of Jesus Christ: An Investigation of
the Narrative Substructure of Galatians 3:1–4:11.* SBLDS
56. Chico, Calif.: Scholars Press, 1983.
Applies A. Greimas's (structuralist) narrative analysis to Gal.
3:1–4:11, in which Hays finds an underlying Gospel story:
"Jesus Christ is the archetypical (or prototypical) hero . . . who,
through his faithfulness unto death on the cross [subjective-genitive interpretation of "faith of Jesus"], wins deliverance
and access to God for his people" (255). A spate of studies on
the interpretation of the genitive relation in πίστις Χριστοῦ has
flowed forth in response to Hays's work, which reinvigorated
the subjective-genitive reading. See now Hays, "*Pistis* and Pauline Christology: What Is at Stake?" in *Society of Biblical Literature 1991 Seminar Papers,* ed. E. Lovering (Atlanta: Scholars,
1991), 714–29.

664 K. Haacker. "Glaube II/3: Neues Testament." Vol. 13, pp.

289–304. *Theologische Realenzyklopädie*. Edited by G. Krause and G. Müller. Berlin: de Gruyter, 1984.

Brief but informative history of research, discussion of Pauline texts, extensive bibliography.

665 A. von Dobbeler. *Glaube als Teilhabe: Historische und semantische Grundlagen der paulinischen Theologie und Ekklesiologie des Glaubens*. WUNT 2/22. Tübingen: Mohr (Siebeck), 1987.

Paul bases faith in an encompassing act of personal engagement: coming to faith is a participation in a pneumatic-charismatic proclamation-event, in the revelation, in the Spirit of God, and in the atonement. Faith is a "threshold phenomenon" that provides a new group identity. The combination of belief in a god, and the profane association of faith with a *Gemeinschaft* (community), would have made Paul's usage understandable to his Hellenistic audience.

666 J. Kinneavy. *Greek Rhetorical Origins of Christian Faith: An Inquiry*. New York and Oxford: Oxford University Press, 1987.

The NT understanding of faith as "persuasion" has its origins in Greek rhetoric, not in the OT or Greek philosophical thought.

667 D. Hay. "*Pistis* as 'Ground for Faith' in Hellenized Judaism and Paul." *JBL* 108 (1989): 461–76.

In passages such as Gal. 3:23, 25, πίστις may express the objective ground for faith ("assurance"), with subjective overtones.

668 G. N. Davies. *Faith and Obedience in Romans: A Study in Romans 1–4*. JSNTSup 39. Sheffield: JSOT Press, 1990.

The center and heart of the Mosaic economy was the response of faith. Fulfillment of promise means that faith in God cannot exist apart from faith in Christ.

669 J. M. Gundry-Volf. *Paul and Perseverance: Staying In and Falling Away*. Louisville: Westminster John Knox, 1991. Original edition: WUNT 2/37. Tübingen: Mohr (Siebeck), 1990.

"Continuity in salvation," which is given to faith alone, takes place through God's triumph in Christ over all obstacles. Paul is confident that even the danger of falling away from faith will be overcome, although he can speak from a human perspective of the loss of salvation. A "dynamic" portrayal of perseverance that has much to commend it.

670 G. Howard. "Faith of Christ." Vol. 2, pp. 758–60 in *The Anchor Bible Dictionary*. New York: Doubleday, 1992.

Argument in favor of subjective-genitive reading by an early proponent in the recent discussion.

671 D. Lührmann. "Faith (New Testament)." Vol. 2, pp. 744–58 in *The Anchor Bible Dictionary*. New York: Doubleday, 1992.

Survey of New Testament usage, bibliography.

672 D. Garlington. *The Obedience of Faith*. WUNT 2/38. Tübingen: Mohr (Siebeck), 1991; idem, *Faith, Obedience, and Perseverance: Aspects of Paul's Letter to the Romans*. WUNT 79. Tübingen: Mohr (Siebeck), 1994.

Paul coined the expression "the obedience of faith" to express his intent of making all people faithful covenant-keepers by virtue of union with Christ and trust in him (and not on the basis of Jewish practices). Paul offers "Christ-fidelity" in place of "Torah-fidelity." Some lack of clarity as to whether faith and obedience are synonymous or whether obedience results from faith.

13.6.9 Justification

Paul's doctrine of justification has long been a matter of controversy in modern scholarship (see the surveys in P. Stuhlmacher, *Gerechtigkeit Gottes bei Paulus*, 2d ed., FRLANT 87 [Göttingen: Vandenhoeck & Ruprecht, 1966], 11–73; M. Seifrid, *Justification by Faith: The Origin and Development of a Central Pauline Theme*, NovTSup 68 [Leiden: Brill, 1992], 6–77). The work of E. P. Sanders has brought further debate. See the entries in chapter 3, "Paul's Conversion," and chapter 6, "Paul and First-Century Judaism." Various challenges to the "new perspective" and its tendency to read justification in terms of ethnic relations in the earliest church have emerged. Perennial questions regarding the "place" of justification in Paul's thought and its relation to obedience undoubtedly will continue. Paul's teaching concerning justification is "grammatically" bound up with his understanding of the Law (§13.6.2) and faith (§13.6.8): the reader should also consult the works listed under those headings.

673 H. Cremer. *Die paulinische Rechtfertigungslehre im Zusammenhange ihrer geschichtlichen Voraussetzungen*. Gütersloh: n.p., 1900.

Important response to Ritschl, which has influenced all subsequent research on the biblical background of Paul's language (particularly that of G. von Rad).

674 A. Schlatter. *Romans: The Righteousness of God.* Translated by S. Schatzmann. Peabody, Mass.: Hendrickson, 1995. German edition: *Gottes Gerechtigkeit: Ein Kommentar zum Romerbrief.* Stuttgart: Calwer, 1935.

Influential interpretation of God's righteousness as God's saving action.

675 E. Käsemann. "The 'Righteousness of God' in Paul." Pp. 168–82 in *New Testament Questions of Today.* Philadelphia: Fortress, 1969. German edition: "Gottesrechtigkeit bei Paulus." Vol. 2, pp. 181–93 in *Exegetische Versuche und Besinnungen.* 2d ed. Göttingen: Vandenhoeck & Ruprecht, 1965 = *ZTK* 58 (1961): 367–78 (additional comments in footnotes).

Seminal essay in which Käsemann rejects Bultmann's anthropological description of justification, arguing that the expression "righteousness of God" derives from apocalyptic Judaism.

676 C. Müller. *Gottes Gerechtigkeit und Gottes Volk: Eine Untersuchung zu Römer 9–11.* FRLANT 86. Göttingen: Vandenhoeck & Ruprecht 1964.

Early dissertation under Käsemann, in which the author argues that Paul replaces the Jewish understanding of "God's righteousness" as "covenant faithfulness" with God's (gracious) judicial claim as Lord of the world.

677 G. Herold. *Zorn und Gerechtigkeit Gottes bei Paulus: Eine Untersuchung zu Röm. 1,16–18.* European University Papers, Series XIII: Theology 14. Bern: Herbert Lang, 1973.

An attempt to read Rom. 1:18 with the preceding context: the wrath of God is revealed in the cross.

678 M. Wolter. *Rechtfertigung und zukünftiges Heil: Untersuchungen zu Röm 5,1–11.* BZNW 43. Berlin: de Gruyter, 1978.

Against Bultmann, Paul's concern is not with the presence of eschatological salvation in Christian existence, but with the assurance that Jesus' death and the justification of the sinner guarantee future salvation. He also rejects Käsemann's insistence that eschatological salvation is presently found exclusively in suffering. A real future eschatology under the category of "hope" is the topic here.

679 J. Reumann. *Righteousness in the New Testament: "Justification" in the United States Lutheran–Roman Catholic Dialogue.* Joseph Fitzmyer and Jerome Quinn, respondents. Philadelphia: Fortress; Ramsey, N.Y.: Paulist, 1982.

Important survey of the New Testament evidence. See also the articles by J. J. Scullion and J. Reumann, *ABD* 5:724–73.

680 J. Piper. *The Justification of God: An Exegetical and Theological Study of Romans 9:1–23.* 2d ed. Grand Rapids: Baker, 1993. Original edition: 1983.
An attempt to understand God's righteousness in terms of God's glory.

681 S. Westerholm. *Israel's Law and the Church's Faith: Paul and His Recent Interpreters.* Grand Rapids: Ecrdmans, 1988.
Insightful interaction with E. P. Sanders, H. Räisänen, and others.

682 O. Hofius. " 'Rechtfertigung des Gottlosen' als Thema biblischer Theologie." Pp. 121–47 in *Paulusstudien*. WUNT 51. Tübingen: Mohr (Siebeck), 1989.
Exposition of the Pauline theme of the justification of the ungodly and its antecedents in the Books of Hosea, Jeremiah, and Isaiah.

683 D. A. Carson, ed. *Right with God: Justification in the Bible and the World.* Grand Rapids: Baker; Carlisle, England: Paternoster, 1992.
Collection of essays sponsored by the Theological Commission of the World Evangelical Fellowship from varying perspectives (including non-Western ones) on the topic of justification.

684 R. Hays. "Justification." Vol. 3, pp. 1129–33 in *The Anchor Bible Dictionary*. New York: Doubleday, 1992.
Useful survey of biblical usage, making the generally accepted (but questionable) assumption that rightcousness language is to be understood in covenantal terms.

685 J. D. G. Dunn and A. M. Suggate. *The Justice of God: A Fresh Look at the Old Doctrine of Justification by Faith.* Grand Rapids: Eerdmans, 1994.
An attempt to apply the doctrine of justification from the new perspective.

686 P. Zahl. *Die Rechtfertigungslehre Ernst Käsemanns.* Calwer Theologische Monographien 13. Stuttgart: Calwer, 1996.
Important analysis of a significant interpreter of Paul's doctrine of justification.

687 T. Laato. "Justification according to James: A Comparison with Paul." *TJ* 18 (1997): 43–84.
Important contribution on a perennial problem.

688 M. Seifrid. *Christ, Our Righteousness: Paul's Theology of*

Justification. New SBT 9. Downers Grove, Ill.: InterVarsity; Leicester, England: Apollos, 2000.
An overview of Paul's teaching. See also Seifrid's *Justification by Faith: The Origin and Development of a Central Pauline Theme,* NovTSup 68 (Leiden: Brill, 1992).

689 P. Stuhlmacher with D. Hagner. *Revisiting Paul's Doctrine of Justification.* Downers Grove, Ill.: InterVarsity, 2001.
Significant interaction with the "new perspective on Paul" from a scholar who has engaged this topic throughout his career. In addition to his other works cited in this volume, see *Gerechtigkeit Gottes bei Paulus,* 2d ed., FRLANT 87 (1965; Göttingen: Vandenhoeck & Ruprecht, 1966).

13.6.10 Reconciliation

The origin of Paul's interpretation of Christ's saving work as "reconciliation," its connection with atonement and justification, and its place within Paul's thought have all been matters of recent debate. Beyond the entries listed below, see also Stuhlmacher (#514) and Ridderbos (#511).

690 J. A. Fitzmyer. "Reconciliation in Pauline Theology." Pp. 162–85 in *To Advance the Gospel.* New York: Crossroad, 1981. Original publication: Pp. 155–77 in *No Famine in the Land.* Edited by J. Flanagan. Missoula, Mont.: Scholars Press, 1975.
Survey of usage and response to Käsemann, "Some Thoughts on the Theme 'the Doctrine of Reconciliation in the New Testament,'" in *The Future of Our Religious Past,* ed. J. M. Robinson (New York: Harper & Row, 1971), 49–64.

691 I. H. Marshall. "The Meaning of 'Reconciliation.'" In *Jesus the Saviour: Studies in New Testament Theology.* Downers Grove, Ill.: InterVarsity, 1990. Original publication: Pp. 108–21 in *Unity and Diversity in the New Testament.* Edited by R. A. Guelich. Grand Rapids: Eerdmans, 1978.
A brief investigation of the NT terms for "reconciliation." Paul's usage represents a correction of the martyr tradition found in 2 Maccabees.

692 O. Hofius. "Sühne und Versöhnung: Zum paulinischen Verständnis des Kreuzestodes Jesu." Pp. 33–49 in *Paulusstudien.* WUNT 51. Tübingen: Mohr (Siebeck), 1989 = Pp. 25–46 in W. Maas, ed., *Versuche, das Leiden und Sterben Jesu zu verstehen.* Munich: Schnell & Steiner, 1983; idem, "'Gott hat unter uns aufgerichtet das Wort von der Versöhnung' (2 Kor 5:19)." Pp. 15–32 in *Paulusstudien*. WUNT 51. Tübingen: Mohr (Siebeck), 1989 = ZNW 71 (1980): 3–20; idem, "Erwägungen zur Gestalt und Herkunft des paulinischen Versöhnungsgedankens." Pp. 1–14 in *Paulusstudien*. WUNT 51. Tübingen: Mohr (Siebeck), 1989 = ZThK 77 (1980): 186–99.

Series of essays which argue that Paul's statements concerning reconciliation are freshly minted from his understanding of the OT, especially Isa. 52:13–53:12 and its context, and that reconciliation is bound up with atonement (understood as inclusive representation).

693 R. P. Martin. *Reconciliation: A Study of Paul's Theology*. Grand Rapids: Academie, 1989. Original edition: London: Marshall, Morgan & Scott, 1980; Atlanta: John Knox, 1981.

Martin commends "reconciliation" as the "center" of Paul's theology, since it has both "vertical" and "horizontal" dimensions. Reconciliation expresses the divine initiative in salvation, entails the restoration of the sinner and the establishment of redeemed (personal) relationships, and reflects the continuity of Paul's message with that of Jesus. See also "Center of Paul's Theology," *DPL* 92–95.

694 H.-J. Findeis. *Versöhnung, Apostolat, Kirche: Eine exegetische-theologische und rezeptionsgeschichtliche Studie zu den Versöhnungsaussagen des Neuen Testaments*. Forschung zur Bibel 40. Würzburg: Echter, 1983.

Thorough study of the Pauline usage.

695 C. Breytenbach. *Versöhnung: Eine Studie zur paulinischen Soteriologie*. WMANT 60. Neukirchen-Vluyn: Neukirchener, 1989.

Useful history of research. Paul draws the language of reconciliation from the (profane) political realm. The terms for "reconciliation" and "atonement" do not belong to the same field, nor do they belong together traditio-historically. Paul is the first to bring the idea of "reconciliation" into connection with the understanding of Christ's death as an atonement (LXX Isa. 52:13–53:12; 2 Cor. 5:21). There was no pre-Pauline Christian interpretation of Jesus' death as an atoning sacrifice. See the response by Stuhlmacher, "Cilliers Breytenbachs Sicht von Sühne und Versöhnung," in *Altes Testament und christlicher Glaube*, ed. I. Baldermann, Jahrbuch für biblische Theologie 6 (Neukirchen-Vlyun: Neukirchener, 1991), 339–54.

696 S. E. Porter. Καταλλάσσω *in Ancient Greek Literature, with Reference to the Pauline Writings*. EFN 5. Cordova, Spain: El Almendro, 1994.

A thorough (affirmative) testing of I. H. Marshall's thesis that Paul uses the term καταλλάσσω in an unattested way, in the active voice, to express God's initiative in reconciling rebellious humanity to himself (2 Cor. 5:18, 19). Various useful exegetical observations along the way. The question nevertheless presses itself as to whether the uses in question are to be read as exceptions after all. See the summary in "Reconciliation and 2 Corinthians 5, 18–21," in Studies on 2 Corinthians, ed. R. Bieringer and J. Lambrecht (Louvain: Louvain University Press, 1996), 693–705.

697 S. Kim. "2 Cor. 5:11–21 and the Origin of Paul's Conception of 'Reconciliation.' " NovT 39 (1997): 360–84.

Beyond the fourth Servant Song (Isa. 52:13–53:12) and Jewish martyr-tradition (2 Maccabees), it was Paul's Damascus-road encounter with the risen Christ that served as the basis for his teaching on reconciliation, which has both a Hellenistic and Hellenistic-Jewish background.

13.6.11 Participation

One of the perennial problems of biblical scholarship of the last century or so has been the relationship between Paul's "participatory" (or "mystical") descriptions of salvation and his teaching concerning justification by faith. In the last couple of decades, Schweitzer's (#21) interpretation of justification as a secondary crater within Paul's primary theory of eschatological participation in Christ has been revived by the work of E. P. Sanders (#106). Some of the debate (and confusion) undoubtedly derives from an excessively narrow conception of justification, which fails to see its roots in the Old Testament, which Paul regards as fulfilled in the risen Christ. Likewise, the participatory dimension of faith in Paul's thought has often been overlooked. As is apparent from the entries below, much attention has been focused on the religio-historical origins of Paul's thought. At this point, the "mystery religions" have been decisively rejected. The appeal to Jewish ideas of "corporate personality" have also been rightly challenged (e.g., S. E. Porter, "Two Myths: Corporate Personality and Language/Mentality Determinism," SJT 43 [1990]: 289–307). See also the entries under §13.9.4, "Baptism."

698 J. Dupont. Syn Christoi l'union avec le Christ suivant saint Paul. Brugge, Belgium: Éditions de l'Abbaye de Saint-André, 1952.

There are two different contexts in which the expression "with

Christ" appears. The first derives from Jewish apocalypticism and the expectation of the coming of the saints with the resurrected Christ. The second, which stresses the element of personal relation with Christ that is already present in Paul's thought, is influenced by Hellenistic thought: to be absent from the body is to be present with the Lord (2 Cor. 5:8; Phil. 1:23).

699 A. Wikenhauser. *Pauline Mysticism: Christ in the Mystical Teaching of St. Paul.* Translated by J. Cunningham. Fribourg, Germany: Herder; Edinburgh and London: Nelson, 1960. German edition: *Die Christusmystik des Apostels Paulus.* 2d ed. Fribourg, Germany: Herder, 1956.

Paul's mysticism is not a "mysticism of faith," but a real fellowship of life with Christ. It differs from the Hellenistic mysteries, particularly in the ethical obligations of the baptized. Can it be said, however, that for Paul faith does not effect real union with Christ?

700 F. Neugebauer. *In Christus: Eine Untersuchung zum Paulinischen Glaubensverständnis.* Göttingen: Vandenhoeck & Ruprecht, 1961.

The expression "in Christ" is bound up with Paul's conception of faith, and is more or less synonymous with "by faith." The former expresses the "indicative" event that the latter intends. Both are essentially ecclesiological and not individualistic in significance. See also "Das paulinische 'in Christo,'" *NTS* 4 (1957–58): 124–38.

701 M. Bouttier. *En Christ Étude d'Exégèse et de Théologie Pauliniennes.* Etudes d'Histoire et de Philosophie Religicuscs 54. Paris: Presses Universitaires de France, 1962.

Both elements of the expression "in Christ" bear a threefold sense. The "in" has an instrumental element, an eschatological sense, and an inclusive or communal idea. "Christ" correspondingly signifies Christ's cross and resurrection, his coming to establish the kingdom, and a mystical sense, according to which he is both exalted to God's right hand and present in God's church.

702 W. Thüsing. *Per Christum in Deum: Studien zum Verhältnis von Christozentrik und Theozentrik in den paulinischen Hauptbriefen.* Neutestamentliche Abhandlungen, n.s., 1. Münster: Aschendorff, 1965.

The union of the elect with the exalted Christ by the Spirit (the "Christocentric" element of Paul's thought) is theocentric in that Christ himself entirely lives and rules for God. Christ is no hindrance to the divine saving purpose of "being all in all": he is no half-god or second God, but rather is the mediator of the "freedom of glory" of the sons of God.

703 R. Tannehill. *Dying and Rising with Christ: A Study in Pauline Theology.* Berlin: Töpelmann, 1967.

The cross is an eschatological and inclusive event. "Mysticism" (participation) is joined to righteousness through faith, and not a separate understanding of salvation for Paul.

704 P. Siber. *Mit Christus Leben: Eine Studie zur paulinischen Auferstehungshoffnung.* ATANT 61. Zürich: Theologischer Verlag Zürich, 1971.

According to Paul, the future resurrection of the dead is the concluding event of the ongoing manifestation of Jesus' resurrection. The basis of hope in the future resurrection is participation in the resurrection of Jesus, which has taken place already.

705 A. J. M. Wedderburn. *Baptism and Resurrection: Studies in Pauline Theology against Its Greco-Roman Background.* WUNT 44. Tübingen: Mohr (Siebeck), 1987.

Paul's understanding of baptism as "dying and coming to life with Christ" was not borrowed from Greco-Roman mystery religions (which did not think in terms of a past death with a deity), but from Jewish traditions of representative figures. The idea of a resurrection which (in some sense) has already taken place (Col. 2:11–13; cf. 2 Tim. 1:17–18) is likely a development of Rom. 6, which speaks of a future resurrection. See also "Some Observations on Paul's Use of the Phrases 'in Christ' and 'with Christ,'" *JSNT* 25 (1985): 83–97.

706 M. Seifrid. "In Christ." Pp. 433–36 in *Dictionary of Paul and His Letters.* Downers Grove, Ill.: InterVarsity, 1993.

Analysis of Paul's usage.

707 W. Barcley. *"Christ in You": A Study in Paul's Theology and Ethics.* Lanham, Md.: University Press of America, 1999.

Such passages speak especially of communal ideas and ethics.

13.6.12 Holiness

708 S. E. Porter. "Holiness, Sanctification." Pp. 397–402 in *Dictionary of Paul and His Letters.* Downers Grove, Ill.: InterVarsity, 1993.

Overview of Paul's usage and understanding of holiness (which has both moral and eschatological aspects). Discussion concerning the relation of "justification" to "sanctification."

709 D. Peterson. *Possessed by God: A New Testament Theol-*

ogy of Sanctification and Holiness. New SBT 1. Grand
Rapids: Eerdmans; Leicester, England: Apollos, 1995.
Sanctification cannot rightly be understood as a mere process
or stage of the Christian life. God has sanctified us wholly in
Christ, therefore we are to become sanctified.

13.6.13 Final Judgment

Just as studies of Paul's concept of sin focus on Rom. 5 and
studies of Pauline anthropology focus on Rom. 7, studies of final
judgment focus on Rom. 2 (along with 2 Cor. 5). Protestant scholarship remains restless concerning the relationship between justification, *sola fide*, and final judgment according to works in
Paul's thought. On this topic, see also the works listed in
§13.6.9, "Justification."

710 H. Braun. *Gerichtsgedanke und Rechtfertigungslehre bei
Paulus.* UNT 19. Leipzig: J. C. Hinrichs'sche Buchhandlung, 1930.
Justification and judgment according to works are irreconcilable. The latter represents a residue of Jewish thought that Paul
did not assimilate.

711 L. Mattern. *Das Verständnis des Gerichtes bei Paulus.*
ATANT 47. Zürich: Zwingli, 1966.
Deals with the discrepancies between justification by faith and
judgment over Christians by postulating three different modes
of judgment: (1) a judgment of destruction over non-Christians;
(2) a judgment whether one is a Christian; and (3) a judgment
that determines how one has lived as a Christian, and hence
that assigns appropriate reward.

712 C. J. Roetzel. *Judgement in the Community: A Study of
the Relationship between Eschatology and Ecclesiology in
Paul.* Leiden: Brill, 1972.
Judgment is related to the community, not the individual.

713 K. P. Donfried. "Justification and Last Judgment in Paul."
ZNW 67 (1976): 90–110.
Justification is a past event, sanctification a present event, and
salvation a future event.

714 E. Synofzik. *Die Gerichts- und Vergeltungsaussagen bei
Paulus.* GTA 8. Göttingen: Vandenhoeck & Ruprecht,
1977.
Rejects the suggestion that Paul's thoughts regarding the last
judgment represent an unassimilated remainder of Jewish and
early Christian theology. The references to judgment and retri-

bution never form a self-standing topic for Paul, but rather are employed only as a "means of argument" in the areas of eschatology, exhortation, and soteriology. The theme of judgment is only one of many in his exhortations. He did not develop a system in the area of eschatology. The saving function of Christ in the final judgment is expressed through Paul's statements on justification.

715 K. Snodgrass. "Justification by Grace—To the Doers: An Analysis of the Place of Romans 2 in the Theology of Paul." *NTS* 32 (1986): 72–93.

Salvation is by grace, but grace effects obedience.

716 S. Travis. *Christ and the Judgment of God: Divine Retribution in the New Testament*. Foundations for Faith. Basingstoke, England: Marshall Pickering, 1986.

The final state will be a confirmation and intensification of the relationship with God or alienation from God that has been experienced in this life. Retributive words point to the fittingness of God's judgments, but the contexts in which they occur generally prevent them from being understood in a strictly retributive sense. See also "Judgment," *DPL* 516–17.

717 K. L. Yinger. *Paul, Judaism, and Judgment according to Deeds*. SNTSMS 105. Cambridge: Cambridge University Press, 1999.

An attempt to integrate justification and final judgment. Paul's conception of judgment is much the same as early Jewish "covenantal nomism," only that the "Christ-event" replaces the giving of the Torah as the expression of electing grace. The works to which Paul refers (in, e.g., Rom. 2) signify "that godly obedience which Paul everywhere expects as the response to grace, and elsewhere terms 'the obedience of faith.'" If early Judaism was characterized by "covenantalism" standing independently alongside "nomism" and not by Sanders's synthetic "covenantal nomism," a different and more complex understanding of final judgment (in Paul and early Judaism) emerges (see Avemarie [#118]).

13.7 Eschatology

The direction of twentieth-century scholarship on "eschatology" was set by A. Schweitzer, who posited that Paul expected "apocalyptic" end-time events and Jesus' return to happen immediately and that Paul invented the "in Christ" formula ("Christ mysticism") as an explanation for the delay-of-the-parousia dilemma (see esp. #21). In reaction to Schweitzer, C. H.

Dodd pointed out that in the life, death, and resurrection of Jesus, the *eschaton* had already entered history (although Dodd initially left no room for Jesus' future return; see esp. #212). Another response came from R. Bultmann, who did away with literal eschatology by redefining it as a Jewish form of self-understanding that expresses the ultimate and transcendent significance of present decision ("demythologizing"; see, e.g., *Jesus Christ and Mythology* [New York: Scribner's Sons, 1958]). O. Cullmann paved the way toward a more balanced appreciation of both present and future aspects of eschatology (see esp. *Christ and Time: The Primitive Christian Conception of Time and History*, trans. F. V. Filson [Philadelphia: Westminster, 1950]). Since "eschatology" can be a very "slippery" term (see, e.g., I. H. Marshall, "Slippery Words: I. Eschatology," *ExpT* 89 [1977–78]: 264–69), note that it is understood here in two senses: (1) as the invasion of the powers of the age to come (esp. the Spirit's coming at Pentecost) in the aftermath of the climactic event of Jesus Christ's death and resurrection, that is, *inaugurated* or *realized eschatology*; and (2) as the future consummation of the judgment of this present evil age and the arrival of the fullness of the new creation in Christ, that is, *futuristic/consistent/apocalyptic* (although the term *apocalyptic* is now generally reserved for a literary genre; see D. Aune, "Apocalypticism," *DPL* 25–35) *eschatology*. Both senses of eschatology are intertwined with God, Christ, the Spirit, salvation, Israel, the church, and ethics (although works in these areas show differing degrees of eschatological awareness), because eschatology involves (1) the climactic, temporal realization of God's eternal purposes in the sending of God's Son to save a people (both Israel and the nations) for himself, through his Son's representative and substitutionary death and resurrection, through which the new creation has entered the world already; (2) the outpouring of the Holy Spirit as the pledge and firstfruits of the inheritance kept in heaven and as the present reality of the new life in Christ; and (3) the imminent return of Christ to judge the world, to deliver his people, and to grant them the inheritance of the new creation. Besides the works below, which cover the whole range of source, nature, meaning, function, alleged development, and eschatologies that Paul opposed, see especially Ridderbos (#511); Beker (#513); Ladd (#516, pp. 397–614); Pate (#518); Hamilton (#558); de Boer (#604); and L. Kreitzer, "Eschatology," *DPL* 253–69.

718 G. Vos. *The Pauline Eschatology.* Phillipsburg, N.J.: P & R, 1994. Original edition: Princeton: Princeton University Press, 1930.

A classic treatment of Paul's eschatology that has withstood the test of time. Deals with the structure of Paul's eschatology, its relation to soteriology, and its religious and ethical motivation before treating the coming of the Lord and its precursors, the man of sin, the resurrection, alleged developments in Paul's thought, chiliasm, the judgment, and the eternal state. Proposed a "semi-eschatology" that appreciated both temporal (present and future) and spatial (in heaven and on earth) elements of eschatology, which anticipated critical scholarship (which had largely ignored Vos's work) by about half a century (see Lincoln [#723]). See also #556.

719 W. Baird. "Pauline Eschatology in Hermeneutical Perspective." *NTS* 17 (1970–71): 314–27.

Finds theories that explain perceived shifts in Paul's eschatological language in terms of gradual development or polemical engagement too simplistic. Argues that, although Paul's eschatological language has undergone change (with concern shifting from the future to the past and present), it is not gradual development from Jewish into Hellenistic forms, since major concepts remain relatively constant. For an opposing view, see C. L. Mearns, "Early Eschatological Development in Paul," *NTS* 27 (1981): 131–51.

720 R. B. Gaffin. *The Centrality of the Resurrection: A Study in Paul's Soteriology.* Baker Biblical Monograph. Grand Rapids: Baker, 1978.

"The resurrection of Christ is *the* pivotal factor" in the whole of Paul's teaching on salvation (135). The various elements of the usual *ordo salutis* (regeneration, justification, sanctification) are, for Paul, various aspects of the single act of God's raising Christ from the dead for us.

721 A. C. Thiselton. "Realized Eschatology at Corinth." *NTS* 24 (1978): 510–26.

Argues that the unifying issue Paul addresses in 1 Corinthians was an overrealized eschatology. Cf. Thiselton (#403, pp. 40–41), in which he reaffirms this thesis but combines it with the "postmodern mood's" infiltration of the social construction of a "virtual" reality. See also P. H. Towner, "Gnosis and Realized Eschatology in Ephesus (of the Pastoral Epistles) and the Corinthian Enthusiasm," *JSNT* 31 (1987): 95–124.

722 G. B. Caird. *The Language and Imagery of the Bible.* Grand

Rapids: Eerdmans, 1997. [See esp. pp. 243–71.] Original edition: London: Duckworth, 1980.

Exposes the problems with various conceptions of eschatology and proposes that eschatological language functions metaphorically for a national Jewish self-understanding of historical teleology. The three propositions of his proposal are (1) "the biblical writers believed literally that the world had had a beginning in the past and would have an end in the future"; (2) "they regularly used end-of-the-world language metaphorically to refer to that which they well knew was not the end of the world"; and (3) "as with all other uses of metaphor, we have to allow for the likelihood of some literalist misinterpretation on the part of the hearer, and for the possibility of some blurring of the edges between vehicle and tenor on the part of the speaker" (256).

723 A. T. Lincoln. *Paradise Now and Not Yet: Studies in the Role of the Heavenly Dimension in Paul's Thought with Special Reference to His Eschatology.* SNTSMS 43. Cambridge: Cambridge University Press, 1981.

Examines the relation of Paul's concept of "heaven" to his eschatology in relevant passages in Galatians, 1 and 2 Corinthians, Philippians, Colossians, and Ephesians. Shows that both temporal and spatial elements are combined in Paul's eschatology and that Christians are to be firmly involved in this present world while sharing in Christ's heavenly session and awaiting the future consummation.

724 M. J. Harris. *Raised Immortal: Resurrection and Immortality in the New Testament.* London: Marshall, Morgan & Scott, 1983. Reprint, Grand Rapids: Eerdmans, 1985.

Examines the themes of resurrection and immortality and their relation to each other. Argues against the immortality of the soul; sees Jesus' resurrected body as essentially invisible and immaterial; and inclines toward the view that individual believers are resurrected at death. See also Harris's *From Grave to Glory: Resurrection in the New Testament, Including a Response to Norman L. Geisler* (Grand Rapids: Zondervan, 1990). For helpful reviews of the controversy that erupted between Harris and N. Geisler, see F. J. Beckwith, "Identity and Resurrection: A Review Article," and S. McKnight, "The Nature of Bodily Resurrection: A Debatable Issue," *JETS* (1990): 369–73, 379–82.

725 W. Meeks. "Social Functions of Apocalyptic Language in Pauline Christianity." Pp. 687–705 in *Apocalypticism in*

the Mediterranean World and the Near East. Edited by
D. Hellholm. Tübingen: Mohr (Siebeck), 1983.

> To illumine the social functions of Paul's apocalyptic belief
> structures, Meeks posits several general characteristics of mil-
> lenarian movements and examines Paul's specific uses of apoca-
> lyptic language in light of alleged analogies in form and function.

726 R. N. Longenecker. "The Nature of Paul's Early Eschatology." *NTS* 31 (1985): 85–95.

> Highlights three factors neglected in analyses of Paul's escha-
> tological statements in the Thessalonian letters: (1) Paul's main
> focus of writing may not be to teach about eschatology, but
> rather to defend his and his companions' conduct among the
> Thessalonians and to encourage the persecuted Thessalonian
> believers; (2) Jesus' resurrection and teachings ground Paul's es-
> chatology rather than an alleged disillusionment with the
> parousia's delay; and (3) the purpose of Paul's statements were
> not primarily didactic but pastoral. Argues that "Paul's basic
> Christian conviction and the starting point for all his theology
> was not apocalypticism but functional christology" (93).

727 P. H. Towner. "The Present Age in the Eschatology of the
Pastoral Epistles." *NTS* 32 (1986): 427–48.

> Shows that the conception of time in the Pastorals is largely
> consistent with the rest of the NT, and that the Christ-event
> has brought in an already-not-yet tension in which there is
> lively anticipation of the climactic return of Christ.

728 L. J. Kreitzer. *Jesus and God in Paul's Eschatology.*
JSNTSup 19. Sheffield: JSOT Press, 1987.

> Explores Paul's eschatology (in comparison to Jewish pseudepi-
> graphal works) in terms of Paul's belief in the parousia and the
> final judgment, and in terms of his understanding of the Mes-
> siah and the kingdom, for its christological content and the re-
> lationship between theocentricity and Christocentricity.

729 E. E. Johnson. *The Function of Apocalyptic and Wisdom
Traditions in Romans 9–11.* SBLDS 109. Atlanta: Scholars
Press, 1989.

> Argues that Paul (in Rom. 9–11) and contemporary Jewish
> apocalyptic writers (250 B.C.E. to 150 C.E.) draw from both apoc-
> alyptic and wisdom traditions. Also examines the function of
> the wisdom traditions in Rom. 9–11. See also Johnson's "The
> Function of Apocalyptic and Wisdom Traditions in Romans
> 9–11: Rethinking the Questions," *SBL Seminar Papers* (1995),
> 352–61, in which she admits that she had made "two separate
> cases for *what* Paul argues and *how* Paul argues and then

wrongly claim[ed] that the former is determined by the latter" (356).

730 A. König. *The Eclipse of Christ in Eschatology: Toward a Christ-Centered Approach.* Grand Rapids: Eerdmans; London: Marshall, Morgan & Scott, 1989.
Brings out the christological nature of eschatology nicely, and rightly argues that this dimension of "the last things" has been overlooked.

731 J. Marcus and M. L. Soards, eds. *Apocalyptic and the New Testament: Essays in Honor of J. Louis Martyn.* JSNTSup 19. Sheffield: JSOT Press, 1989.
See especially R. Sturm, "Defining the Word 'Apocalyptic': A Problem in Biblical Criticism," 17–48, and M. de Boer, "Paul and Jewish Apocalyptic Eschatology," 169–90. For a helpful definition of apocalyptic and insistence on both theological and social functions of apocalyptic language, see also D. N. Scholer, "'The God of Peace Will Shortly Crush Satan under Your Feet' (Romans 16:20a): The Function of Apocalyptic Eschatology in Paul," *ExAud* 6 (1990): 53–61.

732 D. W. Kuck. *Judgment and Community Conflict: Paul's Use of Apocalyptic Judgment Language in 1 Corinthians 3:5–4:5.* NovTSup 66. Leiden: Brill, 1992.
To determine the function of Paul's language of final judgment in 1 Cor. 3:5–4:5, Kuck examines the function of traditions of divine judgment in both Greco-Roman and Jewish sources, analyzes the rhetorical structure and argumentation in 1 Cor. 1:10–4:21, and surveys the functions of future-judgment language in Paul's letters (Pastorals excluded) and other early Christian writings. Concludes that Paul uses apocalyptic language in 3:5–4:5 as part of his rhetorical strategy in 1:10–4:21 to admonish the Corinthian congregation to unity in Christ. Specifically, Paul calls his readers to look to God's future judgment for "the fulfillment of their legitimate aspirations for reward, status, and praise" and thus to "sublimate those community-destroying desires for fulfillment" (236).

733 B. Witherington, III. *Jesus, Paul, and the End of the World: A Comparative Study in New Testament Eschatology.* Downers Grove, Ill.: InterVarsity, 1992.
Compares and contrasts Jesus' and Paul's language of imminence and their teachings on the dominion of God, the community of Christ, the Israel of God, the day of the Lord, the resurrection of the dead, and the end of the world. Contends that the certainty and character of the end account for Jesus' and

Paul's language, so that their statements should neither be demythologized nor mined for the specific timing of the end.

734 M. Silva. "Eschatological Structures in Galatians." Pp. 140–62 in *To Tell the Mystery: Essays on New Testament Eschatology in Honor of Robert H. Gundry.* Edited by T. E. Schmidt and M. Silva. JSNTSup 100. Sheffield: JSOT Press, 1994.

Briefly surveys the redemptive-historical undercurrent running throughout Galatians, showing that a genuine appreciation of its eschatological structures unveils Paul's grounding of "the future triumph of God's righteousness in a carefully developed view of realized eschatology" (161). See also J. L. Martyn, "Apocalyptic Antinomies in the Letter of the Galatians," *NTS* 31 (1985): 410–24.

735 J. Holleman. *Resurrection and Parousia: A Traditio-Historical Study of Paul's Eschatology in 1 Corinthians 15.* NovTSup 84. Leiden: Brill, 1996.

Offers a traditio-historical analysis of three ideas identified as central to Paul's exposition of the eschatological resurrection, claiming to trace the origin of each notion.

736 K. E. Brower and M. W. Elliott. *Eschatology in Bible and Theology: Evangelical Essays at the Dawn of a New Millennium.* Edited by K. E. Brower. Downers Grove, Ill.: InterVarsity, 1997.

A collection of sixteen papers in the categories of biblical theology (two), OT (two), NT (six), Christian doctrine (four), and practical theology (two). On Pauline eschatology, see B. Witherington on transcending imminence and B. Winter on the "seasons" of this life and eschatology in 1 Cor. 7:29–31.

737 J. Plevnik. *Paul and the Parousia: An Exegetical and Theological Investigation.* Peabody, Mass.: Hendrickson, 1997.

Part 1 lays the exegetical foundation for understanding Paul's presentation of the parousia with examination of fundamental concepts and imagery and key texts—1 Thess. 4:13–18; 5:1–11; 1 Cor. 15:23–28, 50–55; and Phil. 3:20–21. Part 2 assembles the concepts discovered through the exegesis of Part 1 and synthesizes it theologically in terms of hope, judgment, conflict with powers and death, living with Christ forever, the church, and Paul's apocalyptic theology.

738 E. E. Ellis. *Christ and the Future in New Testament History.* NovTSup 97. Leiden: Brill, 2000.

See "The Structure of Pauline Eschatology" (originally published in *NTS* 6 [1959–60]: 211–24), in which Ellis argues that 2 Cor. 5 does not deal with the intermediate state, but rather contrasts corporate existence in Adam and in Christ from the standpoint of the consummation. See also "*Soma* in First Corinthians."

13.8 Israel

Since World War II, the discussion of Paul's teaching about the nature and destiny of Israel in Rom. 9–11 has been embroiled in the larger questions over Paul's attitude toward Jews and Judaism as well as Christian-Jewish relations. Together with the distorting influence of modern convictions about multiculturalism and tolerance, this concern with anti-Semitism and interreligious dialogue has resulted in a plethora of revisionist interpretations of Paul. On the one hand, some claim that Christianity and Judaism represent two ways of salvation based on God's promise to Abraham, so that non-Christian Jews are saved by faithfulness to their own covenant without reference to Christ (e.g., Gager [#743] and Stendahl [#741]). On the other hand, some claim that Paul is logically incoherent (e.g., Räisänen [#745]). There are, however, compelling studies showing Paul's coherence (e.g., J. Kim [#316]; B. W. Longenecker, "Different Answers to Different Issues: Israel, the Gentiles, and Salvation History in Romans 9–11," *JSNT* 36 [1989]: 95–123; and D. J. Moo, "The Theology of Romans 9–11: A Response to E. Elizabeth Johnson," 3:240–58 in #316). The exegetical discussion, then, revolves around whether there is a true Israel besides national Israel (a Jewish remnant or the church), whether this true Israel totally displaces national Israel in God's purposes and in inheriting God's promises, and the referent of "all Israel" and the nature of the salvation in Rom. 11:26 (see further Merkle [#755]; see also W. Campbell, "Israel," and J. Scott, "Restoration of Israel," *DPL* 441–46, 796–805; Dunn [#520, pp. 499–532]; Ridderbos [#511, pp. 362–95]; and the commentaries).

739 J. Munck. *Christ and Israel: An Interpretation of Romans 9–11.* Edited by I. Nixon. Philadelphia: Fortress, 1967. Original title: *Christus und Israel.* Copenhagen: Ejnar Munksgaard, 1956.

Forms the exegetical basis for Munck's *Paul and the Salvation of Mankind* (#24). The milieu of Romans is a three-way discussion involving Gentiles, Judaism, and Christianity, and the central problem is the enigma of Israel's rejection of the gospel and the expectation that God will yet save all Israel.

740 P. Richardson. *Israel in the Apostolic Church*. London: Cambridge University Press, 1969.

Examines the development of Christian awareness of the need to appropriate Jewish titles and privileges. Argues that "Israel" is never openly applied to the church until Justin in *Dialogue with Trypho* in 160 C.E. Paul incorporates all Christians into Israel, but does not displace Israel with the church (see pp. 70–158). See also G. Harvey, *The True Israel: Uses of the Names Jew, Hebrew, and Israel in Ancient Jewish and Early Christian Literature*, AGJU 35 (Leiden: Brill, 1996), esp. 225–32, who examines the uses of the names "Jew," "Hebrew," and "Israel" in ancient Jewish and early Christian literature synchronically and argues that "Israel" never connotes a pure community—a true Israel—not even in Rom. 9:6.

741 K. Stendahl. *Paul among Jews and Gentiles and Other Essays*. Philadelphia: Fortress, 1976.

Alleges that Paul was not converted out of Judaism, but was rather called to reach the Gentiles, that he invented the doctrine of justification by faith to "justify" including Gentiles in the kingdom of God, and that Paul's gospel was unique rather than universal. Posits a separate existence of Israel and its final salvation apart from accepting Jesus as the Messiah. See also Stendahl's "Paul and the People of Israel," and "Paul and the Gentiles: A Suggestion Concerning Romans 11:13–24," in *Jewish and Pauline Studies* (Philadelphia: Fortress, 1984), 124–52, 153–63.

742 M. Barth. *The People of God*. JSNTSup 5. Sheffield: JSOT Press, 1983.

Appeals to Eph. 2 as a competent explanation and continuation of Rom. 9–11. Argues that there is only one people of God, but also alleges that this people of God includes the church, the synagogue, the state of Israel, and all secularized Jews.

743 J. G. Gager. *The Origins of Anti-Semitism: Attitudes toward Judaism in Pagan and Christian Antiquity*. Oxford: Oxford University Press, 1983. [See pp. 193–264.]

Agrees with Stendahl and L. Gaston (*Paul and the Torah* [Vancouver: University of British Columbia Press, 1987]) that Paul affirms the validity of the Law and God's promises to Israel and does not envision an end-time conversion of Israel to Christ. Rather Judaism and Christianity are two ways of salvation based on God's promise to Abraham. See also Gager's *Reinventing Paul* (Oxford: Oxford University Press, 2000).

744 S. Hafemann. "The Salvation of Israel in Romans 11:25–32: A Response to Krister Stendahl." *ExAud* 4 (1988): 38–58.

A helpful explanation of Stendahl's paradigm for understanding Paul and a powerful refutation of it (while affirming the future salvation of ethnic Israel, but only by faith in Christ). For a similar refutation of Stendahl, see R. Hvalvik, "A 'Sonderweg' for Israel: A Critical Examination of a Current Interpretation of Romans 11.25–27," *JSNT* 38 (1990): 87–107.

745 H. Räisänen. "Paul, God, and Israel: Romans 9–11 in Recent Research." Pp. 178–206 in *The Social World of Formative Christianity and Judaism*. Edited by J. Neusner et al. Philadelphia: Fortress, 1988.

Alleges that Paul tries to console himself about the nagging problem of Israel's rejection of his message and ends up with an insoluble self-contradiction in his statements about Israel.

746 G. Wagner. "The Future of Israel: Reflections on Romans 9–11." Pp. 77–112 in *Eschatology and the New Testament: Essays in Honor of George Raymond Beasley-Murray*. Edited by W. H. Gloer. Peabody, Mass.: Hendrickson, 1988.

A clear and balanced reflection on Paul's thought on the future of Israel from Rom. 9–11 and its modern implications: the eschatological salvation of ethnic Israel will be a miraculous event that throws further light on justification of the ungodly by grace through faith. See also O. Hofius, "'All Israel Will Be Saved': Divine Salvation and Israel's Deliverance in Romans 9–11," *PSB*, supplement 1 (1990): 19–39.

747 W. S. Campbell. *Paul's Gospel in an Intercultural Context: Jew and Gentile in the Letter to the Romans*. Studien zur interkulturellen Geschichte des Christentums. Frankfurt: Peter Lang, 1991.

A compilation of essays arguing that Paul primarily wrote to the Gentile Christian majority in Rome to defend the continuity of the gospel with God's revelation to Israel and the irrevocability of God's promises to Israel, so as to establish a unity that allows for theological and cultural diversity. See especially "The Freedom and Faithfulness of God in Relation to Israel" (43–59).

748 N. T. Wright. *Climax of the Covenant: Christ and the Law in Pauline Theology*. Edinburgh: T. & T. Clark, 1991; Minneapolis: Fortress, 1992.

See "Adam, Israel, and the Messiah" (18–40) on the close link between Messiah and Israel and how Jesus stands in the place of Israel in his death and resurrection to fulfill Israel's vocation. See "Christ, the Law, and the People of God: The Problem of Romans 9–11" (231–57), in which Wright identifies "all Israel" as the church and the Scripture quotation in 11:26b–27 as referring to the Gentile mission.

749 C. A. Blaising and D. L. Bock. *Progressive Dispensationalism.* Wheaton, Ill.: Victor, 1993.

Helpful survey of the history of dispensationalism. Distinctives of progressive dispensationalism (over against earlier forms) include the adoption of an already-not-yet framework, emphasis on continuity of different phases of the eschatological kingdom (rather than radically discontinuous dispensations), and the existence of one redeemed humanity in the present age (though retaining the future, literal fulfillment of covenant blessings for ethnic Israel).

750 D. J. Harrington. *Paul on the Mystery of Israel.* Zacchaeus Studies: New Testament. Collegeville, Minn.: Liturgical Press, 1992.

Surveys 1 Thess. 2:14–16; Galatians; 2 Cor. 3; Phil. 3; and Romans (esp. 11:25–32), asking why a large part of Israel had rejected the gospel and what God has planned for Israel in the future. Sees Rom. 11:26a as referring to an eschatological mass salvation of ethnic Jews (though not necessarily every Israelite), while rejecting the view that God has a separate way of saving Jews apart from Christ.

751 R. H. Bell. *Provoked to Jealousy: The Origin and Purpose of the Jealousy Motif in Romans 9–11.* WUNT 2/63. Tübingen: Mohr (Siebeck), 1994.

Argues that "jealousy" can be negative or positive, adopting a positive "provoke-to-emulation" interpretation in Rom. 11:11, 14, which builds a "double bridge": "a bridge between the failure of Israel to believe the gospel and her eventual salvation and a bridge between the salvation of Israel and the salvation of the Gentiles" (358).

752 C. J. Schlueter. *Filling Up the Measure: Polemical Hyperbole in 1 Thessalonians 2:14–16.* JSNT 98. Sheffield: JSOT Press, 1994.

Explains Paul's language against the Jews in 1 Thess. 2:14–16 as a use of hyperbolic language to polarize (through comparison to the use of hyperbole in Greco-Roman rhetoric and other Pauline letters).

753 C. H. Cosgrove. *Elusive Israel: The Puzzle of Election in Romans.* Louisville: Westminster John Knox, 1997.

Combines new criticism, reader-response criticism, and canonical criticism in setting out interpretive possibilities for the identity and destiny of Israel in Romans. States that Paul uses the rhetorical device of "co-deliberation" (so that the reader decides Israel's identity and destiny), that Paul's incorporation into the canon has transformed the text's meaning away from his authorial intent (so that Paul's apocalyptic expectation turns out to be a contingent prophecy and is disconfirmed), and that the reader should apply the hermeneutic of love (so that Israel is ethnic Israel in the first instance, but applies to all peoples, thus willing universal salvation).

754   J. N. Aletti. *Israël et la loi dans la Lettre aux romains*. Lectio Divina 173. Paris: Cerf, 1998.
      Considers Rom. 2; 4; 5:12–21; 7:7–25; 9:6–29; 10; 11 on the Law and Israel.

755   B. L. Merkle. "Romans 11 and the Future of Ethnic Israel." *JETS* 43 (2000): 709–21.
      A clear presentation of the three alternative explanations of "all Israel"—all elect Jews and Gentiles; ethnic Israel (either synchronically in one generation or diachronically covering all Israelites who have ever lived); and elect, ethnic Israel throughout history. Argues forcefully for the rarely held elect-Jews-throughout-history view.

13.9 The Church

Although each section of this bibliography only aims at a selective, accurate representation of major options and the state of research, because of space limitations and the vastness of the subject, this section on Paul's conception of the church is even more limited. A generally helpful and up-to-date discussion is found in Dunn (#520; "On Baptism," pp. 442–59; "The Body of Christ," pp. 533–64; "Ministry and Authority," pp. 565–98; "The Lord's Supper," pp. 599–623). The various introductory articles in *DPL* should also be consulted: P. O'Brien, "Church," 123–31; R. Fung, "Body of Christ," 76–82; P. Towner, "Household and Household Codes," 417–19; P. O'Brien, "Fellowship, Communion, Sharing," 293–95; P. Barnett, "Apostle," 45–51; E. Ellis, "Coworkers, Paul and His," 183–89; L. Belleville, "Authority," 54–59; P. Beasley-Murray, "Pastor, Paul as," 654–58; R. Banks, "Church Order and Government," 131–37; J. Everts, "Financial Support," 295–300; T. Schmidt, "Discipline," 214–18; G. Beasley-Murray, "Baptism" and "Dying and Rising with Christ," 60–66, 218–22; I. Marshall, "Lord's Supper," 569–75; B. Blue, "Love Feast," 578–79; R. Martin, "Worship," 982–91; C. Keener, "Man and Woman," 583–92; C. Kroeger, "Head," 375–77; and J. McVay, "Head, Christ as," 377–78. See also Ridderbos (#511, pp. 327–95); §13.12, "Ethics" (see R. Hays, "Ecclesiology and Ethics in 1 Corinthians," *ExAud* 10 [1994]: 31–43, on the ecclesial nature of Paul's ethic); Ladd (#516, pp. 576–94); and E. Best, "Essay 1" (#420, pp. 622–41). Besides works of general orientation, seven additional subcategories are introduced separately below.

13.9.1 General Orientation

756 L. Cerfaux. *The Church in the Theology of St. Paul.* Translated by G. Webb and A. Walker. Fribourg, Germany: Herder & Herder, 1959. French title: *La Théologie de l'Église suivant S. Paul.* Paris: Éditions du Cerf, 1947. Original French edition: 1942. Third French edition: 1965.

Discovers three strands to Paul's conception of the church: (1) adaptation of OT formulas concerning Israel to the church; (2) Christian experience; and (3) evolution in thought in the captivity epistles. The third French edition includes two new chapters that discuss Paul's view of the relationship of the church to the kingdom of God and issues like the Christian ministry, church order, and apostolic succession.

757 R. Schnackenburg. *The Church in the New Testament.* Translated by W. J. O'Hara. London: Burn & Oates, 1965.

A dated but still-useful synthetic treatment of the church in the New Testament. Pages 77–85 examine Paul's personal contribution to the concept of ecclesiology.

758 R. J. Banks. *Paul's Idea of Community: The Early House Churches in Their Historical Setting.* Exeter, England: Paternoster, 1980.

Compares and contrasts Paul's idea of community with that of other religious, philosophical, and social movements. Contentions include: (1) Paul does not conceive of a universal church on earth or of organizational connections; (2) the purpose of gathering is mutual edification, not worship or mission; (3) baptism concerns the individual, not the community; and (4) there were no fixed offices or paid ministry. Sharp dichotomies drawn often lead to strained exegesis (facilitated by treating the Pastorals as non-Pauline). See also V. Branick, *The House Church in the Writings of Paul,* Zacchaeus Studies: New Testament (Wilmington, Del.: Michael Glazier, 1989).

759 D. A. Carson, ed. *The Church in the Bible and the World: An International Study.* Grand Rapids: Baker; Exeter, England: Paternoster, 1987.

Attempts to formulate "some biblically informed and hermeneutically sensitive statements on the doctrine of the church" (vii). Contains E. Clowney, "The Biblical Theology of the Church"; P. O'Brien, "The Church as a Heavenly and Eschatological Entity"; R. Shedd, "Worship in the New Testament Church"; R. Fung, "Ministry in the New Testament"; D. Carson, "Church and Mission: Reflections on Contextualization and the Third Horizon"; S. Sumithra, "Syncretism, Secularization, and Renewal"; and D. Adeney, "The Church and Persecution."

760 E. E. Ellis. *Pauline Theology: Ministry and Society*. Grand Rapids: Eerdmans; Exeter, England: Paternoster, 1989.

Contains a significant treatment of five aspects of ministry in Paul: (1) ministry as a concept; (2) the Spirit's role (and the ascended Christ as the source) in gifts; (3) the role of women; (4) ministry and church order; and (5) place in the social order of the Greco-Roman world.

761 M. J. Wilkins and T. Paige, eds. *Worship, Theology, and Ministry in the Early Church: Festschrift R. P. Martin*. JSNTSup 87. Sheffield: JSOT Press, 1992.

See especially under "Worship" in part 1: L. Morris, "The Saints and the Synagogue," and E. Best, "The Use of Credal and Liturgical Material in Ephesians"; under "Theology" in part 2: J. Dunn, "'The Body of Christ' in Paul," and T. Paige, "Stoicism, ἐλευθερία, and Community at Corinth"; under "Ministry" in part 3: G. Hawthorne, "Faith: The Essential Ingredient of Effective Christian Ministry," C. Kruse, "The Price Paid for a Ministry among Gentiles: Paul's Persecution at the Hands of the Jews," and P. O'Brien, "The Gospel and Godly Models in Philippians."

762 C. S. de Vos. *Church and Community Conflicts: The Relationship of the Thessalonian, Corinthian, and Philippian Churches with Their Wider Civic Communities*. SBLDS 168. Atlanta: Society of Biblical Literature, 1999.

Develops a social-scientific "culture of conflict" model to explain the extent of conflict experienced (or lack thereof) by the churches at Thessalonica, Corinth, and Philippi with their civic communities. See also the seminal essay by J. Barclay, "Thessalonica and Corinth: Social Contrasts in Pauline Christianity," *JSNT* 47 (1992): 49–74.

13.9.2 Metaphors and Other Characterizations

A disproportionate number of studies on metaphors and characterizations of the church have fixated on the phrase "the body of Christ." E. Clowney, however, has persuasively demonstrated the dangers of such a narrow fixation and offered illuminating insights on how biblical models of the church are to be understood ("Interpreting the Biblical Models of the Church: A Hermeneutical Deepening of Ecclesiology," in *Biblical Interpretation and the Church: Text and Context*, ed. D. A. Carson [Exeter, England: Paternoster, 1984], 64–109). Moreover, new light has been shed on many characterizations of the church by the recent focus on the social context of early Christianity (see, e.g., #770 and #771). See also B. Winter. "The Problem with 'Church' for the Early Church," in *In the Fullness of Time: Biblical Studies in Honour of Archbishop Donald Robinson*, ed. D. Peterson and J. Pryor (Homebush West, Australia: Lancer, 1992), 203–17.

763 E. Best. *One Body in Christ: A Study in the Relationship of the Church to Christ in the Epistles of the Apostle Paul.* London: SPCK, 1955.

Argues that the church is a corporate personality in Christ (without losing individual responsibility) and that the "body of Christ" is a metaphor (thus rejecting the conception that the church is an extension of the incarnation). See also J. A. T. Robinson (#609).

764 P. S. Minear. *Images of the Church in the New Testament.* Philadelphia: Westminster, 1960.

Attempts to survey all biblical images of the church. Chapter 2 covers "minor" images; chapter 3, images under "the people of God"; chapter 4, "the new creation"; chapter 5, "fellowship of faith"; chapter 6, the "body of Christ"; and chapter 7, the images' interrelation. See also R. Martin's more limited study, *The Family and the Fellowship: New Testament Images of the Church* (Grand Rapids: Eerdmans, 1979).

765 R. Y. K. Fung. "Some Pauline Pictures of the Church." *EvQ* 53 (1981): 89–107.

Helpful survey of four pictures Paul employs to describe the church—the people of God, the body of Christ, the bride of Christ, and the building in the Spirit—and finds that Christ and Spirit hold these pictures together. See also D. R. Denton, "Further Reflections on 'Some Pauline Pictures of the Church,'" *EvQ* 54 (1982): 147–49, which highlights the dimensions of unity, holiness, life, and growth in these pictures.

766 G. L. O. R. Yorke. *The Church as the Body of Christ in the Pauline Corpus: A Re-examination.* Lanham, Md.: University Press of America, 1991.

Argues that the frequent attempt to find a direct relationship between Christ's personal body and the church as body is unfounded and that the "body" metaphor likens the local and uni-

versal church to the human body (in Colossians and Ephesians, "head" identifies Christ's headship over the church).
767 J. D. G. Dunn. "The 'Body' in Colossians." Pp. 163–81 in *To Tell the Mystery: Essays on New Testament Eschatology in Honor of Robert H. Gundry*. JSNTSup 100. Edited by T. E. Schmidt and M. Silva. Sheffield: JSOT Press, 1994.
Finds four uses of body in Colossians: (1) the body, the church; (2) the fleshly body; (3) the cosmic body; and (4) the eschatological body. See also Dunn's " 'The Body of Christ' in Paul" (#761, pp. 146–62).

768 W. Kraus. *Das Volk Gottes: Zur Grundlegung der Ekklesiologie bei Paulus*. WUNT 85. Tübingen: Mohr (Siebeck) 1996.
A detailed study of Paul's conception of the church in his letters (chapter 2 surveys the OT and Second Temple Jewish material). Argues that Romans is the end of a process in which Paul redefines the people of God in terms of the promise to Abraham, in a way that incorporates both those in Christ and all Israel.

769 J. R. Lanci. *A New Temple for Corinth: Rhetorical and Archaeological Approaches to Pauline Imagery*. Studies in Biblical Literature 1. New York: Peter Lang, 1997.
Argues that in 1 Cor. 3, "rather than inviting the Corinthians to understand themselves as a new temple replacing the one in Jerusalem, Paul uses a metaphor, which both Gentile and Jew could understand, to present and then anchor the motif of community upbuilding which runs throughout the letter" (5). See also Thiselton's discussion of 1 Cor. 3:9c–17 (#403, pp. 307–18); B. Gärtner, *The Temple and the Community in Qumran and the New Testament: A Comparative Study in the Temple Symbolism of the Qumran Texts and the New Testament* (Cambridge: Cambridge University Press, 1965), esp. 49–71; and the general study of R. McKelvey, *The New Temple: The Church in the New Testament* (Oxford: Oxford University Press, 1969), esp. 92–124.

770 H. Moxnes, ed. *Constructing Early Christian Families: Family as Social Reality and Metaphor*. New York: Routledge, 1997.
Part 1 examines the social context of early Christian families; part 2 family as metaphor; and part 3 the impact of asceticism and rejection of sexual desire on family life and metaphors of family. See especially P. Esler, "Family Imagery and Christian Identity in Gal 5:13 to 6:10," and K. Sandnes, "Equality within Patriarchal Structures: Some New Testament Perspectives on the Christian Fellowship as a Brother- or Sisterhood and a Family."

771 I. A. H. Combes. "The Metaphor of Slavery in the New Testament." Pp. 68–94 in *The Metaphor of Slavery in the Writings of the Early Church: From the New Testament to the Beginning of the Fifth Century.* JSNTSup 156. Sheffield: Sheffield Academic Press, 1998.
Looks at the various uses of the metaphor of slavery in the NT and demonstrates that slavery is death to the slave's previous history and identity. As slaves of Christ, Paul and other Christians are "dead to the world and its priorities and are participants in the humiliation and crucifixion of Christ" (89). As slaves of one another, they become not only entirely committed to Christ, but also to one another in love. Calls into question D. Martin's thesis in *Slavery as Salvation* (#154).

13.9.3 Apostle, Church Organization, and Ministry

Central to apostolic and all subsequent ministry is the pointing away from self by the proclamation of the crucified and risen Christ and by a lifestyle that conforms to the pattern of "the cruciform and living Christ," resulting in a holistic witness that announces Christ (see further Thiselton [#403, pp. 663–76, esp. 673]). On the other hand, appeals to the apostle Paul's teaching or practice to ground strict separation between church organization (including office) and ministry are ill-founded: the long-standing consensus that the New Testament shows a process of institutionalization from "charismatic" churches (e.g., in 1 Corinthians) to an institutionalized hierarchical structure in the Pastoral Epistles (see, e.g., E. Käsemann, "Ministry and Community in the New Testament," in *Essays on New Testament Themes* [Naperville, Ill.: Westminster; London: SCM, 1964], 63–94) seems finally to be crumbling from cumulative attack from various fronts (for a survey of the history of that consensus, see #779, pp. 61–179, and #780, pp. 1–19). Besides long-standing exegetical objections that the NT and Pauline writings do not show such a neat development (see, e.g., R. Fung, "Charismatic versus Organized Ministry? An Examination of an Alleged Antithesis," *EvQ* 52 [1980]: 195–214), reevaluation of the NT evidence in light of Greco-Roman and Jewish backgrounds demonstrates that such a division between charism and office/organization is an anachronistic misreading. R. Campbell (#780) challenges the assumption that a defined office of elder was taken over from Judaism in non-Pauline churches (and later crept into Pauline churches) and argues that charismatic gifts operated side by side with a framework of honor and respect (but not office) from the beginning in all churches. Burtchaell (#779), on the other hand, attacks the consensus by arguing that elders and other organizational structures and offices were substantially carried over from Judaism to both Pauline and non-Pauline churches from the beginning. The most significant recent work, however, is A. Clarke's *Serve the Community of the Church* (#784), which is generally persuasive in demonstrating the presence of leadership in the early Christian communities and sheds much light on how Paul corrects different mistaken patterns of leadership in various communities (see esp. chapters 8 and 9). Besides the works listed below, see also Thiselton (#403, pp. 295–307; 318–44); #151; #320; and J. Reumann, "Church Office in Paul, Especially in Philippians," in *Origins and Method: Towards a New Understanding of Judaism and Christianity,* ed. B. H. McLean, JSNTSup 86 (Sheffield: JSOT Press, 1993), 82–91.

772 E. Schweizer. *Church Order in the New Testament.* SBT. Translated by F. Clarke. Naperville, Ill.: Allenson, 1961. Original title: *Gemeinde und Gemeinderordnung im neuen Testament.* Zurich: Zwingli, 1959.

> See especially part I.C, "Paul's Conception of the Church, and Its Development."

773 J. A. Kirk. "Apostleship since Rengstorf: Toward a Synthesis." *NTS* 21 (1974–75): 249–64.

> Argues that the three uses of the term *apostle*—often traced historically to refer to church delegates, Paul, and lastly to the Twelve—are unified in the nature of the call and specific task of proclamation and church planting, differing only in the historical circumstances. Suggests also that the apostolic ministry continues throughout the church age.

774 J. M. Barnett. *Diaconate—A Full and Equal Order: A Comprehensive and Critical Study of the Origin, Development, and Decline of the Diaconate in the Context of the Church's Total Ministry and the Renewal of the Diaconate Today with Reflections for the Twenty-first Century.* Rev. ed. Valley Forge, Pa.: Trinity Press International, 1995. [See esp. pp. 3–42.] Original edition: 1979.

> Definitely reflects an Anglican–Roman Catholic outlook, but it is the most comprehensive work available.

775 B. Holmberg. *Paul and Power: The Structure of Authority in the Primitive Church as Reflected in the Pauline Epistles.* Philadelphia: Fortress, 1980.

Analyzes only the seven undisputed letters. Part 1 is a historical account of the distribution of power in the primitive church (Jerusalem leaders and Paul; Paul and his coworkers and his churches; and relations within local churches). Part 2 subjects the data to further sociological analysis of the authority structure. See also J. H. Schütz, *Paul and the Anatomy of Apostolic Authority*, SNTSMS 26 (Cambridge: Cambridge University Press, 1975).

776 R. Fung. "The Nature of the Ministry according to Paul." *EvQ* 54 (1982): 129–46.

Helpful essay on the relation between the nature of the ministry to the nature of the church, concluding that the ministry is given specifically for the growth of the church. See also the synthesizing conclusion to Fung's four-part series on Paul's understanding of the church and its ministry, "Ministry, Community, and Spiritual Gifts," *EvQ* 56 (1984): 3–20. On Paul as a pastor, see also E. Best, *Paul and His Converts* (Edinburgh: T. & T. Clark, 1988).

777 M. Warkentin. *Ordination: A Biblical-Historical View.* Grand Rapids: Eerdmans, 1982.

Part 1 surveys the OT, rabbinic evidence, and subsequent church history on the rite of ordination. Part 2 explores the NT texts. Finds that the laying on of hands in the NT was "unique, once for all situations" and had "nothing to do with routine installation into office in the church" (156).

778 J. N. Collins. *Diakonia: Re-interpreting the Ancient Sources.* Oxford: Oxford University Press, 1990.

See especially appendix 1. Part 1 examines assumptions about *diakonia*; part 2 surveys non-Christian sources; and part 3 explores the NT and Apostolic Fathers. Argues that the basic notion is not "to wait at table," but rather a general notion of "go-between" (denoting a mode of action rather than the status of the performer of the action, conveying the idea of mandated authority from God, apostle, or church in the NT). "Deacon" is the only distinguishable term, deriving from attendance to the *episkopos*. But see Clarke's criticisms in chapter 9 of #784. See also the old consensus in H. Beyer, "διακονέω, διακονία, διάκονος," *TDNT* 2:81–93.

779 J. T. Burtchaell. *From Synagogue to Church: Public Services and Offices in the Earliest Christian Communities.* Cambridge: Cambridge University Press, 1992.

The first half of the book traces arguments about the origins of Christian ministry from J. Wycliffe to E. Fiorenza and the consensus that emerged out of the nineteenth century that the earliest period of Christianity was free from institutional office. The second half proposes alternatively that there are significant continuities in the organization and offices of the church with the synagogue.

780 R. A. Campbell. *The Elders: Seniority with Earliest Christianity. Studies of the New Testament and Its World.* Edinburgh: T. & T. Clark, 1994.

Examines elders in ancient Israel and early Judaism, Greco-Roman society, Paul, Acts, the Pastorals, and beyond the New Testament. Sees forms of local structure (rooted in households and developing into larger city communities) from the beginning in both Pauline and non-Pauline churches and disputes the "consensus" of a "charismatic period" without such order. Contends that "the elders are those who bear a title of honour, not of office, a title that is imprecise, collective and representative, and rooted in the ancient family or household" (246).

781 T. B. Savage. *Power through Weakness: Paul's Understanding of the Christian Ministry in 2 Corinthians.* SNTSMS 86. Cambridge: Cambridge University Press, 1996.

Considers the meaning of "power through weakness" in light of the social setting of first-century Corinth and the situation in the Corinthian church. Paul teaches that it is through his conformity to the humility and suffering of Christ as a minister of the gospel that God performs his powerful work.

782 A. Bash. *Ambassadors for Christ: An Exploration of Ambassadorial Language in the New Testament.* WUNT 2/92. Tübingen: Mohr (Siebeck), 1997.

Examines the Greco-Roman practice of sending ambassadors (with new attention to inscriptional evidence) and compares this model of ambassadorial communication to the NT. Finds differences in usage in 2 Corinthians; Ephesians; the Pastorals; and Luke-Acts. On the basis of 2 Corinthians, finds that Paul usually exercised power by appeal and supplication.

783 B. Dodd. *Paul's Paradigmatic "I": Personal Example as Literary Strategy.* JSNTSup 177. Sheffield: Sheffield Academic Press, 1999.

Examines Paul's use of personal example as a literary practice in the seven undisputed letters. Argues that Paul's literary practice "reflects his leadership style of modelling and embodying the teaching he propagated" (237). See also A. D. Clarke, " 'Be Imitators of Me': Paul's Model of Leadership," *TynBul* 49, no. 2 (1998): 329–60, in which he convincingly refutes recent claims that Paul's use of the motif of imitation represents a tool of power to bolster his own authority and to shape his social group (e.g., Castelli [#321]; see also Thiselton's critique of Castelli in #403, pp. 371–73 and 795–97).

784 A. D. Clarke. *Serve the Community of the Church: Christians as Leaders and Ministers.* First-Century Christians in the Graeco-Roman World. Grand Rapids: Eerdmans, 2000. Part 1 surveys leadership in Greco-Roman society. Part 2 looks at leadership in the Christian communities. Argues compellingly that different Christian communities were influenced to differing degrees by the theories and practices of organization and leadership in the Greco-Roman city, colony, voluntary associations, Jewish synagogues, and the family, and that Paul opposes many aspects of these patterns of leadership and instead inculcates the notion of service. See also #157.

13.9.4 Baptism

At the beginning of the twentieth century, the history-of-religions school made it fashionable to attribute Paul's understanding of baptism to dependence on the Hellenistic mystery cults. G. Wagner's *Pauline Baptism and the Pagan Mysteries: The Problem of the Pauline Doctrine of Baptism in Romans VI.1–11, in the Light of Its Religio-Historical "Parallels,"* trans. J. Smith (Edinburgh and London: Oliver & Boyd, 1967), disproved direct dependence on these cults. A. Wedderburn (#705) demonstrates the essential dissimilarity in thought-pattern between Christian baptism and the mystery rites and argues for an alternative background of the Jewish tradition of representative figures (see also his "Soteriology of the Mysteries and Pauline Baptismal Theology," *NovT* 29 [1987]: 53–72). Another common assumption is that any reference back to conversion and initiation necessarily alludes to baptism. But see Dunn's cautions (#520, p. 445; developed in more detail in "Baptism and the Unity of the Church in the New Testament," in *Baptism and the Unity of the Church,* ed. M. Root and R. Saarinen [Grand Rapids: Eerdmans; Geneva: WCC Publications, 1998], 78–103); his exegesis on pages 447–57; his *Baptism in the Holy Spirit* (#559), which disproves the assumption of the invariable association of the Spirit with water baptism; and his essay, "'Baptized' as Metaphor" (#790, pp. 294–310), which forcefully demonstrates the necessity of recognizing the metaphorical character of NT baptismal language. Besides the works listed below, see also Thiselton (#403, pp. 135–36, 138–43; 997–1001; 1215–16, 1240–49); Ridderbos (#511, pp. 396–414); Tannehill (#703); and the commentaries on relevant passages (e.g., Rom. 6:1–14; 1 Cor. 1:13–17 [and the more problematic passages in 10:2; 12:13; and 15:29]; Gal. 3:26–29; Eph. 4:4–6; and Col. 2:12). On baptism in the Spirit and issues related to Pentecostalism and the charismatic movement, see also §13.5, "The Spirit." On the believer's baptism/infant baptism debate, see, for example, P. Jewett, *Infant Baptism and the Covenant of Grace: An Appraisal of the Argument That as Infants Were Once Circumcised, So They Should Now Be Baptized* (Grand Rapids: Eerdmans, 1978); M. Kline, *By Oath Consigned* (Grand Rapids: Eerdmans, 1968); V. Poythress, "Indifferentism and Rigorism in the Church: With Implications for Baptizing Small Children," *WTJ* 59 (1997): 13–30; idem, "Linking Small Children with Infants in the Theology of Baptizing," *WTJ* 59 (1997): 143–58; and G. Beasley-Murray, "The Problem of Infant Baptism: An Exercise in Possibilities," in *Festschrift Günter Wagner*, ed. The Faculty of Baptist Theological Seminary Rüschlikon/Switzerland (New York: Peter Lang, 1994), 1–14, who (over against his earlier work [#785]) later advocated a view of the election of the children of believers, such that infant baptism becomes acceptable.

785 G. R. Beasley-Murray. *Baptism in the New Testament.* Grand Rapids: Eerdmans; London: SCM, 1962.
Classic scholarly work that corroborates believers' baptism. But note his rejection of seeing baptism as a purely symbolic rite and advocacy of the Spirit's creative work/regeneration at baptism (but salvation, notes Beasley-Murray, is possible without being baptized). See also R. White, *The Biblical Doctrine of Initiation* (London: Hodder & Stoughton, 1960), especially pp. 127–209, which advocates a similar revised Baptist understanding of baptism.

786 R. Schnackenburg. *Baptism in the Thought of St. Paul: A Study in Pauline Theology.* Translated by G. R. Beasley-Murray. Oxford: Basil Blackwell, 1964. German edition: *Das Heilgeschehen bei der Taufe nach dem Apostel Paulus.* Müchen: K. Zink, 1950.
Does not repudiate the Roman Catholic sacramental view, but generally useful exegesis of texts.

787 E. J. Christiansen. *The Covenant in Judaism and Paul: A Study of Ritual Boundaries as Identity Markers.* Leiden: Brill, 1995.
Part A examines covenantal identity and boundary rites in the OT. Part B deals with Palestinian Judaism and John the Baptist.

Part C analyzes Paul in terms of covenant, baptism, and circumcision. In the OT and the *Book of Jubilees,* covenant identity is ethnocentric; thus, entry is marked by birth and affirmed by circumcision. In the Qumran Temple Scroll, the Damascus Document, and the Rule of the Community, identity is defined by priestly purity; thus, purity rites function as boundary markers. In Paul, Christian identity depends on faith in Christ; thus, baptism symbolizes identification with Christ and incorporation into the church. See also E. Nodet and J. Taylor, *The Origins of Christianity: An Exploration* (Collegeville, Minn.: Liturgical Press, 1998), which traces both baptism and the Lord's Supper back to an Essene background; and R. Averbeck, "The Focus of Baptism in the New Testament," *GTJ* 2 (1981): 265–301, which argues from the background of Jewish water lustrations and baptism that Christian baptism is oriented toward repentance and discipleship.

788 L. Hartman. *"Into the Name of the Lord Jesus": Baptism in the Early Church.* Studies in the New Testament and Its World. Edinburgh: T. & T. Clark, 1997. [See esp. pp. 51–113.]
Christian baptism originated in the christianizing of John's baptism, and its practice manifests recurrent fundamental elements as well as divergent themes. See also Hartman's "Early Baptism—Early Christology" (#543, pp. 191–201).

789 M. O. Fape. *Paul's Concept of Baptism and Its Present Implications for Believers: Walking in the Newness of Life.* Toronto Studies in Theology 78. Lewiston, N.Y.: Mellen, 1999.
Chapter 1 contains a useful review of research on baptism in Paul. Helpfully demonstrates that Paul uses baptism in Rom. 6:1–14; 1 Cor. 12:12–13; and Gal. 3:26–29 to call believers to demonstrate the reality of their new life in Christ by manifesting a corresponding new lifestyle.

790 S. E. Porter and A. R. Cross, eds. *Baptism, the New Testament, and the Church.* JSNTSup 171. Sheffield: Sheffield Academic Press, 1999.
See especially S. Porter and A. Cross, "Introduction: Baptism in Recent Debate"; A. Cross, " 'One Baptism' (Ephesians 4:5): A Challenge to the Church," who argues, against both paedobaptists and believer-baptists, for the importance of a return to the one baptism of the NT as a conversion-initiation rite; A. Campbell, "Dying with Christ: The Origins of a Metaphor?" who highlights the social break in publicly identifying with Christ: "the believer signs his own death warrant so far as acceptance by this world is concerned" (287); and J. Dunn, " 'Baptized' as Metaphor."

13.9.5 Lord's Supper

As with baptism, many modern studies have attempted to trace the source of Paul's theology of the Lord's Supper. There was likewise an attempt to find dependence on death and rebirth rites in the Greek mysteries, although this has given way to more cautious attribution of diverse, limited parallels (see esp. Klauck [#795]). On recent biblical research on the Lord's Supper, see J. Reumann, "Biblical Motifs as Foundations: Jesus, the Hebrew Scriptures, and Early Church Developments," in *The Supper of the Lord: The New Testament, Ecumenical Dialogues, and Faith and Order on Eucharist* (Philadelphia: Fortress, 1983), chap. 1; J. Kodell, *The Eucharist in the New Testament*, Zaccheus Studies: New Testament (Wilmington, Del.: Michael Glazier, 1988); and I. Marshall, "Lord's Supper," *DPL* 569–75. For interaction with older scholarship and a useful highlighting of eschatology, see G. Wainwright, *Eucharist and Eschatology* (London: Epworth, 1971). The most up-to-date survey of research and impressive interpretation of the 1 Corinthian texts, however, is found in Thiselton (#403, pp. 750–79, 848–99). See also Ridderbos (#511, pp. 414–28) and the commentaries on 1 Corinthians 10 and 11.

791 H. Lietzmann. *Mass and Lord's Supper: A Study in the History of the Liturgy (with Introduction and Further Inquiry by R. D. Richardson)*. Translated by D. H. G. Reeve. Leiden: Brill, 1979. Original title: *Messe und Herrenmahl—Eine Studie zur Geshichte der Liturgie*. Berlin: de Gruyter, 1926.

For a discussion of Paul and comparison to the Gospels, see especially pp. 177–87; 321–31; and 596–620. See also E. Mazza, *The Celebration of the Eucharist: The Origin of the Rite and the Development of Its Interpretation*, trans. M. J. O'Connell (Collegeville, Minn.: Liturgical Press, 1999).

792 C. F. D. Moule. "The Judgment Theme in the Sacraments," Pp. 464–81 in *The Background of the New Testament and Its Eschatology: Studies in Honour of C. H. Dodd*. Edited by W. D. Davies and D. Daube. Cambridge: Cambridge University Press, 1956.

Highlights baptism and communion as anticipations of the final judgment (also discusses excommunication), with the longest section on communion.

793 I. H. Marshall. *Last Supper and Lord's Supper*. Grand Rapids: Eerdmans, 1980.

Examines possible Jewish background to Jesus' last meal; attempts to reconstruct the original form of the Last Supper account; and considers questions of history and significance, and the practice of the Lord's Supper in the early church. See especially chapter 5.

794 F. Chenderlin. *"Do This as My Memorial": The Semantic and Conceptual Background and Value of Ἀνάμνησις in 1 Corinthians 11:24–25.* AnBib 99. Rome: Biblical Institute Press, 1982.

Argues that Paul most likely intended "my remembrance" to refer both to reminding the disciples and reminding God. Thus revives in a different form J. Jeremias's interpretation "that God may remember me" (*The Eucharistic Words of Jesus,* trans. N. Perrin [New York: Scribner's Sons, 1966], 237–55). But see Thiselton's assessment in #403, pp. 878–82.

795 H-J. Klauck. *Herrenmahl und hellenistischer Kult: Eine religionsgeshictliche Untersuchung zum ersten Korintherbrief.* 2d ed. NTAbh 15. Münster: Aschendorff, 1986. Original edition: 1982.

Part A covers the history of research. Part B surveys the Greco-Roman milieu (including Jewish and Gnostic meals). Part C interprets the sacred meals reflected in 1 Corinthians. Posits a complex theory of evolution of the words of institution and the contribution of many different religious influences on Paul's formulation. See also Klauck's essay in #796 and "Lord's Supper," *ABD* 4:362–72.

796 B. F. Meyer, ed. *One Loaf, One Cup: Ecumenical Studies of 1 Cor 11 and Other Eucharistic Texts.* New Gospel Studies 6. Louvain: Peeters; Macon, Ga.: Mercer, 1993.

Papers from the Cambridge Conference on the Eucharist in 1988. Contains O. Knoch, " 'Do This in Memory of Me!' (Luke 22:20; 1 Cor. 11:24–25): The Celebration of the Eucharist in the Primitive Christian Communities"; B. Meyer, "The Expiation Motif in the Eucharistic Words: A Key to the History of Jesus?"; W. Farmer, "Peter and Paul, and the Tradition concerning 'The Lord's Supper' in 1 Cor. 11:23–26"; H-J. Klauck, "Presence in the Lord's Supper: 1 Corinthians 11:23–26 in the Context of Hellenistic Religious History"; O. Hofius, "The Lord's Supper and the Lord's Supper Tradition: Reflections on 1 Corinthians 11:23b–25"; and A. Calivas, "The Eucharist: The Sacrament of the Economy of Salvation."

797 B. Witherington, III. " 'Making a Meal of It': The Lord's Supper in Its First-Century Social Setting." Pp. 81–113 in *The Lord's Supper: Believers Church Perspectives.* Edited by D. R. Stoffer. Scottdale, Pa., and Waterloo, Ontario: Waterloo, 1997. A useful survey of the social setting of the Lord's Supper. Suggests that taking the Lord's Supper out of its meal and home context has contributed to the distortion of its essential meaning and function (i.e., expressing union and unity in Christ and in the church).

13.9.6 Discipline

More adequate investigation of church discipline in Paul is partly hindered by three factors: (1) a fixation on 1 Cor. 5:5 to the exclusion of other texts; (2) a related narrowing of Paul's understanding of excommunication/cursing to death; and (3) enchantment with alleged parallels to Greek magical texts, resulting in the so-called curse-of-death interpretation. J. South's monograph and article (#800) and Thiselton (#403) have argued persuasively against this "curse-of-death" view; but see V. G. Shillington, "Atonement Texture in 1 Corinthians 5.5," *JSNT* 71 (1998): 29–50, whose proposal shares similar difficulties with this view, besides the added difficulty of the lack of conceptual parallel between the guilty incestuous man and the substitutionary, sin-bearing scapegoat in Lev. 16. For comparison with Qumran and rabbinic Judaism, see G. Forkman, *The Limits of Religious Community: Expulsion from the Religious Community within the Qumran Sect, within Rabbinic Judaism, and within Primitive Christianity*, ConBNT (Lund: Gleerup, 1972). Because of space limitations and the paucity of full-scale studies of church discipline in Paul, the reader is referred to the survey of research and bibliography in South (#800); Thiselton (#403, pp. 418–38); and T. Schmidt, "Discipline," *DPL* 214–18. See also Rosner (#832, pp. 61–93) on the Deuteronomic background and idem, "OYXI MAΛΛON EΠENΘHΣATE: Corporate Responsibility in 1 Corinthians 5," *NTS* 38 (1992): 470–73, on the need of excommunication to safeguard the church; Roetzel (#712); K. Hein, *Eucharist and Excommunication: A Study in Early Christian Doctrine and Discipline* (Bern: Herbert Lang; Frankfurt: Peter Lang, 1973), 87–132; and the commentaries (esp. on 1 Cor. 5:1–13). A good case for the traditional identification of the offender in 2 Cor. 2:5 and 7:12 with the incestuous man in 1 Cor. 5:3–5 is made by C. G. Kruse, "The Offender and the Offence in 2 Corinthians 2:5 and 7:12," *EvQ* 88 (1988): 129–39 (see likewise chapter 3 of #800).

798   A. Y. Collins. "The Function of 'Excommunication' in Paul." *HTR* 73 (1980): 251–63.
Excommunication functions "to guard the holiness of the community and to avoid offense to the presence of the Holy Spirit" (263). Finds a formal procedural parallel (and partial parallel in meaning) in the death curses in the Greek magic papyri and a parallel in community focus in the Qumran literature.

799   G. Harris. "The Beginnings of Church Discipline: 1 Cor 5." *NTS* 37 (1991): 1–21.
Employs sociological models to interpret 1 Cor. 5: the social construction of reality; reaction to deviance; social norms; and social sanctions.

800   J. T. South. *Disciplinary Practices in Pauline Texts.* Lewiston, N.Y.: Mellen, 1992.
A very useful investigation of all relevant Pauline texts on church discipline. Finds that the Pauline communities "by the exercise of communal discipline guarded their communal boundaries, retained/regained straying members, and kept themselves under the authority of Christ conveyed through Paul" (194). See also South's "A Critique of the 'Curse/Death' Interpretation of 1 Cor. 5:1–8," *NTS* 39 (1993): 539–61.

13.9.7 Worship

D. G. Peterson's *Engaging with God: A Biblical Theology of Worship* (Grand Rapids: Eerdmans, 1992) compellingly shows that the NT and Paul (see esp. pp. 166–93 and 194–227) portray worship as a total life orientation that encompasses both everyday life and congregational worship. The everyday-life aspect of worship is thus expressed in God-honoring ethics (see §13.10). The congregational aspect of worship encompasses the entire life of the community in its mutual upbuilding (including the exercise of gifts and office toward this end; thus see the other subsections of §13.9). The most up-to-date bibliography may be found in Hurtado (#805, pp. 119–38; see also D. Aune, "Worship, Early Christian," *ABD* 6:973–89). On worship practices in the Pauline churches, see also Meeks (#145, pp. 140–63) and A. Cabaniss, *Patterns in Early Christian Worship* (Macon, Ga.: Mercer; Louvain: Peeters, 1989), 43–67. On prayer, see #331; #330; and D. Peterson, "Prayer in the Writings of Paul," in *Teach Us to Pray: Prayer in the Bible and in the Church*, ed. D. A. Carson (Grand Rapids: Baker; Exeter, England: Paternoster, 1990), 84–101. For possible hymns, see §9.2, "Hymns and Creeds." On the Sabbath–Lord's Day controversy, see D. A. Carson, ed., *From Sabbath to Lord's Day: A Biblical, Historical, and Theological Investigation* (Grand Rapids: Zondervan, 1982). For a reconstruction of music in the earliest Christian worship services, see W. Smith, *Musical Aspects of the New Testament* (Amsterdam: Uitgeverij W. Ten Have, 1962). On the exercise of spiritual gifts, see §13.5, "The Spirit."

801 R. Corriveau. *The Liturgy of Life: A Study of the Ethical Thought of St. Paul in His Letters to the Early Christian Communities.* Studia 25. Brussels and Paris: Desclée de Brouwer; Montreal: Les Editions Bellarmin, 1970.

A very helpful exegetical study that highlights Paul's notion of the entire Christian life as worship. Covers 1–2 Thessalonians, 1–2 Corinthians, Philippians, Romans, and Ephesians in their epistolary context and chronological sequence.

802 F. Hahn. *The Worship of the Early Church.* Translated by D. E. Green. Philadelphia: Fortress, 1973. Original title: *Der urchristliche Gottesdienst.* Stuttgart: Katholisches Bibelwerk, 1970.

A wealth of information, but be wary of the alleged schematic periodicization of early Christianity in the sequence of Palestinian Christianity, Hellenistic-Jewish Christianity, and Gentile Christianity. A process of development is also proposed by R. Martin, "Patterns of Worship in New Testament Churches," *JSNT* 37 (1989): 59–85, yielding four alleged liturgical models (Paul, Luke, the Pastoral Epistles, and John).

803 R. P. Martin. *The Spirit and the Congregation: Studies in 1 Corinthians 12–15.* Grand Rapids: Eerdmans, 1984.

A concise exposition of 1 Corinthians 12–15 that brings out Paul's perspective on the church, worship, and charismatic gifts in the context of the centrality of the gospel and the resurrection hope. See also Martin's more wide-ranging *Worship in the Early Church*, rev. ed. (Grand Rapids: Eerdmans, 1974), and *The Worship of God: Some Theological, Pastoral, and Practical Reflections* (Grand Rapids: Eerdmans, 1982).

804 P. F. Bradshaw. *The Search for the Origins of Christian Worship: Sources and Methods for the Study of Early Liturgy.* Oxford: Oxford University Press, 1992.

See "Worship in the New Testament" (30–55) for useful survey and critique of scholarly reconstructions of liturgy (including baptism and the Lord's Supper).

805 L. W. Hurtado. *At the Origins of Christian Worship: The*

Context and Character of Earliest Christian Devotion.
Grand Rapids: Eerdmans, 1999.
    A most helpful discussion of the characteristics of earliest
    Christian worship against the religious environment of the
    Roman world, highlighting its exclusivity (monotheism) and
    "binatarian" character (worship of Jesus side by side with God).

13.9.8 Male and Female Relations and Women in Ministry

    Three questions in this controversy form the framework of
L. Belleville's *Women Leaders and the Church* (Grand Rapids:
Baker, 2000): (1) "In which ministries can women be involved?";
(2) "What roles can women assume in the family and in society?"; and (3) "What, if any, positions of authority can women
hold in the church?" (16). Arguing an egalitarian position, Belleville concludes that "God gifts women in exactly the same ways
he gifts men"; "God intended the male-female relationship to be
equal and mutual"; and the New Testament nowhere defines
church roles on the basis of gender (181). Three distinct hermeneutical planks (with many holding to different combinations)
appear to ground the egalitarian position: (1) revisionist attempts
to reinterpret Paul's historical meaning in the relevant passages,
such that notions of hierarchy or subordination are removed
(even among egalitarians who retain this plank, emphasis has increasingly shifted to the second plank; for critiques, see #806 and
#811); (2) attempts to ground Paul's historical meaning in a spe-
cific situation or cultural milieu (often in conjunction with some
reinterpretation, but retaining some notions of hierarchy or subordination in its original setting; see, e.g., #809 and #817), such
that his injunctions do not hold in a new context; and (3) a subtle development from view 2 to a view of organic development
in the New Testament and in subsequent history in interaction
with and as restricted by culture (Longenecker [#823] emphasizes
the external constraints of culture; Dawes [#816] thinks that the
biblical author simply mistakenly shared his culture's views).
Two distinct hermeneutical planks ground the complementarian
position: (1) the constituted order of God's creation of male and
female involves role differentiation and the functional subordination of women (on the basis of both Gen. 1–3 and Paul's appeal
to it); and (2) the historical meaning of the Pauline passages applies for all time in the church and the home (although more explanation is needed as to how or why they do not apply to all of

life [since they are grounded in creation] and as to how redemption or eschatology factors into Paul's injunctions and practice). The trend is toward the position that Paul is neither a full-fledged egalitarian nor traditional hierarchicalist (see esp. C. Blomberg, "Neither Hierarchicalist nor Egalitarian: Gender Roles in Paul" [#820, pp. 329–72]). There is also greater appreciation of the mutual interplay of creation, redemption/eschatology, and culture in Paul's theology of male-female relations and of women's roles in the church (see esp. Thiselton [#403, pp. 607; 799–848; and 1146–62]). Thus both egalitarians and complementarians need to account adequately for Paul's theology of creation (gender distinction involves sameness or complementariness of roles?), the fall and redemption (transcending creation or transforming fallen creation or elements of both?), and cultural engagement/witness (were Paul's instructions and practices culturally specific or culturally constrained?). Because of the vastness of the literature, only a representative sample of more recent, noteworthy works were chosen (esp. since older works of merit are usually adequately cited). See also #144; #146; #319; and #830. For a brief overview of the larger world of feminist interpretation with bibliography, see W. W. Klein, C. L. Blomberg, and R. L. Hubbard, Jr., *Introduction to Biblical Interpretation* (Dallas: Word, 1993), 453–57.

806 W. A. Grudem. "Does *Kephalē* Mean 'Source' or 'Authority Over' in Greek Literature? A Survey of 2,336 Examples." *TJ* 6 (1985): 38–59.
   Finds forty-nine examples with notions of authority, but no instances of the meaning "source" or "origin." See also Grudem's "The Meaning of *Kephalē* ('Head'): A Response to Recent Studies," *TJ* 11 (1990): 3–72 (reprinted as appendix 1 in #808), in which he critiques arguments for the meaning "source"; idem, "The Meaning of *Kephalē* ('Head'): An Evaluation of New Evidence, Real and Alleged," *JETS* 44 (2001): 25–65; and J. A. Fitzmyer, "Another Look at *Kephalē* in 1 Cor 11:3," *NTS* 35 (1989): 503–11, which shows the Hebrew and LXX evidence for "head" expressing authority.

807 B. Witherington, III. *Women in the Earliest Churches.* SNTSMS 59. Cambridge: Cambridge University Press, 1988. [See esp. pp. 24–117.]
   A generally informative and helpful study of the NT and post-NT, pre-Nicene evidence. The treatment of the Pastorals and

the suggestion that the authors of Matthew and Luke-Acts were less able to deal with eschatological tension are less satisfactory.

808 J. Piper and W. Grudem, eds. *Recovering Biblical Manhood and Womanhood: A Response to Evangelical Feminism.* Wheaton, Ill.: Crossway, 1991.

A comprehensive response to challenges to gender-based role differences by evangelical feminists (see esp. section II). Sets forth a vision of manhood and womanhood in equality of status but complementarity in the home and the church. See also R. Saucy and J. Tenelsof, eds., *Women and Men in Ministry: A Complementary Perspective* (Chicago: Moody, 2001).

809 C. S. Keener. *Paul, Women, and Wives: Marriage and Women's Ministry in the Letters of Paul.* Peabody, Mass.: Hendrickson, 1992.

Part 1 covers 1 Cor. 11:1–16; 14:34–35; and 1 Tim. 2:9–15. Part 2 covers Eph. 5:22–31; 6:5–9. Argues for full equality of function in both ministry and the home by limiting Paul's commands to a specific congregational or cultural situation and emphasizing the need to contextualize any underlying principles.

810 J. M. Gundry-Volf. "Male and Female in Creation and New Creation: Interpretations of Galatians 3:28c in 1 Corinthians 7." Pp. 95–121 in *To Tell the Mystery: Essays on New Testament Eschatology in Honor of Robert H. Gundry.* Edited by T. E. Schmidt and M. Silva. JSNTSup 100. Sheffield: JSOT Press, 1994.

Argues that two opposing interpretations (by the Corinthian sexual ascetics and by Paul) are found in 1 Cor. 7: the Corinthian ascetics' view resulted in the simple obliteration of established relationships and roles; Paul's view holds creation and eschatology/redemption in dynamic interrelation. See also Gundry-Volf's "Gender and Creation in 1 Corinthians 11:2–16: A Study in Paul's Theological Method," in *Evangelium—Schriftauslegung—Kirche: Essays in Honor of P. Stuhlmacher,* ed. O. Hofius (Göttingen: Vandenhoeck & Ruprecht, 1997), 152–71; and "Paul on Women and Gender: A Comparison with Early Jewish Views" (#60, pp. 184–212).

811 A. J. Köstenberger. "Gender Passages in the NT: Hermeneutical Fallacies Critiqued." *WTJ* 56 (1994): 259–83.

A critique of egalitarian reinterpretations of Paul. Köstenberger lists the shortcomings as "(1) underestimating the power of presuppositions; (2) lack of balance in hermeneutical methodology; (3) underrating the importance of the use of the OT in the

NT; (4) improper use of background information; (5) an arbitrary distinction between 'paradigm passages' and 'passages with limited application'; (6) isolationist exegesis; and (7) leveling the distinction between historical exegesis and modern contextualization" (282).

812 R. T. France. *Women in the Church's Ministry: A Test Case for Biblical Interpretation.* Grand Rapids: Eerdmans, 1995. Reveals the hermeneutical issues involved in the debate. Restricts submission to within marriage and claims that Gal. 3:28 represents a long trajectory of the outworking of God's ultimate purpose in Christ that was not fully achievable in the first-century situation (i.e., with the change in situation, women should be in the authoritative and teaching ministry). See also A. Perriman, *Speaking of Women: Interpreting Women* (Leicester, England: Apollos, 1998), and William J. Webb, *Slaves, Women, and Homosexuals: Exploring the Hermeneutics of Cultural Analysis* (Downers Grove, Ill.: InterVarsity, 2001) (see the review by T. R. Schreiner, *SBJT* 6 [spring 2002]: 46–64).

813 A. J. Köstenberger, T. R. Schreiner, and H. S. Baldwin, eds. *Women in the Church: A Fresh Analysis of 1 Timothy 2:9–15.* Grand Rapids: Baker, 1995. The consensus of the contributors is that 1 Tim. 2:9–15 prohibits women from teaching or exercising authority over men in the church (with some differences of interpretation and application). Includes essays on background, genre, word and syntactical studies, a synthetic dialogue with scholarship, and reflections on hermeneutics and the history of interpretation, which are intended to refute egalitarian works such as R. and C. Kroeger, *I Suffer Not a Woman: Rethinking 1 Timothy 2:11–15 in Light of Ancient Evidence* (Grand Rapids: Baker, 1992).

814 T. Schmeller. *Hierarchie und Egalität: Eine sozialgeschichtliche Untersuchung paulinischer Gemeinden und grieschisch-römischer Vereine.* SBS 162. Stuttgart: Katholische Bibelwerk, 1995. Investigates status differentiation in the Greco-Roman associations and in the Pauline communities. Concludes that both departed from the hierarchical patterns of their social milieu, while combining both hierarchical and egalitarian elements. On women's roles in the culture of specific cities, see W. Cotter, "Women's Authority Roles in Paul's Churches: Countercultural or Conventional?" *NovT* 36 (1994): 350–72.

815 C. Niccum. "The Voice of the Manuscripts on the Silence of Women: The External Evidence for 1 Cor 14:34–35." *NTS* 43 (1997): 242–55.

Defense of the textual originality of 1 Cor. 14:34–35 and refutation of P. Payne's "Fuldensis, Sigla for Variants in Vaticanus, and 1 Cor. 14:34–35," *NTS* 41 (1995): 240–62.

816 G. W. Dawes. *The Body in Question: Metaphor and Meaning in the Interpretation of Ephesians 5:21–33.* Biblical Interpretation Series. Leiden: Brill, 1998.

Helpful discussion of the interpretative debate over Eph. 5:21–33 and the functioning of the metaphors "head" and "body." Finds that "there is no doubt that the traditional, hierarchical interpretation of this passage is correct" (199). But proposes that the author of Ephesians was not consistent in his use of metaphor and logic and that the interpreter is justified in "correcting" the author.

817 R. G. Gruenler. "The Mission-Lifestyle Setting of 1 Timothy 2:8–15." *JETS* 41 (1998): 215–38.

Attempts to limit Paul's restrictions to immature Christian women who are "out of order as to proper mission style" (237) and claims that mature Christian women were not excluded from teaching and leading. But see an alternative treatment of women in the Pauline mission by A. Köstenberger, "Women in the Pauline Mission" (#658, pp. 221–47).

818 K. Giles. "A Critique of the 'Novel' Contemporary Interpretation of 1 Timothy 2:9–15 Given in the Book *Women in the Church.*" *EvQ* 72 (2000): 151–67 and 195–215.

A two-part essay critiquing the claim of the authors of *Women in the Church* (#813) to upholding the historic interpretation of 1 Tim. 2:9–15. Not all the critiques are of equal weight, but Giles points out: (1) a shift in basis from inherent inferiority of women (from the chronological order of creation) to a constitutive order given by God with male leadership and female subordination; (2) gender differentiation in itself does not necessarily support a differentiation of roles; and (3) the authors avoid imputing inherent inferiority or subordination to women. See also A. J. Köstenberger, "Women in the Church: A Response to Kevin Giles," and K. Giles, "Women in the Church: A Rejoinder to Andreas Köstenberger," *EvQ* 73 (2001): 205–24 and 225–45.

819 J. M. Holmes. *Text in a Whirlwind: A Critique of Four Exegetical Devices at 1 Timothy 2.9–15.* JSNTSup 196. Sheffield: Sheffield Academic Press, 2000.

Reexamines four exegetical devices commonly applied to 1 Tim. 2:9–15: immediate context; broader context; parallel with 1 Cor. 14:34–35; and 1 Tim. 2:13–14 as theological foundation for verse 12. Contends that the prohibition in verses 11–

12 applies to a general-life rather than a congregational context; that Paul intended it to be normative everywhere; that 1 Cor. 14:34–35 presents an opposing viewpoint rather than being a parallel teaching; and that 1 Tim 2:13–15 concludes the whole of chapter 2, and verses 8–12 in particular. Useful bibliography and interaction with modern scholarship (often highlighting weaknesses in arguments from both sides of the debate).

820 J. R. Beck and C. L. Blomberg, eds. *Two Views on Women in Ministry.* Counterpoints. Grand Rapids: Zondervan, 2001.
Essays by a pair of male and female egalitarian (C. Keener and L. Belleville) and complementarian (T. Schreiner and A. Bowman) writers, with questions and reflections by the editors and an appendix by Blomberg.

13.10 Ethics

Although each section of this bibliography only aims at a selective, accurate representation of major options and the state of research, because of space limitations and the vastness of the subject, this section on Pauline ethics is even more limited. B. Rosner (#832) has helpfully suggested that Paul's ethics may be examined from seven angles: (1) origin (whether dependent on scriptural and Jewish sources); (2) context (social history of the Greco-Roman world); (3) social dimension (using sociological models and tools to analyze a text); (4) shape (forms such as catechisms, catalogs, and codes); (5) logic (relation of the indicative and the imperative); (6) foundations (motivations, norms, and criteria); and (7) relevance. The reader should consult the two essays under each of these headings in Rosner's excellent volume. Besides general works that cover multiple angles, the "General Orientation" subsection below highlights some works that deal with the origin (e.g., #832 and #826); social dimension (e.g., #827); logic (e.g., #831 and #830); foundations (e.g., #822); and relevance (e.g., #823) of Pauline ethics. See also Dunn (#520, pp. 626–712); #234; #347; #489; #505; #507; #707; J. Gundry-Volf, "Conscience," and S. Mott, "Ethics," *DPL* 153–56, 269–75; and §13.9, "The Church." Works relevant to the context and shape of Paul's ethics may be found in chapter 7, "Paul and the Greco-Roman World." The subsections on sexual ethics (note that women in ministry is under §13.9.8); homosexuality; marriage/celibacy and divorce and remarriage; and relation to civil authorities are merely suggestive. The reader should consult the bibliographies in the works cited, the works under "General Orientation," and the commentaries on the primary Scripture passages involved. Bibliography for other ethical issues may be similarly traced. On slavery, see especially Thiselton's superb treatment of 1 Cor. 7:17–24 (#403, pp. 544–65), in which he rightly stresses that slavery and freedom both matter and do not matter. "These do *not promote or impede spiritual status*. But the gospel is lived out *through* earthly institutions and constraints, *not in spite of* them" (558). On issues arising in 1 Cor. 8:1–11:1, there is likewise no better starting point than Thiselton's commentary (e.g., on conscience, pp. 640–44).

13.10.1 General Orientation

821 V. P. Furnish. *Theology and Ethics*. Nashville: Abingdon, 1968.

Examines the seven undisputed letters and deals with the sources, form and function, theme, and character of Paul's exhortations. Paul's ethics are radically theocentric, Christocentric, and eschatological, and his exhortations call forth a deliberate response to God's claim (but not as the actualization of a mere possibility). Includes a useful appendix surveying interpretations of Paul's ethics from 1868 to the 1960s. See also Furnish's *The Love Command in the New Testament* (Nashville: Abingdon, 1972), 91–131.

822 T. J. Deidun. *New Covenant Morality in Paul*. AnBib 89. Rome: Biblical Institute Press, 1981.

Examines the theological context, the ground and formal content, the nature of Christian love, and the relationship between love and Law in new-covenant morality in the seven undisputed letters. Attempts a balanced synthesis that upholds both divine initiative and human response, love and Law, spontaneity and principle, and the Spirit's interior activity and external law.

823 R. N. Longenecker. *New Testament Social Ethics for Today*. Grand Rapids: Eerdmans, 1984.

Chapter 1 describes four ways of using the NT and their shortcomings and proposes seven basic biblical perspectives toward an eclectic model of ethics. Chapter 2 sets forth Longenecker's understanding of the Bible and Christian theology as a story of organic development. He proposes his understanding of the cultural mandate (neither Jew nor Greek), the social mandate (neither slave nor free), and the sexual mandate (neither male nor female) in chapters 3, 4, and 5 (with Gal. 3:28 understood as "the Magna Carta of the New Humanity"). Provocative, but very debatable premises and conclusions.

824 R. Mohrland. *Matthew and Paul: A Comparison of Ethical Perspectives.* SNTSMS 48. Cambridge: Cambridge University Press, 1984.

Summarizes the ethical structures of Matthew and Paul (Law, reward and punishment, relationship to Christ, and the role of grace, love, and inner forces) and compares them. Finds that Matthew's ethics are oriented toward submission to authority while Paul's ethics rest on God's grace in Christ, but sees both as complementary.

825 V. P. Furnish. *The Moral Teaching of Paul: Selected Issues.* Nashville: Abingdon, 1985.

Opposed to both strict adherence to the Scriptures as eternally and universally binding and relegation of the Scriptures to irrelevance. Devotes a chapter each to marriage and divorce, homosexuality, women in ministry, and relation to governing authorities.

826 A. Malherbe. *Moral Exhortation: A Greco-Roman Sourcebook.* LEC 4. Philadelphia: Westminster, 1986.

A useful compilation of primary texts that illustrate typical features in which Christianity may be indebted to the Greco-Roman moral tradition. See also #439 and #500.

827 W. A. Meeks. *The Moral World of the First Christians.* LEC 6. Philadelphia: Westminster, 1986.

An important attempt to reconstruct the symbolic and social universe (with attention to the traditions of Greece, Rome, and Israel) within which the moral teachings of the early Christians made sense. See also Meeks's *The Origins of Christian Morality: the First Two Centuries* (New Haven: Yale University Press, 1993).

828 J. M. G. Barclay. *Obeying the Truth: Paul's Ethics in Galatians.* Edinburgh: T. & T. Clark, 1988; Minneapolis: Fortress, 1991.

A fine study of Paul's ethics in Galatians that includes a helpful survey of views on the paraenesis of Gal. 5:13–6:10 and discussion of mirror-reading (i.e., reconstructing the situation of the letter). Argues that Paul appeals specifically to the Galatians to be directed by the Spirit, gives assurance concerning the Spirit's sufficiency, and warns against moral danger.

829 W. Schrage. *The Ethics of the New Testament.* 2d ed. Translated by D. Green. Edinburgh: T. & T. Clark, 1995. Original edition: Philadelphia: Fortress, 1989. German title: *Ethik des Neuen Testaments*. Göttingen: Vandenhoeck & Ruprecht, 1989. Original German edition: 1982. See "The Christological Ethics of Paul" (163–239), which deals with the basis of Pauline ethics, the nature and structure of the new life, the material criteria of ethics, and concrete ethics (individual morality; man and wife/marriage and divorce; work, property, slavery; and Christians and the state), and "The Ethics of Responsibility in the Deutero-Pauline Epistles" (241–78).

830 P. H. Towner. *The Goal of Our Instruction: The Structure of Theology and Ethics in the Pastoral Epistles*. JSNTSup 34. Sheffield: JSOT Press, 1989.

Chapter 2 reconstructs the situation of the Pastorals; chapters 3–6 examine their theological structure; chapters 8–10 elucidate their ethical structure. By considering the use of particular emphases to redress the influence of false teaching and overrealized eschatology, Towner's book demonstrates the untenability of the modern "Christian Good Citizenship/bourgeois Christianity" interpretation, shows that the Christ-event and salvation serve as indicative grounding to the imperative of response, and highlights the missions motif in the outworking of faith in particular situations.

831 J. P. Sampley. *Walking between the Times: Paul's Moral Reasoning*. Minneapolis: Fortress, 1991.

A useful introduction to how Paul approaches moral issues. Part 1 describes the two time frames of Paul's symbolic universe (the death and resurrection of Christ and Christ's return). Part 2 deals with Paul's moral reasoning, and part 3 covers the means and motives of believers' knowledge and practice.

832 B. S. Rosner. *Paul's Scripture and Ethics: A Study of 1 Corinthians 5–7*. Reprint, Biblical Studies Library. Grand Rapids: Baker, 1999. Original edition: AGJU 22. Leiden: Brill, 1994.

Examines 1 Cor. 5–7 for the extent to which Paul depends on the Scriptures for practical/pragmatic/*halakhic* authority. Attempts to highlight indirect and subtle dependence on the OT (besides explicit quotations), often as mediated by early Jewish moral teaching, to demonstrate that the Scriptures are not only witnesses to the gospel, but also guides for ethical conduct.

833 B. S. Rosner. *Understanding Paul's Ethics: Twentieth-Century Approaches*. Grand Rapids: Eerdmans; Carlisle, England: Paternoster, 1995.

Besides a helpful introduction and conclusion by Rosner, the essays are: (1) A. Harnack, "The Old Testament in the Pauline

Letters and in the Pauline Churches," and T. Holtz, "The Question of the Content of Paul's Instructions"; (2) E. Judge, "Interpreting New Testament Ideas," and B. Winter, "Civil Litigation in Secular Corinth and the Church: The Forensic Background to 1 Corinthians 6:1–8"; (3) G. Theissen, "The Strong and the Weak in Corinth: A Sociological Analysis of a Theological Quarrel," and G. Harris, "The Beginning of Church Discipline: 1 Corinthians 5"; (4) A. Seeberg, "Moral Teaching: The Existence and Contents of 'the Ways,'" and L. Hartman, "Code and Context: A Few Reflections on the Parenesis of Colossians 3:6–4:1"; (5) R. Bultmann, "The Problem of Ethics in Paul," and M. Parsons, "Being Precedes Act: Indicative and Imperative in Paul's Writing"; (6) E. Lohse, "The Church in Everyday Life," and E. Schnabel, "How Paul Developed His Ethics"; and (7) W. Schrage, "The Formal Ethical Interpretation of Pauline Paraenesis," and R. Longenecker, "New Testament Social Ethics for Today."

834 R. B. Hays. *The Moral Vision of the New Testament: A Contemporary Introduction to New Testament Ethics.* New York: HarperCollins, 1996. [See esp. pp. 16–72.]

An ambitious attempt to combine the descriptive, synthetic (finds three focal images: community, cross, and new creation), hermeneutical, and pragmatic tasks. Deals with five test cases: violence in defense of justice, divorce and remarriage, homosexuality, anti-Judaism and ethnic conflict, and abortion.

835 R. N. Longenecker, ed. *Patterns of Discipleship in the New Testament.* McMaster New Testament Studies. Grand Rapids: Eerdmans, 1996.

See especially J. Weima, " 'How You Must Walk to Please God': 1 Thessalonians," on the gift of and call to holiness; L. Belleville, " 'Imitate Me, Just as I Imitate Christ': Discipleship in the Corinthian Correspondence"; L. Jervis, "Becoming Like God through Christ: Discipleship in Romans"; G. Hawthorne, "The Imitation of Christ: Discipleship in Philippians," on the imitation of Paul, God, and Christ, respectively; and M. Knowles, " 'Christ in You, the Hope of Glory: Discipleship in Colossians," on the christological and cosmological underpinnings of right behavior.

836 E. H. Lovering and J. L. Sumney, eds. *Theology and Ethics in Paul and His Interpreters: Essays in Honor of Victor Paul Furnish.* Nashville: Abingdon, 1996.

Part 1, "Theology and Ethics in Paul," contains L. Keck, "The Accountable Self"; R. Scroggs, "Paul and the Eschatological Body"; R. Hays, "The Role of Scripture in Paul's Ethics"; J. Martyn, "The Crucial Event in the History of the Law (Gal

5:14)"; J. Dunn, " 'The Law of Faith,' 'the Law of the Spirit,' and 'The Law of Christ' "; M. Hooker, "A Partner in the Gospel: Paul's Understanding of His Ministry"; B. Gaventa, "Mother's Milk and Ministry in 1 Corinthians 3"; J. Sampley, "Reasoning from the Horizons of Paul's Thought World: A Comparison of Galatians and Philippians"; P. Achtemeier, "The Continuing Quest for Coherence in St. Paul: An Experiment in Thought"; and E. Lohse, "Changes of Thought in Pauline Theology? Some Reflections on Paul's Ethical Teaching in the Context of His Theology." Part 2, "Pauline Theology and Ethics in Canonical and Early Post-canonical Context," contains C. Barrett, "Deuteropauline Ethics: Some Observations"; J. Bassler, " 'He remains faithful' (2 Tim 2:13a)"; C. Black, "Christ Crucified in Paul and in Mark: Reflections on an Intracanonical Conversation"; D. Smith, "The Love Command: John and Paul?"; and H. Attridge, "Paul and the Domestication of Thomas." Part 3 contains four essays on theology and ethics in Paul's modern interpreters.

837 F. J. Matera. *New Testament Ethics: The Legacies of Jesus and Paul*. Louisville: Westminster John Knox, 1996.

A pioneering volume that describes the ethical teaching of the New Testament writings as distinct, literary products (the Four Gospels as the legacy of Jesus and the letters of Paul as the legacy of Paul), rather than on the basis of diachronic reconstruction or synchronic synthesis.

13.10.2 Sexual Ethics and Homosexuality

The best starting point for studying Paul's teaching on sexual ethics and homosexuality is Thiselton (#403). In "Union with Christ and the Theology of the Body (6:12–20)" (pp. 458–79), Thiselton makes manifest Paul's teaching that sexual intercourse is an intimate act involving the whole person and that what it means to be "in Christ" emerges from one's acts in the body and in everyday life. In "Vice Lists, Catechesis, and the Homosexual Debate (6:9–10)" (pp. 440–53; bibliography on pp. 421–23), Thiselton argues forcefully for the importance of the OT and Christian catechetical background (over against the current focus on the Greco-Roman setting) and demonstrates the invalidity of attempts to limit Paul's condemnation of homosexuality to pederasty (Scroggs) or prostitution (Boswell). See also Thiselton's "Can Hermeneutics Ease the Deadlock?" in *The Way Forward: Christian Voices on Homosexuality and the Church* (London: Hodder & Stoughton, 1997), 145–96. For a more concise introduction, which properly recognizes sexuality as an expression of the whole human self, the goodness of sex in marriage, and Paul's restriction of sexual activity to heterosexual, monogamous marriage, see D. F. Wright, "Sexuality, Sexual Ethics," *DPL* 871–75.

838 R. Scroggs. *The New Testament and Homosexuality: Contextual Background for Contemporary Debate.* Philadelphia: Fortress, 1983. [See esp. pp. 99–122.]

Alleges that Rom. 1:26–27; 1 Cor. 6:9–10; and 1 Tim. 1:9–10 condemn only pederasty and not homosexuality in general. See also J. Boswell, *Christianity, Social Tolerance, and Homosexuality: Gay People in Western Europe from the Beginning of the Christian Era to the Fourteenth Century* (Chicago: University of Chicago Press, 1980), esp. 106–17, 335–53, who alleges that Paul only condemns male prostitution and heterosexuals who commit homosexual acts.

839 R. B. Hays. "Relations Natural and Unnatural: A Response to John Boswell's Exegesis of Rom 1." *JRE* 4 (1986): 184–215.

A decisive refutation of J. Boswell's exegesis of Rom. 1. See also #834.

840 J. S. Siker, ed. *Homosexuality in the Church.* Louisville: Westminster John Knox, 1994.

See especially R. Hays, "Awaiting the Redemption of Our Bodies: The Witness of Scripture Concerning Homosexuality," who affirms the Scripture's teaching that homosexuality is a sin; and V. Furnish, "The Bible and Homosexuality: Reading the Texts in Context," who attempts to remove the Bible's condemnations of homosexuality by stressing its historical and cultural particularity and alleged ignorance of the complex conditions of natural homosexual orientation.

841 A. J. Malherbe. "On Marriage, 4:3–8." Pp. 224–41 in *The Letter to the Thessalonians.* AB 32B. New York: Doubleday, 2000.

Helpful discussion of 1 Thess. 4:3–8 with abundant citation of relevant ancient Greco-Roman and Jewish primary sources as well as interaction with modern secondary sources. Interprets *ktasthai skeous* as "acquiring a wife" and sees Paul discussing marriage in language similar to his philosophic contemporaries, but modified in the framework of a sanctified life.

13.10.3 Marriage/Celibacy and Divorce and Remarriage

The best starting point for studying Paul's teaching on marriage/celibacy and divorce and remarriage is Thiselton (#403). On pages 483–543 and 565–606, Thiselton provides an excellent exegesis of 1 Cor. 7:1–16 and 25–38 and survey of the range of positions, as well as abundant bibliography. He argues persuasively that Paul finds both marriage (with affection and erotic love included) and celibacy to be good, according to the gift that God has given to each, although celibacy has advantages over marriage if it is one's gift. After a judicious weighing of the arguments, Thiselton concludes that remarriage after divorce is permissible, depending on the circumstances and one's gift. For a concise introduction with helpful bibliography, see G. F. Hawthorne, "Marriage and Divorce, Adultery and Incest," *DPL* 594–601. See also H. W. House, ed., *Divorce and Remarriage: Four Christian Views* (Downers Grove, Ill.: InterVarsity, 1990).

842 O. L. Yarbrough. *Not Like the Gentiles: Marriage Rules in the Letters of Paul.* SBLDS 80. Atlanta: Scholars Press, 1985.

Provides helpful comparative study of marriage and sexual morality in Jewish and Greco-Roman moral traditions and pays close attention to 1 Thess. 4:3–8 (taking the "to obtain a wife" interpretation) and 1 Cor. 7 to determine their meaning and function. Emphasis on Jewish background. For a contrary emphasis on Hellenistic background, see Deming (#162).

843 C. S. Keener. . . . *And Marries Another: Divorce and Remarriage in the Teaching of the New Testament.* Peabody, Mass.: Hendrickson, 1991.

Addressed particularly to "those who would judge or penalize the innocent party" (xii). Contains good interaction, especially with primary sources (rabbinic and classical). On Paul, see chapters 5–7 (on divorce, marriage, and remarriage of ministers, respectively). See also R. F. Collins, *Divorce in the New Testament* (Collegeville, Minn.: Liturgical Press, 1992), 9–64, which interacts extensively with modern scholarship.

13.10.4 Relations to Civil Authorities

The best starting point for Paul's teaching on relations with civil authorities is D. J. Moo, "The Christian and Secular Rulers (13:1–7)" (#396, pp. 790–810). Moo properly stresses that civil government is an institution established by God and that it is normally the Christian's duty to submit to civil authorities, the only exception being when their authority conflicts with God's authority. See also Schreiner (#397, pp. 677–89) and S. Mott, "Civil Authority," *DPL* 141–43.

844 R. H. Stein. "The Argument of Romans 13:1–7." *NovT* 31 (1989): 325–43.

Shows clearly that Rom. 13:1–7 forms a cohesive argument and affirms the traditional interpretation of subjection to rulers (i.e., because they possess divine authority and support what is good but punish what is evil).

845 S. E. Porter. "Romans 13:1–7 as Pauline Political Rhetoric." *FN* 6 (1990): 115–37.

Sees Rom. 13:1–7 as a diatribe, in which Paul defines obedience as willing submission—with the unstated assumption of restriction to a just power—and legitimate authority as ruling consistent with God's justice. Also argues that the participle *huperechō*, modifying "authorities," refers to superior in a qualitative sense, that is, according to their justness. Concludes that Rom. 13:1–7 is a call to action—to be subordinate to just authorities, to do what is right and receive appropriate praise, with the converse implication that unjust authorities are not authorities at all and deserve no obedience.

846 N. Elliott. *Liberating Paul: The Justice of God and the Politics of the Apostle.* Maryknoll, N.Y.: Orbis, 1994; Sheffield: Sheffield Academic Press, 1995.

Attempts to "liberate" Paul from the shackles of misinterpretation that support political oppression, and to paint a portrait of Paul as a preacher of (political) good news to the poor.

Name Index

Aageson, J. W., 108
Achtemeier, P, 230
Adeney, D., 205
Aiken, David, 10
Aland, K., 100, 104
Albl, M. C., 108
Aletti, J. N., 203
Alexander, L. C. A., 35
Allison, D., Jr., 59
Alsup, J. E., 69, 76
Anderson, R. D., Jr., 90
Archer, G. L., 105
Aretas IV, 35
Aristotle, 128
Arnold, C. E., 134, 137, 152
Asher, J. R., 131
Attridge, H. W., 81, 230
Augustine, 81
Aune, D. E., 49, 96–97, 193, 218
Avemarie, F., 45
Averbeck, R., 214

Baarda, T., 172
Babcock, W. S., 81, 105
Badenas, R., 163
Baeck, L., 43
Bahnsen, G., 161
Bailey, D. P., 175–76
Bailey, J., 71
Baird, W., 194
Balás, D. L., 81
Balch, D., 49–53
Balchin, J., 150
Baldermann, I., 187

Baldwin, H. S., 223
Balz, H., 70, 159
Bandstra, A. J., 161
Banks, R. J., 28, 176, 203–4
Barclay, J. M. G., 61, 74, 165,
    205, 227
Barcley, W., 190
Barker, M., 151
Barnabas, 82
Barnett, J. M., 209
Barnett, P., 75, 115, 203
Barrett, C. K., 40, 73, 110,
    113–14, 230
Bartchy, S., 51
Barth, M., 117, 121, 200
Barton, S., 165
Bash, A., 211
Bassler, J. M., 142, 147, 230
Batey, R., 161
Bauckham, R., 81, 101, 148, 150,
    152, 154
Bauer, W., 79–80
Baur, Ferdinand Christian,
    20–21, 73, 100
Beasley-Murray, G. R., 203, 213
Beasley-Murray, P., 69, 203
Beck, J. R., 225
Becker, J., 40
Beckwith, F. J., 195
Beker, J. C., 81, 142, 166
Bell, R. H., 128, 202
Belleville, L. L., 132, 203, 220,
    225, 229
Ben-Chorin, S., 43

Berger, K., 51, 72, 143
Berger, P., 54
Berkley, T. W., 128
Best, E., 25, 71, 118, 122, 204–6,
   210
Betz, H. D., 40, 49, 87–88, 92,
   114, 116
Betz, O., 76
Beutler, J., 138
Beyer, H., 210
Bieringer, R., 129, 131, 188
Billerbeck, P., 46
Black, C., 167, 230
Black, D. A., 85, 167
Blackman, E., 64
Blaising, C. A., 202
Blanke, H., 121
Blocher, H., 168
Blomberg, C. L., 221, 225
Blomkvist, V., 134
Bloomquist, L. G., 135
Blue, B., 203
Bock, D. L., 202
Bockmuehl, M., 44, 78, 119
Boers, H., 127
Bolt, P. G., 180
Bonhöffer, A., 48
Bonsirven, J., 105
Borchert, G., 18
Borgen, P., 154
Boring, M. E., 51, 74
Bormann, L., 55
Bornkamm, G., 28, 39
Bosch, D., 179
Boswell, J., 230–31
Bousset, W., 21, 23
Bouttier, M., 189
Bowden, J., 36, 41, 64, 70, 149,
   172
Bowers, P., 179
Bowman, A., 225
Boyarin, D., 45
Bradshaw, P. F., 219
Brandenburger, E., 166
Branick, V., 204
Brauch, M., 25
Braun, H., 191
Brewer, D. Instone, 106

Breytenbach, C., 36, 187
Bring, R., 161
Brockhaus, U., 54
Bromiley, G. W., 111, 159, 181
Brower, K. E., 198
Brown, C., 159
Bruce, F. F., 34, 39, 52, 59, 110,
   113, 116–17, 120, 122
Bruner, F. D., 156
Buber, Martin, 43
Bultmann, R., 21, 23–24, 38–39,
   58, 127, 141, 156, 167, 169,
   181, 184, 193, 229
Burke, K., 93
Burtchaell, J. T., 209–10
Burton, E. D. W., 115
Buttolph, P., 123
Byrne, B., 150, 176

Cabaniss, A., 218
Cadbury, H. J., 63–64
Caird, G. B., 194
Calivas, A., 216
Calvin, John, 164
Campbell, A., 214
Campbell, R. A., 208, 211
Campbell, T. H., 32
Campbell, W. S., 199, 201
Campenhausen, H., 80
Cannon, G. E., 136
Capes, D., 149
Carson, D. A., 35, 47, 85–86, 98,
   102, 107, 142, 157, 185,
   204–6, 218–19
Casey, P. M., 151, 154
Castelli, E. A., 93, 212
Cerfaux, L., 204
Charlesworth, J. H., 29
Chenderlin, F., 216
Cheung, A. T., 130
Chilton, B., 75
Chirichigno, G., 105
Chow, J. K., 129
Christiansen, E. J., 213
Chrysostom, John, 81–82
Ciampa, R. E., 133
Clarke, A. D., 36, 55, 81, 209–12
Clarke, F., 24, 38, 178

Classen, C. J., 88, 90–91
Clement of Rome, 103
Clines, D. J. A., 149, 168
Clowney, E., 205
Collins, A. Y., 218
Collins, J. N., 210
Collins, R. F., 137, 232
Colpe, C., 51
Combes, I. A. H., 208
Conzelmann, H., 24, 113, 123
Corley, B. C., 33
Corriveau, R., 219
Cosgrove, C. H., 26, 202
Cotter, W., 223
Cousar, C., 173
Crafton, J. A., 93
Cranfield, C. E. B., 112, 161
Cremer, H., 183
Cross, A. R., 214
Crouch, J. E., 52, 136
Cullmann, O., 67, 178, 193
Cunningham, J., 189

Dahl, N. A., 23, 134, 146–47, 178
Danove, P., 87
Dassmann, E., 80
Daube, D., 178, 215
Davids, P. H., 14, 77, 110
Davies, G. N., 182
Davies, W. D., 24, 42, 44, 178, 215
Davila, J. R., 154
Davis, C. J., 152
Davis, C. W., 87, 136
Dawes, G. W., 220, 224
Dean, O. C., Jr., 40, 171
de Boer, M. C., 151, 167, 197
Deichgräber, R., 68
Deidun, T. J., 226
Deines, R., 44, 46
Deissmann, A., 32, 48, 95
de Jonge, M., 71, 172
de Lacey, D. R., 70, 150
Delling, G., 24, 146
DeMaris, R., 137
Deming, W., 55, 232
den Heyer, C. J., 41
Denton, D. R., 206

de Vos, C. S., 205
de Witt, J. R., 142
Dibelius, M., 38, 123
DiCicco, M. M., 132
Dietzfelbinger, C., 28
Dittmar, W., 105
Dodd, B. J., 72, 211
Dodd, C. H., 67, 105, 156, 171, 192–93
Dölger, F. J., 52
Donaldson, T. L., 29, 46
Donelson, L. R., 100
Donfried, K. P., 35, 126–27, 138, 191
Doty, W. G., 95–96
Douglas, Mary, 55
Downing, F. G., 57
Dungan, D. L., 59
Dunn, J. D. G., 29, 42, 60, 69, 74, 80, 101, 112, 117, 121, 144, 146, 149–52, 155–56, 159, 164–65, 174, 185, 203, 205, 207, 212, 214, 230
Dupont, J., 188

Eckstein, H.-J., 170
Eco, Umberto, 128
Eichholz, G., 76
Ellingworth, P., 152
Elliott, M. W., 46, 198
Elliott, N., 127, 233
Ellis, E. E., 24, 72–73, 101, 106, 151, 154, 198, 203, 205
Engberg-Pedersen, T., 56–57
Enroth, A.-M., 163
Erickson, R., 86
Ericksson, A., 92
Ernest, J., 159
Eskola, T., 46
Esler, P., 207
Espy, J. M., 163
Eusebius, 81
Evans, C. A., 10, 14, 42–43, 49, 75, 82, 102, 108
Everts, J., 203

Fanning, B., 85
Fape, M. O., 214

Farmer, W. R., 95, 175, 216
Fee, G. D., 71, 113, 119, 152,
    155–56, 158
Ferguson, E., 64
Filson, F. V., 193
Findeis, H.-J., 187
Finegan, J., 32
Fiore, B., 49–50, 139
Fiorenza, E., 210
Fitzgerald, J., 49–50
Fitzmyer, J. A., 34, 39, 70, 112,
    121, 151, 179, 184, 186, 221
Flanagan, J., 186
Forbes, C., 129
Forkman, G., 217
Fornberg, T., 134
Fortna, R. T., 35
Foucalt, M., 93
Fowl, S. E., 71, 110
France, R. T., 150, 223
Francis, F. O., 136
Frankemölle, H., 77
Fredriksen, P., 29
Freedman, D. N., 13, 35, 65
Friedrich, G., 181
Fung, R. Y. K., 116, 203, 205–6,
    208, 210
Funk, R. W., 67, 95
Furnish, V. P., 60–61, 114, 152,
    226–27, 231

Gaffin, R. B., Jr., 155, 157, 194
Gager, J. G., 200
Gamble, H. Y., 103–5, 127
Gardner, P. D., 129
Garlington, D., 183
Garrett, S., 50
Gärtner, B., 207
Gasque, W. W., 147
Gaston, L., 200
Gaventa, B. R., 29, 35, 230
Geertz, Clifford, 53
Geisler, N., 195
Gempf, C., 34, 55
Geoffrion, T. C., 136
Georgi, D., 74
Giddens, A., 130

Giles, K., 224
Gill, D., 55
Gilmour, S., 24
Girard, René, 174
Gloer, W. H., 71, 201
Gnilka, J., 41
Goetius, E. V. N., 181
Goodspeed, E. J., 103
Goppelt, L., 69, 76, 106
Gorday, P., 81
Grayston, K., 173
Green, D. E., 219, 227
Green, J. B., 152
Greig, J., 162
Greimas, A., 181
Grieschen, C. A., 148, 153
Grieve, A., 95
Grobel, K., 23
Grudem, W. A., 157, 221–22
Gruenler, R. G., 224
Guelich, R. A., 186
Gundry, R. H., 163, 169
Gundry-Volf, J. M., 171, 182,
    222, 225
Gunkel, H., 21–22, 38
Gunther, J. J., 73
Guthrie, D., 100, 146
Guthrie, G., 85–86
Guthrie, S., 67
Güting, E. W., 93

Haacker, K., 28, 32, 40, 65, 78,
    181
Haase, W., 18, 32, 41, 50–52, 56,
    59, 65, 72
Haenchen, E., 109, 111
Hafemann, S. J., 25, 61, 131,
    165–66, 200
Hagner, D. A., 43, 70, 103–4, 186
Hahn, F., 67, 146, 178, 219
Hall, C., 67
Halliday, M., 91
Hamerton-Kelly, R., 174
Hamilton, Jim, 12
Hamilton, N. Q., 156
Hannah, D. D., 154
Hansen, G. W., 88, 133

Hanson, A. T., 106
Harding, M., 140
Hardy, B., 68
Hare, D. R. A., 32
Harrill, J., 56
Harrington, D. J., 202
Harris, G., 218, 229
Harris, H., 25
Harris, M. J., 43, 62, 70, 149, 195
Harris, W. H., 134
Harrisville, R. A., 22
Harrisville, R. A., III, 181
Hartman, L., 214, 229
Harvey, G., 200
Harvey, J. D., 94
Hasel, G., 141–42
Hata, G., 81
Haubeck, W., 70, 177
Hauser, A. J., 89
Hawthorne, G. F., 14, 18, 76,
    118, 205, 229, 232
Hay, D. M., 142–43, 182
Hays, R. B., 107–8, 145, 165, 181,
    185, 204, 229, 231
Heckel, T., 170
Hegel, Georg W. F., 20
Heiligenthal, R., 162
Hein, K., 217
Heitmüller, 21, 23–24
Hellholm, D., 134, 196
Helmbold, A., 69
Hcmer, C. J., 34–35
Hengel, M., 36, 44, 56, 64, 70,
    76–77, 149, 165, 172
Hennecke, E., 79
Herold, G., 184
Hester, J. D., 160
Hill, C., 65
Hill, D., 176
Hock, R., 52
Hofius, O., 61, 69, 165, 176,
    185–86, 201, 216, 222
Holladay, C. R., 50, 74
Holland, G. S., 90, 138
Holleman, J., 198
Holmberg, B., 54, 209
Holmes, J. M., 224

Holmstrand, J., 86
Holtz, T., 60, 146, 229
Homer, 107
Hooker, M. D., 168, 175, 230
Horbury, W., 153, 175
Horn, F. W., 158
Horrell, D. G., 130, 154
Horsley, R. A., 57
House, H. W., 232
Howard, G., 182
Hoyle, R. B., 156
Hubbard, R. L., Jr., 221
Hübner, H., 18, 105, 162, 165
Hughes, F., 138
Hultgren, A., 18, 28, 149, 180
Hurd, J. C., Jr., 32–33, 59, 129
Hurst, L. D., 29
Hurtado, L. W., 30, 148–50, 154,
    219
Hvalvik, R., 201
Hyatt, J., 24
Hyldahl, N., 34

Ignatius, 66, 103

Jackson, F. J. F., 63
Janowski, B., 176
Jeal, R. R., 135
Jeremias, J., 76, 216
Jervell, J., 110, 169
Jervis, L. A., 97, 229
Jewett, P., 213
Jewett, R., 33–34, 138, 169
Johanson, B. C., 84
Johnson, E. E., 142–43, 196
Johnson, L. T., 77, 99, 124–25
Josephus, 90
Jostein, Å., 61
Judge, Edwin, 49, 51–53, 229
Juel, D. H., 107, 147
Jüngel, E., 58

Kabisch, R., 21–22
Kalin, E. R., 28, 70, 173
Käsemann, Ernst, 21, 24–25,
    67–68, 111–12, 145, 167,
    169, 172–73, 184, 186, 208

Keck, L. E., 25, 151, 229
Kee, H., 24
Keener, C. S., 203, 222, 225, 232
Keesmaat, S. C., 145
Kennedy, G. A., 87, 91
Kennel, G., 72
Kern, P. H., 90
Kertelge, K., 60, 81, 165
Kidd, R. M., 139
Kiley, M., 137
Kim, J. D., 92
Kim, Seyoon, 27–28, 61, 188
Kinneavy, J., 182
Kirk, J. A., 209
Kittel, G., 159
Klauck, H-J., 216
Klausner, J., 43
Klein, M., 77
Klein, P., 33
Klein, W. W., 135, 221
Kleinknecht, K., 173
Kline, M., 213
Klumbies, P. G., 147
Knauf, E. A., 35
Knight, G. W., III, 124
Knight, H., 67
Knoch, O., 216
Knowles, M., 229
Knox, John, 32–33, 35, 103
Koch, D., 107–8
Kodell, J., 215
Koester, Helmut, 24
Kohl, M., 55, 169, 172
König, A., 197
Koperski, V., 161
Köstenberger, A. J., 180, 222–24
Kraft, R. A., 79
Kramer, W., 68
Kraus, W., 65, 174, 207
Krause, G., 182
Kreitzer, L. J., 149, 168, 193, 196
Krodel, G., 79
Kroeger, C., 203, 223
Kroeger, R., 223
Kruse, C. G., 165, 205, 217
Kuck, D. W., 197
Kümmel, W. G., 24, 27, 38, 168

Kuss, O., 39
Kuula, K., 166

Laato, T., 45, 78, 185
Ladd, G. E., 143, 146
Lake, K., 63
Lambrecht, J., 131, 165, 188
Lamp, J. S., 130–131
Lanci, J. R., 207
Lane, W., 132
Larsson, E., 65
Lategan, B., 51
Lau, A., 152
Lautenschlager, M., 77
Legasse, S., 39
Leitch, J. W., 113
Lentz, J., 110
Levinsohn, S., 85–86
Lewis, G. S., 154
Lichtenberger, H., 165
Lietzmann, H., 48, 215
Lightfoot, J. B., 20, 76
Lincoln, A. T., 118, 195
Lindemann, A., 80
Litfin, D., 89
Litwak, K. D., 108
Logan, A. H. B., 50
Lohfink, G., 81
Lohse, E., 41, 120, 171, 229–230
Longenecker, B. W., 134, 165, 181, 199
Longenecker, R. N., 30, 39, 69, 98, 106, 116, 152, 196, 220, 226, 229
Louw, J. P., 85–86
Lovering, E. H., 181, 229
Luckmann, T., 54
Lüdemann, G., 33–36, 74
Lüdemann, H., 23, 32
Lührmann, D., 50, 183
Lull, D. J., 34, 157
Lummis, E., 22
Luter, A., 149
Lyonnet, S., 172

Ma, W., 158
Maas, W., 186

MacDonald, D. R., 81
MacDonald, M., 54
Machen, J. G., 23
Mack, B. L., 88
Malherbe, A. J., 50–51, 97, 123,
    138, 151, 227, 231
Malina, B., 56, 89
Marcion, 105
Marcus, J., 197
Marsh, J., 67
Marshall, I. H., 64, 122, 124, 150,
    176, 186, 188, 193, 203, 215
Marshall, P., 53
Martin, B., 164
Martin, D. B., 54, 130, 208
Martin, R. P., 14, 18, 67–68, 72,
    110, 115, 146–47, 150, 187,
    203, 206, 219
Martin, T. W., 65, 137
Martín-Asensio, G., 91
Martyn, J. L., 117, 198, 229
März, C.-P., 60
Matera, F. J., 154, 230
Matlock, B., 26
Mattern, L., 191
Mattill, A. J., Jr., 110
Mazza, E., 215
McKelvey, R., 207
McKnight, S., 195
McLean, B. H., 96, 175, 209
McNeil, B., 175
McVay, J., 203
Meade, D. G., 99, 101
Mealand, D. L., 93
Mearns, C. L., 194
Meeks, W. A., 25, 50, 52–53, 136,
    151, 195–96, 227
Melanchthon, Philip, 88
Menzies, A., 21
Menzies, R. P., 158
Merk, O., 18
Merkle, B. L., 203
Metzger, B. M., 19, 100
Meyer, B. F., 216
Michel, O., 105
Middendorf, M. P., 128
Miller, J. C., 129

Miller, J. D., 139
Mills, W., 18
Minear, P. S., 206
Minor, M., 83
Mitchell, M. M., 82, 91
Mitton, C. L., 103
Mohrland, R., 227
Montefiore, C. G., 43
Montgomery, W., 22–23
Moo, D. J., 35, 112, 161–62, 199,
    232
Moores, J. D., 127
Moritz, T., 135
Morland, K. A., 133
Morris, L., 35, 122–23, 146–47,
    166, 173, 205
Mott, S., 225, 232
Moule, C. F. D., 95, 149, 215
Mounce, W. D., 124
Mouton, E., 90
Moxnes, H., 147, 207
Müller, C., 184
Müller, G., 182
Müller, M., 98
Mullins, T. Y., 95
Munck, Johannes, 20, 24, 199
Murphy-O'Connor, J., 98

Neill, S., 25
Neirynck, F., 59
Neudorfer, H.-W., 65
Neugebauer, F., 189
Neusner, J., 64, 73, 201
Newman, C. C., 151, 154
Neyrey, J., 50, 54, 56
Niccum, C., 223
Niebuhr, R. R., 95
Nixon, I., 199
Nodet, E., 214
Norden, E., 48, 66
Norris, R. A., Jr., 81, 181

O'Brien, P. T., 47, 96, 118–20,
    147, 149, 179–80, 203, 205
O'Connell, M. J., 215
Odgen, S., 58
O'Donnell, M., 87, 99

Ogg, G., 32, 67
O'Hara, W. J., 204
Olbrechts-Tyteca, L., 92
Olbricht, T. H., 50, 88–91
Ollrog, W.-H., 178
O'Mahony, K. J., 92
Oostendorp, D. W., 73
Origen, 81
Oss, D., 157
Overbeck, Franz, 79, 82

Pagels, E. H., 80
Paget, J. C., 81
Paige, T., 49, 71, 101, 205
Painter, J., 75
Parsons, M., 229
Parunak, H., 85
Pate, C. M., 143, 151, 166, 168
Patrick, D., 91
Patterson, S., 60
Patzia, A. G., 105
Payne, P., 224
Perelman, C., 92
Perkins, P., 170
Perriman, A., 223
Perrin, N., 216
Pervo, R. I., 110
Pesch, R., 64
Peterlin, D., 136
Peterman, G. W., 136
Petersen, P., 18
Peterson, B. K., 132
Peterson, D. G., 147, 190, 206, 218
Peterson, N., 53
Philo of Alexandria, 43, 90, 162, 170
Piper, J., 185, 222
Plato, 170
Plevnik, J., 25, 198
Pliny the Elder, 66
Plummer, A., 113
Plutarch, 90
Pogoloff, S. M., 129
Polhill, J. B., 41
Polycarp, 103
Porter, S. E., 14, 26, 42, 49,

83–91, 102, 110, 138, 187–88, 190, 214, 233
Poythress, V., 213
Pratscher, W., 75
Prior, M., 139
Pryor, J., 206

Quanbeck, P., II, 22
Quinn, J. D., 123–24, 184

Rabinowitz, Noel, 12
Rainbow, P., 150
Räisänen, H., 29, 65, 163, 165–66, 185, 201
Ramsay, W., 22
Rapske, B., 55
Reasoner, M., 128
Reed, J. T., 85–87, 96, 138
Reeve, D. H. G., 215
Reid, D. G., 18
Reitzenstein, R., 21
Rengstorf, K., 24
Renwick, D. A., 132
Reumann, J., 76, 184–85, 209, 215
Richard, E., 151
Richards, E. R., 97
Richardson, N., 148
Richardson, P., 45, 59, 200
Richardson, R. D., 215
Ridderbos, H., 142, 146
Riesner, R., 31, 34, 36, 61
Rigaux, B., 24
Ritschl, Albrecht , 20
Robertson, A., 113
Robinson, J. A. T., 169–70, 206
Robinson, J. M., 186
Roetzel, C. J., 41, 161, 191
Röhser, G., 167
Roloff, J., 69, 76
Root, M., 212
Rordorf, W., 68
Rosner, B. S., 217, 225, 228
Rowdon, H. H., 70, 150
Russell, W. B., III, 133

Saarinen, R., 212
Sabourin, L., 172

Sampley, J. P., 52, 228, 230
Sand, A., 169
Sanders, E. P., 25, 28, 40,
    42–44, 46–47, 59, 112, 163,
    166, 183, 185, 188,
    192
Sanders, J. A., 82, 108
Sanders, J. T., 69
Sandmel, S., 43
Sandnes, K., 132, 207
Sappington, T. J., 137
Sass, G., 160
Saucy, R., 157, 222
Savage, T. B., 211
Scharlemann, M., 64
Schatzmann, S. S., 158, 184
Schelkle, K., 17
Schlatter, Adolf, 21, 24, 181, 184
Schleiermacher, Friedrich D. E.,
    20
Schlueter, C. J., 202
Schmeller, T., 223
Schmidt, D., 85
Schmidt, T. E., 198, 203, 207,
    217, 222
Schmithals, W., 50
Schnabel, E., 163, 229
Schnackenburg, R., 204, 213
Schneemelcher, W., 79
Schneider, G., 70, 159
Schnelle, U., 51, 171
Schoeps, H. J., 43
Scholer, D. N., 197
Schrage, W., 50, 227, 229
Schreiber, S., 110
Schreiner, T. R., 112, 144, 165,
    223, 225
Schubert, P., 96
Schütz, J. H., 210
Schweitzer, A., 22–25, 156, 188,
    192
Schweizer, E., 59, 209
Schwemer, A. M., 36
Scott, J. M., 45, 177, 180, 199
Scroggs, R., 64, 229–31
Scullion, J. J., 185
Scult, A., 91

Seeberg, A., 229
Seeley, D., 173
Segal, A., 29, 44
Seifrid, Mark A., 12, 30, 47, 170,
    183, 185–86, 190
Senior, D., 179
Sevenster, J., 49
Shedd, R., 205
Sherwin-White, A. N., 51, 54
Shillington, V. G., 217
Siber, P., 190
Siker, J. S., 231
Silva, M., 85, 108, 119, 133, 164,
    198, 207, 222
Simon, M., 64
Sinclair, S. G., 150
Smith, D. M., 107, 230
Smith, J., 212
Smith, L., 58
Smith, W., 219
Snodgrass, K., 192
Soards, M. L., 197
Soderlund, S. K., 126
Söding, T., 175
South, J. T., 218
Spicq, C., 159
Stacey, W. D., 169–70
Stalker, D. M. G., 39
Stambaugh, J., 53
Stamps, D. L., 87–89, 91
Stanley, C. D., 107–8
Stanton, G., 165
Stauffer, E., 67
Steely, J., 23
Stegner, W., 45
Stein, R. H., 233
Stendahl, K., 27, 163, 200–201
Stettler, H., 153
Still, T. D., 138
Stirewalt, M. L., Jr., 98
Stoffer, D. R., 217
Storms, C. S., 157
Stott, D., 36
Stowers, S. K., 50, 93, 96, 127
Strachan, L. R. M., 95
Strecker, G., 51
Strelan, R., 56

Stuhlmacher, P., 28, 70, 78, 142, 164, 172, 178, 183, 186–87
Stuhlmueller, C., 179
Sturm, R., 197
Suggate, A. M., 185
Suhl, A., 32
Sumithra, S., 205
Sumney, J. L., 74–75, 229
Sykes, S., 174
Synofzik, E., 191

Taartz, I., 97
Tajra, H., 54
Talbert, Charles H., 109–10
Tan, Randall K. J., 12
Tannehill, R., 190
Taylor, J., 35, 56, 214
Taylor, S. S., 82
Temporini, H., 18, 32, 41, 50–52, 56, 59, 65, 72
Tenelsof, J., 222
Tenney, M. C., 69 .
Tertullian, 80
Theissen, G., 55, 170, 229
Thielman, F., 43, 165
Thiselton, A. C., 114, 126, 194, 207, 212, 216, 226, 230–32
Thompson, M. D., 60, 180
Thomson, I. H., 93
Thrall, M. E., 115
Thurén, L., 166
Thüsing, W., 189
Tombs, D., 83, 86, 89
Tomson, P., 44, 165
Towner, P. H., 49, 194, 196, 203, 228
Trajan, 66
Travis, S., 192
Trilling, W., 122
Trobisch, D., 103–4
Tuckett, C. M., 29, 154, 171
Turner, M., 152, 159

Vander Broek, L., 71
van Dülmen, A., 161
Vanhoye, A., 29, 60, 181
Van Roon, A., 134
Verner, D., 53

Vielhauer, P., 109–11
Vincent, J., 168
Vollenweider, S., 71, 177
von Harnack, A., 67, 79, 82, 228
von Dobbeler, A., 182
von Rad, G., 183
Vos, G., 155, 194

Wacker, W. C., 124
Wagner, G., 201, 212
Wainwright, G., 215
Walker, A., 204
Wall, R. W., 102
Walter, N., 146
Walton, S., 111
Wanamaker, C. A., 94, 122
Wansbrough, H., 60
Wansink, C., 57
Warfield, B. B., 64
Warkentin, M., 210
Watson, D. F., 89–91
Weaver, P., 92
Webb, G., 204
Webb, W. J., 132, 223
Weber, Max, 46, 54
Wedderburn, A. J. M., 50, 60, 127, 167, 190, 212
Weima, J. A. D., 98, 138, 229
Weiss, J., 48
Welborn, L. L., 130
Wendland, H., 48
Wengst, K., 69
Wenham, D., 36, 61, 152
Werline, R., 82
Westerholm, S., 45, 164–65, 185
Wettstein, Johann Jakob, 51
White, J. L., 95–97
White, M., 50
White, R., 213
Whiteley, D. E. H., 142
Wiens, D., 50
Wikenhauser, A., 189
Wilckens, U., 28, 46, 109, 162
Wilder, W. N., 134
Wiles, G. P., 96
Wilk, F., 108
Wilkins, M. J., 71, 101, 205
Wilkinson, J., 92

Williams, H. H. D., 131
Williams, S., 172, 181
Williamson, H. G. M., 107
Wilson, A. N., 41, 143
Wilson, R. McL., 49, 79
Wilson, S. G., 59
Wilson, W. T., 137
Winger, M., 165
Winter, B. W., 36, 55, 57, 81, 88, 198, 206, 229
Wire, A. C., 92
Witherington, B., III, 41, 56, 145, 149, 153–54, 197–98, 216, 221
Wolter, M., 184
Woodbridge, J. D., 98
Wrede, W., 21–24, 41
Wright, D. F., 231

Wright, N. T., 25, 29, 44, 71, 126, 143–45, 149, 165, 201
Wycliffe, J., 210

Yamauchi, E., 49
Yarboro, A., 123
Yarbrough, O. L., 232
Yinger, K. L., 192
Yoder Neufeld, T. R., 135
Yonick, S., 24
Yorke, G. L. O. R., 206

Zahl, P., 185
Zahn, T., 103
Zeller, E., 21
Zscharnack, L., 38

2899